Democratic Accountability, Political Order, and Change

Democratic Accountability, Political Order, and Change

Exploring Accountability Processes in an Era of European Transformation

Johan P. Olsen

OXFORD
UNIVERSITY PRESS

OXFORD
UNIVERSITY PRESS

Great Clarendon Street, Oxford, OX2 6DP,
United Kingdom

Oxford University Press is a department of the University of Oxford.
It furthers the University's objective of excellence in research, scholarship,
and education by publishing worldwide. Oxford is a registered trade mark of
Oxford University Press in the UK and in certain other countries

First Edition published in 2017

Impression: 1

Published in the United States of America by Oxford University Press
198 Madison Avenue, New York, NY 10016, United States of America

British Library Cataloguing in Publication Data
Data available

Library of Congress Control Number: 2016954544

ISBN 978–0–19–880060–6

Printed in Great Britain by
Clays Ltd, St Ives plc

For James G. March
a great friend, teacher, colleague, and co-author
throughout half a century

Preface and Acknowledgments

Accountability regimes are crucial for the legitimacy of a polity and this book examines democratic accountability as a mechanism by which citizens are supposed to influence and control their elected representatives, non-elected officials, and other power holders. More precisely, I focus on the interrelations between democratic accountability, political order, and orderly change, that is, how democratic accountability processes are affected by and affect political association and the social basis of political order, political organization and the institutional basis of order, and political agency and the behavioral basis of order.

I see the growing number of accountability demands in contemporary representative democracies as part of a legitimacy crisis, a loss of confidence in institutions and leaders, and a struggle over the terms of political order. I hold that accountability theory is only likely to be useful for making sense of those accountability processes if there is a re-examination and reassessment of the possibilities and limitations of the key ideas and assumptions of mainstream rational choice, principal–agent approaches to democratic accountability.

Aspiring to make a modest contribution to such a development I offer an institutional approach that assumes that political orders can be more or less settled. Accountability processes can be order transforming as well as order maintaining. Events are not necessarily a product of the deliberate choices of identifiable actors, it is not always easy to conclude who is responsible and should be held to account, and rational adaptation based on experiential learning is not guaranteed. Representative democracies struggle to reconcile a culture assuming human control and accountable actors with the observation that it is notoriously difficult to identify objectively who is responsible for specific events in a political world of interdependency, interaction, and compromises. A possible consequence of this tension is that political talk and political action are separated and inconsistent, sometimes creating demands for reducing the gap between talk and action and sometimes not. Mass mobilization related to the terms of political order is rare and takes place only under specific conditions, rather than being commonplace.

Based upon these assumptions I argue that we can learn two things from accountability processes, especially in an era of major changes in terms of political order. First, our understanding of the interrelationship between accountability, political order, and orderly change can be improved. Second, I claim that accountability processes can teach us something about political life in general. New insight invites reconsideration of standard understandings and the vocabulary of democratic organization and governance, including what terms such as accountability, democracy, politics, the sovereign state, and constitutional choice come to mean and imply under different and shifting circumstances.

This book, then, can be read in relation to two different aims and time and space frames. The first, reflected in the subtitle of the book, is to shed light on the politics of accountability in a specific era of European institutional transformation. The second is to explore what studies of accountability processes can tell us more generally about political order and orderly change, and how they bring up enduring and foundational democratic challenges: how and why humans constitute themselves in political communities; how peaceful coexistence, cooperation, and conflict resolution can be secured among people with competing conceptions of good society and good governance; how shared purposes, trust, solidarity, deserved legitimacy, and allegiance for the political order can be built and maintained; how different institutional arrangements contribute to democratic politics as a way to rule divided societies without undue violence or elimination of diversity, individual freedom, and influence; and how a heterogeneous and pluralistic society can be transformed into a viable political community constituted on principles and rules that have normative validity in themselves, beyond their specific policy outcomes.

Although this book is centered on Europe, worries about the health of representative democracy and its key institutions and leadership are not limited to Europe. For instance, the US Social Science Research Council's program "Anxieties of Democracy," launched in June 2015, is motivated by a concern about whether the core institutions of established democracies that connect citizens and civil society to the political system—elections, mass media, political parties, interest groups, social movements, and legislatures—can capably address large problems in the public interest (<http:/www.ssrc.org/programs/view/anxieties-of-democracy/>). And, of course, the need to rethink and reassess the actual *organization, working,* and *change* of formal legal institutional arrangements labeled "democracy" is even greater in other parts of the world.

This is my third book with Oxford University Press in the last decade and there are both continuities and changes between the books. All of them start out from an organization theory-based institutional perspective on political organization and organizing. They try to make sense of the European Union as a grand-scale experiment in political organization, while also aiming to explore some general theoretical and conceptual issues in an empirically informed way on the basis of lessons from the European Union as an unsettled and dynamic polity.

The first book, *Europe in Search of Political Order* (2007), provided a discussion of how democratic polities try to cope with a variety of tensions that do not have any universally accepted and enduring solutions, yet have the potential to change the political organization of Europe. These include tensions between unity and diversity, citizens and their helpers, democratic design and historical drift, and between different types of coexisting political orders. In the second book, *Governing through Institution Building* (2010), I argued that if the future of democracies depends on the quality of their political institutions, improved understanding of how institutions of government are organized, work, and change may be achieved by studying large-scale institutional designs and reforms. This third book builds on the two others, but here I give priority to understanding the interaction between democratic accountability, political order, and orderly change.

A major difference between the two first books and this one is related to the changing political climate in the Western world. The vision of liberal constitutional democracy and a capitalist market economy as the end of history has been replaced by disillusion with representative democracy and pessimism about the future. Over the last decade, public opinion in Europe has, due to a variety of crises, changed from fairly widespread optimism about the European project to an atmosphere characterized by indifference, or discontent and protest. As has often been the case, there has been no lack of big words to describe the problems facing the European Union. There is perceived disintegration, a systemic crisis of confidence in political institutions and leaders, renewed nationalism, increasing socioeconomic inequality, growing polarization, and extremism. There is hate speech, violence, half-truths, and lies rather than honest and fair debate. Most recently, the Brexit referendum has been interpreted as a turning point in the history of European integration and even in the history of Western democracy.

While there is fairly broad agreement that something has gone wrong in the union, opinions differ as to where the problems are located, what caused them, and how they can be mended. Most Europeans report that they believe in "democracy," but they disagree about what the term means and implies and there is limited trust in the institutions and leaders of polities that aspire to democratic legitimacy. For example, for some Brexit represents a verdict on the elites both in Brussels and Westminster. Leaders are divorced from the everyday life of ordinary people and in particular from the situation of people struggling with unemployment, poverty, and insecurity. It is dangerous to continue to ignore or explain away their discontent, anger, distrust, and protests. The vision of an ever closer union has to be buried. For others, Brexit shows the extent to which ordinary people are ill-informed and manipulated. They do not understand the complexity and dynamics of the problems facing Europe. They do not appreciate the many benefits that follow from the union, but take them for granted. "The people" should not be trusted with important decisions about complex issues such as whether a country should join or exit the European Union. For those in this camp, the way forward is still moving towards "more Europe."

From an institutional perspective, the Brexit referendum is not likely to be the last word in either European integration and disintegration processes or in Britain's relations with the EU. The referendum is more likely to be the start of a complex political change process where much will depend on how the new situation is handled by a variety of potential participants and whose outcome is impossible to predict. There are pleas for pragmatism and finding workable solutions that all parties can accept. But there are also deep divides. For instance, when taking on the EU presidency (July 1, 2016), Slovakia declared its ambition to reshape Europe and change the balance of power between levels of governance by scaling back the powers of Brussels and supranational institutions and strengthening the role of member states and intergovernmental cooperation. Poland has demanded a new treaty, a suggestion that met with little enthusiasm from most European leaders. In brief, the current situation poses big and scary questions and huge challenges and offers few unifying answers. Demagogues can address citizens outside established political institutions, providing radical and simple solutions to complex problems, a situation that in several ways resembles the Europe of the 1930s.

However, an optimistic democratic view is that even though democracies make mistakes, there is no reason to be alarmed. Democracies learn from experience. They are able to rationally adapt to shifting circumstances, correct their mistakes, recover, and make progress. For example, in a recent study of four crises of American democracy, Alasdair Roberts (2017) concludes that American democracy has always risen to new challenges, reforming its institutions and redefining itself. Arguably, the history of European democracy invites somewhat less optimistic conclusions, as do studies of experiential learning and adaptation in formal organizations and formally organized institutions (March and Olsen 1975, March 2010). A key question facing accountability theory is to what degree accountability processes contribute in practice, and not only in theory, to experiential learning and improvement in situations such as the one Europe faces now.

I admit that this book raises more questions than answers. However, I believe that students of democratic accountability, like most social scientists, should spend more time formulating important questions and possibly a little less time on finding precise answers to not-so-important questions. Accountability theorists still have a long way to go, but my attempt to address the relations between democratic accountability, political order, and orderly change has been based upon the optimistic view that a political phenomenon "is unique when we have failed to develop a theory that will make it non-unique. Thus, uniqueness is less a bar to future theoretical success than a confession of past theoretical failure" (Cyert and March 1963: 287).

This book project started on 4 November 2015, when Dominic Byatt at Oxford University Press sent me an email. He had found an article of mine interesting (Olsen 2015b) and he asked whether I had any thoughts on developing the argument into a book. I had not planned to do so, but his message tempted me to try. Chapters 1, 5, and 7 were written specifically for this book. The four other chapters to some degree draw on previously published material, and I am thankful for the publishers' permission to reuse this material. Chapter 2 draws on an article entitled "The institutional basis of democratic accountability" that appeared in *West European Politics* (2013, 36 (3): 447–73, <http://www.tandfonline.com/doi/full/10.1080/01402382.2012.753704>). Chapter 3 borrows from the article in *Governance* (2015, 28 (4): 425–40) that motivated Dominic's inspiring message: "Democratic order, autonomy, and accountability." Chapter 4 is adapted from my 2014 chapter "Accountability and ambiguity," printed in *The Oxford Handbook of Public Accountability*. Finally, Chapter 6 is based on "Democratic accountability and the terms of political order," published in the *European Political Science Review* in 2016 (<http://journals.cambridge.org/repo_A10AIFaP8vXONk>).

As usual, there are many people to thank. Papers related to the book have been presented at seminars at Comenius University in Bratislava, Slovakia and at Utrecht University, the Netherlands, and as a keynote speech at the Structure and Organization of Government (SOG) Conference *Accountability and Welfare State Reforms* in Bergen, Norway, 19 February 2015. I have also had the pleasure of presenting some preliminary thoughts related to the book in lectures and seminars at several Norwegian institutions: in Bergen, Bodø, Kristiansand, Oslo, Tromsø, and Volda. I thank the participants at these events for their comments and questions. In addition to Dominic, the godfather of the book, I want to thank Jozef Batora, Mark Bovens, Madalina Busuioc, Morten Egeberg, Jon Erik Fossum, Åse Gornitzka, Karin Lillehei, Per Lægreid, Margo Meyer, Helene Olsen, Olof Petersson, Dawn Preston, Thomas Schillemans, Vaishnavi Venkatesan, Olivia Wells, and several anonymous reviewers. Robert E. Goodin deserves special thanks for being a helpful colleague in several phases of this book process, and I also thank Arena, Centre for

European Studies at the University of Oslo for providing good working conditions for an emeritus.

Since this is the last book I will write, I want to dedicate it to James G. March—a great friend, teacher, colleague, and co-author throughout (nearly) half a century. His footprints are all over this book as well as everything else I have written. And for that I am thankful!

Johan P. Olsen

Oslo
August 2016

Contents

1

Democratic Accountability and the Terms of Political Order

Exploring Democratic Accountability

In contemporary representative democracies accountability is seen as an ideal and an achievement and also as partially constitutive of democratic government. Democratic accountability implies governance based on feedback, learning from experience, and the informed consent of the governed. Citizens are neither the initial authors of laws and budgets nor the designers of the political order under which they live. But they are not powerless. Although most decisions are made by elected representatives, appointed officials, and other power holders, rulers still have an obligation to be appropriately accountable to the ruled. In well-functioning democracies it is difficult for decision makers *not* to respond to calls for accounts without losing legitimacy. Power without accountability is illegitimate, and unaccountable government implies a democratic deficit and an illegitimate political order. Those acting on behalf of the population must describe, explain, and justify their actions and face possible consequences. Power holders are expected to act in anticipation of having to account for their actions (Pitkin 1967), and expecting to be held responsible makes a difference in both behavior and the way behavior is explained and justified (Tetlock 1992, Lerner and Tetlock 1999).

What is involved in demanding, rendering, assessing, and responding to accounts is subject to disagreement, both academically (Bovens et al. 2014) and politically (Verhey et al. 2008). There are different interpretations of (a) what relevant normative standards and effective accountability institutions are; (b) what the appropriate role of rank-and-file citizens is; (c) to what degree citizens are motivated to and capable of holding power holders to account; (d) how accountability regimes affect the democratic legitimacy of a polity; and (e) how regimes and orders emerge and change.

Democratic accountability regimes and processes involve issues ranging from whether a rule has been broken or a budget misused to contestations over the cognitive, normative, and power foundations of political order and the institutions that legitimize an order as the rightful political organization and form of government. Academic efforts to make sense of accountability relations include approaches ranging from bookkeeping and the discipline of accountancy to approaches viewing the development and contestation of accounts as related to fundamental issues in democratic politics and governance.

Some scholars prefer a restricted use of accountability linked to formal systems of accounting, auditing, and scrutiny. For them, the term is limited to specific institutional spheres with predetermined authorized roles and relationships, normative success criteria, and formalized enforcement mechanisms and sanctions. This book, in contrast, presents a wide and dynamic conception of what accountability means and implies under varying and shifting circumstances. In exploring democratic accountability processes—what generates accountability demands and with what consequences—I take an institutional approach that takes seriously the idea that democratic citizens have a right to call their rulers and each other to account at any moment.

A viable political order needs legitimacy and support from its citizens. The essence of morality lies in the right of each citizen to demand an account from others of what they have done and to discuss what are good reasons for accepting behavior and accounts as satisfactory (Goodin 2016). Political actions, institutions, and outcomes require explanation and justification, and accountability demands are linked to what is seen as legitimate in a political culture, that is, what citizens in a specific setting and time period see as an appropriate arrangement of governmental institutions, and what behavior, outcomes, explanations, and justifications are viewed as acceptable. Specifically, democratic legitimacy is based on the voluntary consent of the governed, and in that context legitimacy can also refer to what normative democratic theories define as good arguments for justifying a belief in the rightfulness of a political order, ideas often linked to assumptions regarding what citizens would accept if fully informed.

A distinction is made between effectiveness and legitimacy (Lipset 1963: 22, 64). Effectiveness implies that citizens believe in the authority of an order because of its performance and consequences. Legitimacy refers to a belief in the use of appropriate principles and procedures for preparing, making, implementing, and enforcing decisions. In this book, it is assumed that withdrawal of legitimacy and an increasing number of accountability demands related to the terms of political order will depend on (a) technical–instrumental performance and effectiveness in solving agreed-upon problems and providing important collective services; (b) normative procedural validity, as defined by a community and its ways of doing things, such as free opinion formation and elections, the rule of law, and enlightened decision making; and (c) who gets what, who contributes what, and the distribution of life chances.

A rising number of demands for explanations and justifications indicates the limits of popular acceptance, allegiance, and support. Accountability demands can be triggered when something goes wrong, such as when institutional routines have not worked as expected or there have been deviations from agreed-upon rules, goals, and contracts. Demands can also be triggered by political conflict over what constitutes a rightful political order, generating requests for reassessment and change. Accountability theory needs to address how properties of a political order affect, and are affected by the number and types of accountability demands; what the demands are all about and whether they involve a single rule, act or actor, or the terms of political order; how many and who are activated in accountability processes; the perceived acceptability of accounts; and the responses to accounts.

The goal of this book is to outline elements of an analytical framework for thinking about these interrelations between democratic accountability, political order, and orderly change, including the peaceful succession of power, that is, how democratic accountability processes are affected by an existing political order and how they, in turn, affect that order. Political accounts are seen as both the product of a political order and a force in its creation, maintenance, and change (March and Olsen 1995: 180). I explore the relationships between democratic accountability, as one principle for organizing relations between rulers and the ruled, and political orders founded on varying forms of political association, organization, and agency.

On the one hand, it is assumed that democratic orders are organized, integrated, and institutionalized to different degrees and in different ways, with different consequences for accountability processes. How do the institutional arrangements within which accountability processes take place affect what democratic accountability is all about, what accountability demands are generated, and for whom? What connections are there between how political orders are organized and their ability to foster, sustain, and improve democratic accountability? What specific institutions support effective accountability regimes?

On the other hand, it is assumed that democratic accountability regimes and processes affect the established political order. Are accountability regimes and processes order maintaining or order transforming? How crucial are they for institutional continuity or orderly change? Do accountability processes affect an order's cognitive, normative, and power foundations? Do they foster democratic legitimacy and the ability to learn from experience and adapt to shifting circumstances?

The basic argument is simple. Theorizing relationships between democratic accountability, political order, and orderly change brings political science back to its roots by calling attention to the kinds of activities democratic politics and governing are, the institutional contexts within which they typically take place, and the role of ordinary citizens. Theories of democratic accountability, and in particular theories that aim to capture the role of accountability processes in dynamic and transformative periods, need to relax several key assumptions in the mainstream rational choice, principal–agent accountability literature (Waterman and Meier 1998, Miller 2005, Gailmard 2014). Accountability is a many-faceted phenomenon and to make sense of how accountability processes are affected by and affect the political order, it is necessary to reassess what is to be treated as endogenous and exogenous to democratic politics and governance. The importance of this kind of reassessment is increased due to a rising attention to accountability issues and a perceived democratic deficit. Accountability has become a buzzword and an "obsession." It has been hailed as a democratic panacea, securing learning, improvement, and progress, and a threat to trust relations, effectiveness, and efficiency (Lerner and Tetlock 1999, Borowiak 2011, Dubnick 2011, Pollitt and Hupe 2011, Bovens et al. 2014, Wright 2015).

The main frame of reference for understanding the upsurge in accountability demands is Europe in an era of institutional uncertainty and contestation. The political organization of the European continent is currently in transformation. There are simultaneous processes of political integration and disintegration. There are attempts to build "an ever closer union" as well as resistance to further integration, "Brexit" and possible new exits from the European Union (EU), and separatist movements at the nation-state level. Accountability demands address the terms of political order, territorial borders, identities, agendas, and institutions. They involve reassessments of the role of the sovereign territorial state and of democratic politics in society, how unity and diversity and power relations between institutions shall be balanced, and how orderly change can be legitimately achieved. In contrast, mainstream principal–agent approaches are primarily based upon American and American-inspired studies in an era of fairly stable institutions and interinstitutional relations.

I hold that some central assumptions of mainstream principal–agent approaches, and the formal legal normative democratic assumptions in which they are embedded, are unlikely to capture key aspects of democratic accountability in contemporary Europe and other polities in transformative periods. This is so simply because too many aspects of political order and change, as well as accountability regimes and processes, are taken for granted and treated as exogenous to democratic politics and governance. A wide and dynamic conception of politics, governance, and accountability relations is likely to be more useful, or so I argue.

Political Association, Organization, and Agency

Democratic politics is ideally a way to rule divided societies without undue violence (Crick 1982: 32) and possibly civilize institutions, individuals, and conflicts (Elias 1982 [1939]). Democracies try to combine a quest for order and unity with flexibility and acceptance of freedom of expression and organization, legitimate organized opposition, a strong civil society, and civil disobedience. The doctrine of limited constitutional government holds that it is important to keep some things above or outside politics. The doctrine justifies restricting the use of binding collective decisions and democratic accountability in the defense of individual autonomy. Majority government does not guarantee legitimacy and peaceful coexistence. In polarized societies, majority decisions and winner-takes-all regimes are likely to create polarization and confrontation if there are no institutions protecting minorities and individuals. Democracy may lead to violence if it lacks an institutional framework to control passions, force reflection, balance powers, regulate conflict, and reduce discontent to "bearable dissatisfaction" (Hall 2004: 135, 138).

Democratic politics involves interaction between the mutual dependencies of the whole and some sense of independence of the parts, and one of its challenges is to hold divided societies together without destroying diversity. The private realm needs to be protected from political intervention as does the public realm from the private one. There are limits beyond which a government should not go in maintaining or creating unity. It is, however, difficult to say exactly where to locate those limits, and nothing can forever be exempted entirely from political intervention and influence (Crick 1982: 142, 170). Because integration into a larger order competes with the desire for autonomy among the order's constituent parts, all polities face the question of how much and what forms of integration the components can tolerate, and how much and what forms of diversity the order can tolerate (Olsen 2007: 24). The legitimacy of a political order, and variations in the number and type of accountability demands and their effects, is likely to depend on success in balancing unity and diversity, that is, combining divergent interests, perspectives, histories, cultures, powers, and resources into a reasonable coherent political order while maintaining a sense of individual and local autonomy (March and Olsen 1995: 66). Ongoing European integration and disintegration processes typically illustrate the challenges of organizing unity in diversity.

Integration is a process that turns previously separated units into components of a relatively coherent and consistent order. The term also signifies some measure of the density and intensity of relations among the constitutive elements of an order, for example, the degree of coherence, consistency, and coordination among the parts (March 1999: 134–5). Political orders are organized by different mixes of functional, social, cultural, and organizational–institutional integration. *Functional integration* refers to causal interdependence among the parts and the degree to which decisions and events in one part of a system have an immediate and direct impact on other parts. *Social integration* refers to structural connectedness, a socio-metric measure of linkages such as communication, travel, and trade. *Cultural integration* implies that the causal and normative beliefs of a social group fit together and make sense. There is trust and solidarity and conflicts are equally likely within the component units as between them. *Integration as political organization and institutionalization* refers to codes of appropriate behavior, structures of meaning that explain and justify the behavioral prescriptions, and common resources that create capability and capacity to act in a coordinated way (March and Olsen 1995: 66, March 1999: 134–5, Egeberg 2004, Olsen 2007: 23).

The approach used in this book gives primacy to the possible explanatory power of organizational–institutional factors and how a political order is integrated, rather than to macro-societal processes and individual actors. Yet, it takes into account that both the society to be governed and how individuals are associated and political agency have a role to play.

Political association and the social basis of political order refer to what group of individuals constitutes "the people" and the political community. Democracy is premised on the existence of a polity with members—the Demos—as the constituent power that authorizes representatives and officials to exercise binding power on their behalf and legitimizes their decisions (Weiler 1996: 111). The idea of an undivided and indivisible people, the belief that individuals shall not be subjected to or affected by decision makers beyond their control, and the claim that conflicts shall be resolved through the free formation of public will and authoritative legislative decisions, have high normative standing in democracies. Nevertheless, democracy, as a legitimation principle, does not prescribe precisely the proper territorial borders of a democratically constituted political community and the terms of association. How borders should be drawn, who qualifies as a citizen, who shall decide who is to be included, and how this can be legitimately done in the face of disagreement and competing boundary claims are all contested. One example of such uncertainty is whether demos should be constituted on the basis of territoriality, history, nationality, ethnicity, commitment to specific political principles, or being subjected to or affected by government rule and laws (Goodin 2007, Näsström 2011).

What unifies a group of individuals and what divides it and tears it apart? Are individuals primarily integrated by expediency and mutual advantage? Is there a collective identity, loyalty, solidarity, and trust? Are citizenship and membership in the *polis* the dominant factors for belonging and identity? Are there shared democratic ideals providing a common conception of what constitutes reasonable, just, and desirable forms of political governance and human coexistence? These questions are relevant because "the people" can be a community sharing basic norms and understandings or a collection of groups and individuals divided as friends and enemies by stable disagreements and cleavages, and because it is commonplace to argue that individuals who differ fundamentally in their normative and causal beliefs will find it difficult or impossible to communicate and reason together. They will have a limited ability to act as an organized, coherent collectivity in a way that fosters political order, solidarity, and shared rules for living together (MacIntyre 1988, Frazer 1992). John Stuart Mill even argued that "free institutions are next to impossible in a country made up of different nationalities" (Mill 1962: 309). However, the assumption that democratic government requires a pre-existing demos is challenged by the belief that democratic politics can integrate a multicultural society and create a demos that respects shared political principles (Habermas 1998).

Political organization and the institutional basis of political order refer to formal and informal behavioral codes prescribing appropriate conduct; structures of meaning, explanations, and justifications of behavioral codes; and structures of power and authority, rights, and resources that enable and constrain actors differently and make it more or less possible for them to follow the prescribed codes of conduct.[1] Democracy is a doctrine that regards how polity and society shall be organized and governed and how conflicts shall be dealt with. Normative democratic theory brings hope for citizens' influence based on norms of political self-governance, equality, and freedom. Institutional arrangements create organized action capacities in political life and make it possible to cope with the tensions that come with different forms of political association.

[1] "Institution" refers to a collection of rules and organized practices, embedded in structures of meaning and resources that are relatively invariant in the face of turnover of individuals and changing external circumstances (March and Olsen 1989, 2006). Rules prescribe codes of appropriate behavior for specific roles in specific situations. Structures of meaning explain, justify, and legitimate behavioral rules. Structures of resources create capabilities for acting. Resources are routinely tied to rules, empowering and constraining actors differently and making them more or less capable of acting according to codes of behavior. *Institutionalization* implies: (a) Increasing clarity and agreement about rules. Standardization and formalization of practice reduce uncertainty and conflict concerning who does what, when, and how. As some ways of acting are perceived as natural and legitimate there is less need for using incentives or coercion in order to make people follow prescribed rules; (b) increasing consensus concerning how behavioral rules are to be explained and justified, with a common vocabulary, expectations, and success criteria. There is a decreasing need to explain and justify why modes of action are appropriate; (c) that the supply of resources becomes routinized. It takes less effort to obtain the resources required for acting in accordance with prescribed rules. As a corollary, deinstitutionalization implies that identities, roles, authority, explanations, justifications, and resources become contested. There is increasing uncertainty, disorientation, and conflict. New actors are mobilized. There are demands for new explanations and justifications of existing practices. Outcomes are more uncertain, and it is necessary to use more incentives or coercion to make people follow prescribed rules.

Modern democracies are, however, composite political orders with built-in enduring institutionalized tensions (Olsen 2010, 2014a). A demos, as a group of people who claim the right to self-governance based on political equality among citizens, may be more or less in agreement regarding how they want to be organized and governed politically and what kind of society is desirable. Political orders impose exclusions, distribute burdens and sacrifices asymmetrically, and create losers, hurting those who do not "fit in" (Connolly 1987: 138). No order is unanimously accepted and supported. Differences and conflicts, rather than perfect harmony and consensus, are normal and legitimate. Democratic polities, like most formal organizations, most of the time exist and thrive with considerable tensions and quasi-resolution of conflict. Except at the level of non-operational goals, there is no internal consensus (Cyert and March 1963). It easier to get support for principles such as democracy, rule of law, and human rights than agreement about what the principles should mean and imply in specific contexts.

Democratic polities are communities of collective decision making. They are also communities of reasoned debate and argumentation, education, and socialization with a potential for internalization of expectations, explanations, justifications, criteria of good arguments, and principles of legitimate persuasion (March and Olsen 1995). Accountability processes involve the search for meaning and truth, as well as decision making, and a challenge for democracies is to develop deserved respect for political order, public authority, and consensually valid norms of duty (Weber 1978: 31), that is, to develop and maintain citizens' and rulers' allegiance to the foundational principles of democratic self-governance and to inculcate ethical standards of equality, freedom, representation, modes of appropriate conduct, and accountability.

Institutions impact accountability processes through opportunity and incentive structures, by influencing identities, normative standards, and causal beliefs, and by providing resources and action capabilities. Different institutions are, however, carriers of competing identities, behavioral logics, beliefs, and capabilities. They themselves represent a possible source of tension as accounts are trying to fit into competing frameworks of normative and cognitive beliefs and power structures. Institutions may be carriers of a history of peaceful problem solving and compromises, or violent confrontations and coercion. They may be more or less legitimate and trusted, generating few or many accountability demands. They may be founded on a logic of consequentiality, expediency, and calculated advantage, relating accountability demands and assessments to performance and results, or on a rule-bound logic of appropriateness, collective identity, and felt belonging to a community that makes actors rise above the pursuit of economic/material self-interest and advantage. In the latter case, institutions are the expression of a moral and cognitive community. Accountability demands are made and accounts are assessed on the basis of a shared cultural heritage that prescribes how one shall conduct one's life and specific roles in ways that are characteristic of, and consistent with, dominant normative beliefs and understandings of that culture (March and Olsen 1995).

Political agency and the behavioral basis of political order refer to how a political order operates in practice—the actual use of institutionalized access opportunities, what is attached to and detached from politics, and what is made an object of political dialogue and compromise or confrontation and domination. Formal legal institutions have limited democratic value if citizens are not motivated to use and capable of effectively using available access opportunities. Citizenship refers not only to a legal status providing rights and a civic identity and belonging, but also to political agency, participation, and influence.

An institutional approach holds that institutions create order, but an imperfect and temporary order. They affect, but do not determine, action (March and Olsen 1989). In democracies, political accounts and responses to accounts are often constructed in encounters among contending accounts (March and Olsen 1995: 175). In other words, accounts and responses to accounts are negotiated and politically constructed. Actors, issues, and relevant resources may or may not be activated. Nevertheless, in polities emphasizing human will, understanding, and control, accountability norms seem to require an "adequately blameworthy agent" (Shklar 1990: 62); this is also the case when there are multiple actors, ambiguous cognitive uncertainty, normative standards, limited control, and vague compromises, rather than clear-cut chains of authorization and accountability.

A focus on the relations between democratic accountability and orderly change draws attention to the role of political agency and deliberate choice in processes of institutional development. A core democratic norm is that the terms of political order must ultimately be decided by and addressed to the individuals who are to be governed by them. The democratic hope is that citizens and their representatives shall be able to design and reform institutions at will, making governing through organizing and reorganizing an important aspect of political agency (Olsen 2010). A standard assumption is that structural choice, like all political processes, involves competing interests and power struggles (Moe 1990). Winning elections provides control of public authority. Winners are in a position to design and impose whatever structures they like and the losers have to accept what the winners impose, even if it makes them worse off (Moe 1991: 123, 124, Moe and Caldwell 1994: 173).

The role of institutional design and the conditions under which political actors can get beyond existing arrangements have, however, been questioned (March and Olsen 1983, 2006, Olsen 2010). Political and social developments are only partly under political control and an institutional approach does not see history as "efficient." Adaptation to reform efforts and to changes in functional or normative environments is neither precise, nor rapid, nor cost-free. Equilibrium cannot be guaranteed among co-evolving institutions. Institutions are likely to defend their identity and resist changes that threaten their foundational normative and organizational principles (March and Olsen 1989). Human actors learn from experience, but experience is often a poor teacher. Actors are easily confused and led astray by their interpretations of history (March and Olsen 1975, March 2010).

Rather than a founding moment, when a polity and its accountability regime are constituted through deliberate decisions by "we the people" (Ackerman 1993), there may be historical drift and path dependency. While an exceptional, unprecedented crisis situation may facilitate radical change and create a new beginning, normally institutions "are not created all at once, in accordance with a single ordering principle; they are created instead at different times, in the light of different experiences, and often for quite contrary purposes" (Orren and Skowronek 2004: 112). History evolves by simultaneous processes of fragmentation and fusion of polities rather than through a progressive movement toward any particular type of polity. Thus, history does not inevitably produce larger and more inclusive or multifunctional polities. Large entities often contain the seed of their own dissolution. There is a propensity for polities to become too large to remain efficient and viable, especially as internal conflicts grow and old identities resurface. Bloated entities fracture into micro-polities that are too small to be economically, culturally, politically, or militarily viable. At any given moment, there exist numerous actual and potential political forms that attract and sometimes compete for human loyalties (Ferguson and Mansbach 1996: 52–4).

One implication for accountability theory is the need to go beyond the assumption that political orders and accountability regimes emerge, are maintained, and change as a result of the structural choices of predetermined principals. *If*, for example, political democracy is seen to have emerged as a kind of net consequence of a vast multitude of responsive adjustments to a vast number of particular situations, and attributing the result to a single force or principle amounts to mythologizing (Dewey 1927: 84), it may be fruitful to study in some detail how processes of institutionalization and deinstitutionalization, integration and disintegration, are related to accountability processes. Accountability theorists have to address how democratic accountability is defined and attributed in varying institutional settings, as well as through what processes agents are made responsible and called to account and under what conditions accountability processes are likely to foster orderly change.

This book certainly does not aim to provide definitive answers to the questions of how political orders affect accountability processes and how accountability processes affect established orders. While I have no intention of reviewing the substantial literature (Bovens et al. 2014), I will challenge some key assumptions of mainstream rational choice, principal–agent approaches and suggest alternative assumptions that treat more aspects of accountability processes as endogenous to democratic politics and governance. The competing assumptions are seen as supplementary, rather than as exclusive alternatives. The spirit is to take some modest steps towards understanding areas of application for competing approaches and their different assumptions: To discuss how helpful the different assumptions are for understanding the relationships between accountability and the terms of political order, and to invite debate and empirical studies of the organizational–institutional basis of accountability.

I address six themes that shed some light on why it may be fruitful to move beyond key assumptions of mainstream principal–agent approaches:

- Political order: How accountability processes may take place in more or less settled political orders and in orders integrated in different ways.
- Continuity and change: How accountability processes may be order maintaining or order transforming, and how change may be more or less orderly as a result of deliberate design and reform.
- Political agency and ambiguity: Democratic accountability requires agents with discretion as well as criteria of non-authorized behavior and unacceptable explanations and justifications. Yet, political life is often characterized by ambiguity, uncertainty, and limited control. It can be problematic to identify who is responsible for what has happened and attribute accountability objectively; improvement through rational adaptation can be difficult to achieve; and accountability processes can provide an occasion for accountability politics, blame games, and image management.
- Political talk and political action: Effective democratic accountability requires that actors speak the truth and that there be consistency between what is said and done. Separation of and inconsistency between talk and action is, however, common in political life, and some polities, more than others, are perceived as legitimate and thus avoid accountability demands related to the terms of order, in spite of a disconnect between rhetoric and practice.
- Political attention and participation: Accountability processes sometimes attract many participants and issues. At other times they take place without much public attention. Whereas it is often assumed that the relevant actors are constantly active, the degree of attention and participation may change over the process studied.
- Lessons to be learnt: An institutional approach, based upon the assumptions above, suggests two things that can be learnt from accountability

processes. The first is related to how accountability, political order, and orderly change are interconnected. The second is related to what accountability in an era of transformation can tell us about political life, organization, and governance in general.

Beyond Mainstream Assumptions

Political Order

Mainstream principal–agent approaches usually assume a settled political order, with predetermined agents and principals/forums/constituencies. There is fairly broad agreement regarding what roles, rights, and duties different institutions and actors are supposed to have in a political order. Some make the rules; others apply them. There are imposed or contractual agreements regarding who is accountable to whom, for what, under what circumstances, and according to what criteria of authorized behavior and desirable results. There is also agreement regarding legitimate mechanisms for enforcing accountability, sanctioning agents, and promoting effective accountability, for instance, electoral control of representatives by voters and political and legal control over "the bureaucracy." Analyses often build on idealized formal legal normative conceptions of the institutions and actors of representative democracy—the legislature, the executive, the judiciary, and the elected representative, the bureaucrat, the judge, and the citizen.

An institutional approach challenges mainstream assumptions and official presentations of accountability mechanisms in representative democracies. There is a need to study empirically how institutional arrangements assumed to secure democratic accountability differ and how they work in practice. It is likely to be fruitful to see polities as more or less settled, institutionalized, and integrated. A political order may be well established, emerging, or on the edge of disintegration. The institutions organizing common affairs may be more or less legitimate and trusted, with varying capacities for organized action, problem solving, and conflict resolution. Authorization and accountability relations, identities, and roles, and normative standards for assessing behavior and results, may be more or less specified and agreed upon.

There is then a need to theorize accountability relations and processes in unsettled polities with weak or contested institutions, as well as in settled polities with well-entrenched institutions and an agreed-upon, stable institutional arrangement prescribing how authority and power are to be legitimately allocated, exercised, controlled, and made accountable. It is also reasonable to take into account that the societies to be governed involve different mixes of unity/diversity, trust/mistrust, confidence/fear, historical experiences, cleavage patterns, and coalitions. Individuals associate and dissociate in a variety of ways, and demands for and effects of accountability processes are likely to be affected by what unites and divides a population. It is, furthermore, reasonable to differentiate between normal times and exceptional times. There are times when accountability processes take place within the framework of institutions and regimes that are taken for granted, as well as times when established arrangements are challenged and a variety of participants and issues are mobilized.

Continuity and Change

Mainstream principal–agent approaches usually assume that accountability processes are instruments for controlling and disciplining agents in order to secure compliance. Their focus is on detecting and correcting deviance from authoritative commands and agreements and sanctioning unruly agents and agents who do not deliver acceptable explanations and justifications. Accountability processes are part of policing, sustaining, or strengthening a political order with well-defined rules, roles, and power relations, or implementing orderly change consistent with the preferences of principals.

Democracies, however, need to foster both continuity and change (Olsen 2009a) and accountability processes can be order transforming as well as order maintaining (Eisenstadt 1995: 306). Accountability processes can challenge an existing order or help establish order where none exists. They can contribute to a shifting balance between institutions and roles constituted according to different purposes and normative and organizational principles. They can challenge established facts, causal models, success criteria, and power relations, rather than take them for granted. Such processes may or may not be consistent with the will of established principals and the order's rules of change. There are periods of continuity and orderly change when rulers are called to account through peaceful institutional contestation, for example, competitive free elections. There can also be periods with coups d'états or riots and violence in the streets, causing breakdowns in institutions and identities, in solidarities and cleavages, organized action capabilities and coalitions, and in learning and adaptation capacities.

Under some conditions experience leads to learning, improved understanding, and adaption to new circumstances. Facts and causality are beyond doubt, as are agreed-upon normative criteria defining appropriate behavior and outcomes. It is obvious where responsibility and accountability are located. Identifiable actors have clear authorization and mandates and they have adequate resources to fulfill the prescriptions of an identity or role. Unacceptable behavior is a result of incompetence, an accident, misuse of power, or a criminal act. Malpractice can be prevented.

At other times, facts and causality are not that clear and there are ambiguous or contested success criteria. New and unknown situations challenge a community's self-understanding and established accounts. Rather than a shared analysis of experience, there are different interpretations with competing assessments and narratives. Specific policies, actors, positions, or institutions may be contested. There may be disagreement about whether powers and public money have been used inappropriately, and what legitimate and orderly change is. There may also be struggle over, and major shifts in, the vocabulary of politics and government (Ball et al. 1989, Richter 1995). It is commonplace to observe that power and status relations between professions, political parties, and institutions of government affect which narratives win the day.

One implication for accountability theory is the need to understand the processes through which knowledge comes to be politically established as reality and norms accepted as valid (Berger and Luckmann 1967: 3). A political tradition dating back to Aristotle claims that public debate, contestations, and political judgment improve learning and understanding. A competing tradition argues that learning from experience and improvement requires a technical–scientific process and the absence of politics. "The learning effort must be de-politicized. It is impossible to draw the correct lessons in an environment beset by impression management, blame avoidance, protection of the status quo, and potentially politically motivated advocacy of change" (Boin and 't Hart 2016: 15).

For accountability theory it becomes vital to clarify what political struggles over accounts are all about and the conditions under which accountability processes are order maintaining or order transforming. It is also important to take into account that dividing lines are not necessarily between predetermined principals, who control opportunity structures and incentives, and agents, who have superior information and expertise. One challenge is to observe actual dividing lines, how cleavages and coalitions change, and the possible room for political agency and leadership, discretion, and creativity.

Political Agency and Ambiguity

Mainstream approaches, as well as the normative theories of representative democracy in which they are embedded, assume that accountability requires identifiable, blameworthy actors who possess discretion and choice. The search for a responsible agent is founded on a belief in political agency and history determined by deliberate choice. Democratic ideals prescribe informed citizens and officials and celebrate human will, understanding, and control. Action is assumed to build on reason and experience. Progress is seen to be achieved through the moral and cognitive lessons of history, and not through political or religious dogmas. In principal–agent approaches, the core element of accountability processes is decision making where rational actors demand, render, assess, and sanction accounts based on calculation of expected advantage. There are authorized and non-authorized alternatives. Actors are obliged to explain and justify what they have done and not done, and there are clear ideas about what are acceptable explanations and justifications.

Theories of accountability are, however, likely to benefit from taking into account that the nature of collective decision making varies. There are alternatives to assuming rational strategic actors with predetermined preferences and resources, engaged in non-cooperative games, and calculating individual utility. Human actors are boundedly rational, and rational theories prescribing how intelligent people should choose and act among available alternatives under ideal circumstances do not necessarily coincide with how presumably intelligent people actually choose and act under real circumstances (March 2015). Processes of decision making, deliberation, reason giving, sense making, and learning are imperfect. Political aspirations vary, and so do policy styles. Political actors may emphasize what unites or divides a population. Decision making may involve different behavioral logics (March and Olsen 1998), and sometimes political actors act under conditions of factual and causal uncertainty, normative ambiguity, and limited control (Cohen et al. 1972, Lomi and Harrison 2012). It is, for example, not unusual to see authorization and accountability processes based upon vague compromises create unclear mandates for action, success criteria, and power relations, rather than processes formulating a clear-cut public will, authoritative decisions, and binding mandates. Decisions just seem "to happen" (March 1994). Outcomes occur as chance results of the concurrence of events and an ecology of loosely coupled processes outside the control of any identifiable decision makers (Cohen et al. 1972).

Such conditions make it difficult to objectively attribute accountability, but they create the conditions for blame games and image management. Responsibility is also attributed and rewards and punishments are allocated when it is problematic to agree upon who made decisions and caused events to happen. It may be easier to make sense of the enduring belief in, and pursuit of, accountability in the face of the problems of establishing causality and attributing credit and blame if we take into account that more things are going on in accountability processes than establishing facts and causality, making authoritative decisions, and responding to unacceptable explanations and justifications from agents.

Vague and slippery concepts, uncertain events, and long-term consequences foster contestation and the politics of accountability. Ambiguity and uncertainty provide opportunities for using accountability demands and responses as a rhetorical device in partisan battles (Hood 2014), and agents do not necessarily want to avoid accountability. Accounts are also given when they are not called for. Rather than being compelled to render accounts, agents volunteer accounts as a means of managing their image. Accountability processes provide opportunities for justifying oneself and cultivating one's reputation and legitimacy, as well as to search for scapegoats. Giving accounts voluntarily may be part of an effort to create legitimacy in the eyes of a variety of forums or stakeholders that can affect an agent's performance and success. Accounts may be motivated by (a) internalized democratic values and a civic ethos; (b) socio-cultural norms embedded in specific institutions, professions, identities, or communities; (c) a desire for feedback, learning, and improvement; (d) a search for recognition; and (e) political–strategic reasons such as convincing an audience, reducing opposition, structuring attention and accountability relations, and increasing one's room for maneuver (Karsten 2015).

For accountability theory it may be worthwhile to assume that accountability processes, under some conditions, can be understood as ceremony and ritual. They provide occasions for storytelling that celebrate myths and self-understanding—socially integrating myths that generate pride of belonging, or divisive myths that foster hatred and confrontation. Indeed, some people primarily associate "politics" with myth making, propaganda, and deception. Cynics argue that all power corrupts and that politics is the art of deceiving people. Yet, accountability processes provide an occasion for exercising values, non-operational goals, emotions, worldviews, and symbols—for expressive behavior and possibly catharsis. Reputations are defended and attacked. Actors may search for and test virtue, collective purpose, and understandings and question what are appropriate authority and power relations. They may distribute glory or blame for what has happened and exercise, challenge, or reaffirm friendship or trust relationships, antagonisms, power, or status relationships (March and Olsen 1976: 11, 1995). Sense making may be as important as decision making. Accountability processes are influenced by what agents have done and the kinds of accounts they render. It is also influenced by the interpretations, motivations, and capabilities of those demanding and assessing accounts and by the relationship between democratic rhetoric and practice.

Political Talk and Political Action

Accountability is a democratic virtue (Bovens 2010) and democratic norms prescribe that elected representatives and public officials have a duty to give truthful accounts to the public. Informed citizens and policymaking require transparency, reliable information, and consistency between behavior and how behavior is explained and justified. Arguing, decision making, and outcomes are assumed to be tightly intertwined. Deliberative democratic theories hold that a legitimate political order requires that actors speak the truth. They give one another mutually acceptable reasons, explanations, and justifications, and what is said is consistent with what is done. In rational choice, principal–agent approaches portray accountability as a matter of control and compliance. Information and expertise are strategic resources and a source of power for agents. One problem facing principals is that agents cannot be trusted to act in the best interest of principals (Strøm 2000, Strøm et al. 2003, Gailmard 2014). Political talk and political action may be separated, and achieving consistency between what is said and what is done is a question of getting incentives right.

Accountability processes provide a possible link between democratic rhetoric and practice. But the link is not always strong. A challenge for accountability theory is that narratives explaining and justifying the terms of political order do not necessarily coincide with how an order operates and changes in practice. Political systems create myths about themselves in attempts to cultivate a belief in their legitimacy and to secure obedience (Weber 1978: 213). Democracies, like all other systems, live on a body of dogma, self-justification, and self-glorification (Schattschneider 1960: 99). There are narratives celebrating popular self-governance and majority rule, but also non-majoritarian institutions. An example is courts and the "enormous intellectual energies and resources poured into the official myth that judges only carry out law and never make it, a lie so powerful and yet so unbelievable" (Shapiro 2008: 772).

An institutional approach to democratic accountability explores the possible separation of rhetoric and practice. The world of talk—ideologies, theories, principles, visions, and ideas about what is true and morally right—may be more or less loosely connected to the world of action—how a polity actually operates, its capabilities and capacities, routines, and standard operating procedures (Meyer and Rowan 1977, March 1984, Brunsson 1989). Public officials are often asked to take action when the demands placed on them are beyond the capabilities of their office (March and Olsen 1995: 134, Fukuyama 2014), and separation of talk and action may, under some conditions, contribute to legitimacy and support. For example, political deliberation, decision making, and acting may be separated when there are discrepancies between, on the one hand, what forms of organization fit technical–functional requirements and produce the best substantive results and, on the other hand, what forms fit normative environments and cultural prescriptions of appropriate organization and governance (Meyer and Rowan 1977, Brunsson 1989, 2007).

Talk provides meaning, signals intention, and expresses hope, ambition, and fear. Because it is important to be *seen* as doing well, narratives are inspired by what is normatively praiseworthy in a political culture (or in an academic theory or professional ideology), and in contemporary democracies discourse is usually based on concepts of purposeful action and ideals such as rationality, control, coherence, accountability, trustworthiness, and progress. Such ideals are, however, sometimes unrealistic and impossible to realize. Simple and ambiguous ideas may mobilize support, but they may not be feasible in practice or offer precise guidance for action (Cyert and March 1963: 43, 117). They have little effect upon what is done, how it is done, and what is achieved. Issues are deliberated and decisions are made, but with limited results. There is also action without much preceding deliberation or formal decision making. Institutional routines reflect what is doable in a practical situation more than what is desirable in the best of all worlds. Action is driven by routines and standard operating procedures or by unexpected events and the pressure of the moment—by what seems to be possible and efficient under existing circumstances.

Possibly, the separation of talk and action can be seen as a way representative democracies try to cope with cultural demands for a responsible actor in a dynamic, interdependent, and complex world where it is often difficult to identify objectively who is responsible for what. One of the puzzles for accountability theory is why some polities more than others thrive over extended periods with a separation of political talk and political action—between, on the one hand, official narratives that explain and justify the terms of political order and, on the other hand, how governmental institutions are actually organized, work, and change in practice. Why is it that some polities in which rhetoric and practice are separated and inconsistent are perceived as legitimate by citizens and largely avoid accountability demands related to the normative, cognitive, and power bases of order while others face accountability demands, including demands for a reduction of talk/action gaps and the democratic deficit they are seen to produce? Generally, why does the political significance of and public attention paid to accountability processes vary and change?

Political Attention and Involvement

Most principal–agent approaches and the normative democratic theories in which they are embedded view or prescribe accountability processes as a mechanism for citizens to have influence, either directly or through elected representatives. Standard accounts assume that a settled parliamentary order or a checks-and-balances order determines who is considered legitimate principals and agents, how they are related, and when they are supposed to be activated. Usually, principal–agent approaches also assume that the relevant actors are mobilized throughout the accountability processes they are studying. One complication of this approach is that formal legal institutions are sometimes empty shells or window dressing. They do not guarantee popular attention, participation, or control; nor do they guarantee democratic accountability and legitimacy.

Consequently, students of democratic accountability need to relate accountability processes to the *actual* role of democratic politics, citizens, and elected representatives, and not solely to formal legal norms regulating the distribution of power and responsibility. There is a need for a conception of democracy and democratic accountability that recognizes the limitations of the public and its powers (Schattschneider 1960: 140–1), that is, a conception that takes into account that time and energy are scarce resources and that attention to accountability processes competes with other things these resources can be used for. It cannot be taken for granted that all relevant actors are active, or that attention and participation are constant over the accountability processes studied (Cohen et al. 1972). Neither can accountability be limited to holding to account those who formally act on behalf of the public. It is necessary to include all powerful actors affecting the democratic quality of the polity and society.

It is important for accountability theory to explain the varying significance of, and attention to, accountability processes. Why do accountability processes sometimes attract public attention and generate mass mobilization and at other times escape public notice? Why does the degree of attention and mobilization change over the course of a given process? It may be worthwhile to ask whether citizens have the motivation and capability to use institutionalized opportunities for action and how actors including political leaders, public administration, accountants, auditors, ombudsmen, the police, courts, and mass media interact in accountability processes. Part of the answer is related to the nature of accountability processes, what effects they have, and what lessons they teach us.

Possible Lessons

Mainstream principal–agent approaches assume that the effects and effectiveness of accountability regimes are measured by the degree to which they make agents act in accordance with the interests and desires of the principal. An alternative is to assume that the most important outcome of accountability processes under some conditions is their effects upon an order's cognitive, normative, and power foundations, including who shall be accepted as legitimate principals and agents.

At transformative moments of history, institutionalized ways of constructing accounts—the basic conceptions, categories, and presumptions on which they are based—are no longer helpful in making sense of experience and they may break down (March and Olsen 1995: 185). The same may be the case for codes of appropriate behavior, cleavages, power relations, and coalitions. Accountability processes may involve contestations over who should belong to "the people" as full citizens, how political borders should be drawn, what migration flows are acceptable, and what are legitimate accession criteria for membership. There may be struggles over (a) collective identities and loyalties; (b) how authority, power, responsibility, and accountability should be organized; (c) what power democratic institutions and actors should have; (d) how tensions between majority rule and minority protection should be balanced; and (e) the role of ordinary citizens when it comes to authorizing power holders and holding them to account.

Democracy is currently the key normative, ethical standard used to assess the legitimacy of political orders and forms of governance. However, democratic development is an open process. Democratic politics can settle the unsettled and unsettle the settled—they can create order and challenge order (Connolly 1987: 15, 141). Historically there have been debates and struggles over the content of "democracy" and what priority democratic concerns (such as equality, freedom, transparency, participation, and representation) should have in different institutional contexts compared to, for example, security, prosperity, maintaining order, and community. The content and the relative importance of normative/ethical and organizational principles have been reinterpreted over time. Current accountability processes can turn out to be part of an historical struggle between order and reform (Mill 1956: 57–8), and represent a possible transition to a new and yet unrealized or unrecognized political order (Bendix 1968: 9).

When theorizing the effects of democratic accountability processes on political order and orderly change, it is likely to be more useful to start out with a dynamic concept of democracy than to assume that the term implies a static set of normative and organizational principles prescribing clear institutional arrangements, predetermined principals and agents, forms of governance, success criteria, and codes of appropriate behavior. Democracy means different things to different actors and its meaning changes over time. It is not obvious how the term will be defined and what importance it is likely to have in accountability processes in different institutional contexts and over time. There is no guarantee that democratic concerns will always trump other concerns. Far from being a universal conception, democracy is contextual and embedded in time, space, and specific institutional settings. Possible lessons from studies of accountability processes are not limited to insight into the interaction between predetermined principals and agents, control and compliance. There are also lessons to be learnt about political organization and governance and the varying and shifting meanings of terms such as accountability, democracy, politics, the sovereign state, and constitutional choice.

Accountability as Order-Maintaining Routines and Order-Transforming Politics

Together, these competing assumptions suggest that understanding how democratic accountability processes are influenced by the political order within which they take place, and how they, in turn, influence that order, requires a menu of assumptions and ideas about what is actually going on in accountability processes. The long list of competing assumptions indicates a large number of possible combinations and patterns. There are many questions, and few answers, and accountability theorists have a long way to go, in particular when it comes to understanding democratic accountability in dynamic, compound polities with complex combinations of political association, organization, and agency. From an institutional perspective, two (stylized) patterns can be outlined: Accountability as order-maintaining routines and accountability as order-transforming politics.

Order-Maintaining Routines

In settled and legitimate political orders, accountability processes are highly institutionalized and routinized and are, for example, related to elections, annual reports, auditing, inspections, and routine scrutiny and hearings. Accountability regimes are based on shared norms and understandings, such as the ideals of democracy, the rule of law, an ethos of public service, and professional norms, or upon strong incentives for following rules and routines. Citizens trust institutions and agents to do what they are supposed to do. Priority is given to securing impartiality, competence, and integrity in public affairs (Holmberg and Rothstein 2012). Public attention is modest and ordinary citizens are unlikely to be mobilized in large numbers.

Calls for explanations and justifications, and responses to such calls, are taken care of by specialized personnel in specialized institutional contexts. They are founded on correct assumptions about where authority, power, responsibility, and accountability are located. Identifiable actors can legitimately be called to account because they have chosen an action and caused an event. There are adequate resources for monitoring, analyzing, and responding to the behavior and non-behavior of agents. It is also fairly easy to anticipate what will be accepted as appropriate behavior, outcomes, and accounts, a fact likely to reduce the likelihood of major deviance from authorized behavior and conventions and to reduce the need to call decision makers to account and correct unacceptable behavior.

Accountability processes are primarily order-maintaining instruments of management control. Focus is on oversight, scrutiny, monitoring, and evaluating performance in order to increase efficiency and eliminate waste, fraud, and the abuse of power. Non-routine calls for accountability are triggered when something is seen to have gone wrong: When there are breaches of the existing order, when expectations, goals, rules, and standards are not met, or when behavior is seen to be dysfunctional, unethical, or illegal. Discontent and accountability demands are likely to be related to a single event, decision, actor, or institution, rather than to the foundations of the political order as a whole.

Integration in terms of interdependence and contact has the potential to create a perceived need for coordination, collective decision making, and shared rules. Cultural integration and a community based on a shared collective identity and agreed-upon norms for living together are likely to facilitate shared institutions and an extended political agenda. These are conditions that often will activate accountability demands. However, the more homogeneity and consensus in terms of shared norms and understandings there is in a population, the more likely that accountability processes will be of an order-maintaining nature. Trust gives decision makers a relatively wide margin of discretion, and the more citizens trust governmental institutions and their fellow citizens, the less likely there is to be mass mobilization in accountability processes.

Polities can provide few or many institutionalized opportunities for citizens to challenge rulers and demand explanations and justification for their behavior. Organizational mechanisms such as sequential attention to goals, decentralization and local rationality, and conflict resolution, as well as slack resources, buffer inconsistencies and tend to reduce the perceived need for coordination (Cyert and March 1963). As a result, the likelihood of accountability demands with order-transforming implications is reduced. Accountability demands directly related to the terms of the political order are also less likely in polities where institutions provide opportunities for airing discontent and resolving conflicts through compromises. Examples are well-working institutions with authorization of rulers, citizen representation and participation, transparency, and legitimate criticism and opposition. Fairly stable institutional settings make it possible to learn from experience and adapt to shifting circumstances through deliberate design and reform, in accordance with institutionalized rules for orderly change. And the more capable political institutions are when it comes to learning from experience and solving problems sequentially through incremental reforms rather than allowing historical cleavages to accumulate (Lipset 1963: 71, 79), the less likely it is that accountability processes will involve mass mobilization and demands for radical change in the established order.

When there is agreement on normative success criteria and power relations, accountability processes are dominated by *analysis*—clarifying facts and causality and re-establishing control and order. When there is disagreement about cognition and what normative yardsticks shall be used, but acceptance of power relations, accountability processes tend to be dominated by *bargaining* among predefined actors. The politics of accountability—debates, contestations, and conflict resolution over what behavior and results are authorized and desirable, or how orders, rules, and roles are to be interpreted in a specific case—takes place within a settled institutional order and there is orderly change.

Politics of Accountability and Shifting Terms of Order

In less settled and less legitimate polities where facts, causal understandings, normative standards, and power relations are complex, diffuse, fluid, and contested, accountability processes make room for the politics *of* political order and not only for politics *within* an existing order. It is difficult to attribute responsibility objectively and say who can legitimately be held democratically accountable. At the same time, ambiguity and uncertainty foster blame games and image management. Behavior and outcomes may be interpreted as necessary and unavoidable, as desirable, as regrettable mistakes, or as the result of incompetence or of inadequate resources, in instances where the agents have done everything they could possibly do. Whereas some observers argue that there is an accountability deficit, others perceive an accountability overload reducing trust, risk taking, innovation, and improvement. Accountability demands are frequent, and accountability processes are likely to involve mass mobilization and contestation of the legitimacy of the political order. There may be calls for comprehensive institutional reform, reduced information asymmetries, new success criteria, and redistribution of resources and capabilities, with order modification or replacement as a possible result.

This pattern is most likely to be observed in polities combining, on the one hand, strong interdependencies and high frequency of contacts with, on the other hand, weak cultural integration and limited trust in governmental institutions and their ability to solve problems. The pattern tends to materialize in periods of exceptional conditions, disorder, unpredictable government, and arbitrary use of powers. It is fostered by major scandals, performance crises, and human suffering, and especially in situations with clear-cut reality checks: That is, when there is broad agreement that the established political order is dysfunctional and does not work in an acceptable way or when there is a general performance crisis and traditional explanations and justifications do not make sense, but there are competing accounts and no agreement regarding what causes the problems and what should be done.

In such cases, trust in the order is reduced or withdrawn. The margin of discretion for decision makers becomes narrower. The chances of popular mobilization and demands for changes in the normative and organizational principles of the order increase. Gaps between accountability and practice are less likely to be accepted. Political orders legitimated solely by expediency, a logic of consequentiality, calculation of advantage, and continuous performance are most vulnerable. Orders based on a shared collective identity and loyalty to a political community and its institutions, a variety of historically developed ties, and a logic of appropriateness are likely to be more path-dependent, robust, and capable of sustaining a variety of enduring tensions.

The more power is centralized and the more discretion and capabilities an institution or actor has, the more important it is to hold them to account. The probability of accountability demands, public attention, mass participation, and effects upon the political order increases when power is centralized. Such developments are also more likely when political leaders emphasize what splits a population rather than what ties it together, and when they use confrontation and a winner-takes-all style, rather than giving priority to dialogue and searching for integrating narratives and compromises. This is especially likely to be the case where there are permanent minorities. Disagreement about the terms of political order and threats to well-established identities, mindsets, interests, and power and trust relations may either reflect a changing power balance or contribute to such a shift. There may be struggles over what constitutes good government and acceptable terms of political order. The politics of accountability may transform accountability regimes as well as the political order and the rules for living together.

Demands for reform of a political order are, however, not always successful. Accountability processes related to the terms of political order are resource-demanding activities and citizens may not have the resources necessary for demanding, assessing, and sanctioning accounts. Ambiguity, uncertainty, and political contestation make learning from experience problematic. Citizens may lack relevant information or be overwhelmed by information, often of a technical character. Massive power inequalities are likely to reduce the number of accountability demands and their effects upon the existing order and its cognitive, normative, and power foundations. Critical accounts may be ignored and nobody is made accountable because powerful actors successfully protect themselves and their institution, profession, or the political order at large from criticism. Power asymmetries and attempts to protect an existing regime may lead to operators being made accountable while people higher up in the hierarchy—those in charge of recruitment and training and top leaders responsible for systems—avoid responsibility, blame, and sanctions. The space for democratic institutional design and reform is thus reduced.

What Will Follow

These are preliminary speculations that will be explored further in the following chapters. Particular attention will be paid to the politics of accountability and the shifting terms of order. The six themes outlined above are interrelated and most of them are dealt with in more than one chapter. Some overlapping is unavoidable. Still, each chapter focuses on one of the themes and provides a basis for the following chapters.

The next two chapters further develop an institutional perspective on democratic accountability. In Chapter 2 the main focus is on the organizational–institutional basis of accountability and how an established order affects accountability processes, with reference to both settled and unsettled polities and polities integrated in different ways. Chapter 3 expands the perspective by attending to how an established order (at T1) affects accountability processes, which in turn affect the terms of political order (at T2). Different political orders and accountability regimes are seen to make different forms of popular participation possible, making it more or less likely that accountability processes become order-maintaining and order-transforming processes.

Chapter 4 addresses the assumption that there is a strong link between accountability and decision making. In mainstream principal–agent theory, as well as in much democratic theory and organization theory, accountability is linked to a belief in human agency and history determined by human will, causal understanding, and control. An institutional approach gives rational choice and rational adaptation a less heroic role by taking into account that ambiguity, uncertainty, and limited control are inherent to political life. The fluidity and unresolved conflicts of political life make it difficult to correctly assign causal responsibility and learn from experience. Accountability theory therefore has to take into account that ambiguity is intrinsic to political life and that there is more to accountability processes than decision making, control, and compliance.

Chapter 5 explores factors that contribute to making it possible for a polity to thrive despite a separation between official narratives and organized practice and still avoid accountability demands challenging the legitimacy of the political order. This is done using Norway as an example of a fairly settled and legitimate polity integrated by several different ties and the EU as an example of an emerging order and an unsettled polity with problematic legitimacy and still in search of a unifying narrative.

Chapter 6 analyzes the varying public attention to accountability processes and the actual use of institutionalized opportunities for participation—why accountability processes sometimes attract considerable attention, whereas at other times they do not. Increased demands for accountability are likely to reflect discontent with the established order or its development, and I interpret the recent obsession with accountability as part of a struggle over the terms of political order and the rules for living together. The chapter attends to the explanatory power of *political association* involving different mixes of unity/diversity, trust/mistrust, and historical experiences; *political organization* and the ordering routines, ideas, and resources of institutions; and *political agency* and the motivation and action capabilities of individual citizens.

The final chapter addresses some possible lessons from studies of accountability processes in the context of the European continent in an era of discontent and reduced trust in representative political institutions and leaders. European integration and the ostensible erosion of state sovereignty have opened the way for accountability politics related to the terms of political order, and institutional contestations and reassessments can have potentially order-transforming effects. The politics of accountability involve competing interpretations of democracy and how to democratically settle crises and conflicts. There is disagreement over what a legitimate political order is, including how the territorial borders of political communities are drawn; what are considered common affairs; the role of democratic politics in society; how authority and power are allocated, exercised, controlled, and made accountable between levels of government and between institutional spheres; and what the legitimate role of citizens is.

The aim of this book is therefore twofold. The first is to contribute to the theorization of democratic accountability. The second is to discuss what accountability processes in contemporary Europe tell us about political order and orderly change in general. The discussion is organized around the indeterminacy and dynamics of "democracy," the importance of accountability processes for rank-and-file citizens, the challenges of democratic politics and the territorial nation-state, and the role of constitutional choices and evolving historical practices in orderly change.

2

The Organizational Basis of Accountability: Settled and Unsettled Polities

Theorizing Accountability

An institutional approach to accountability in contemporary representative democracies gives priority to the organizational basis of democratic accountability and attends to how properties of a political order affect, and are affected by, accountability processes. Political orders are more or less institutionalized and they are integrated in different ways. In addition, they change over time, increasing or decreasing the degree of order. There are stable periods, with settled orders, and there are exceptional and transformative periods when the major institutions and their purpose, organization, and role are challenged. An institutional approach assumes that theorizing accountability comprises both settled polities with well-entrenched institutions and unsettled polities with weak or contested institutions.

This view challenges key assumptions of mainstream rational choice, principal–agent approaches regarding what accountability is all about—what is involved in demanding, rendering, assessing, and responding to accounts and assigning responsibility, and how accountability regimes work and change (Chapter 1). Mainstream approaches usually assume settled polities with predetermined principals and agents related by clear chains of authorization, delegation, and accountability. Stable institutionalized rules, roles, success criteria, and power relations specify what different actors are authorized to do, and what codes of good conduct and account giving they are expected to meet. Institutions are portrayed as instruments of management and control, and priority is given to securing the compliance of agents and the interests of principals. An institutional approach holds that these assumptions are unlikely to apply to accountability in unsettled orders and in exceptional and dynamic situations, namely, when facts and causality interpretations, the normative standards of assessment, and authority and power relations of an order are in flux, which is the case in Europe today.

Most approaches, however, agree that accountability regimes are an important property of representative democratic orders. Representation and accountability are core democratic values and the idea that representative government requires accountability to the general public is an important part of the democratic creed. Informed consent is the foundation of legitimacy and it is supposed to be implemented through the development of accounts and the enforcement of accountability. Accountability matters because many actors—elected and non-elected—make decisions on behalf of a political community and because there is the suspicion that power is likely to be misused. Therefore, the people, as a body of self-governing free citizens, equal in political participation, consideration, and worth, need to hold power holders to account.

There is also fairly widespread agreement that democratic accountability requires well-developed institutions and that a lack of effective accountability relations and processes undermines democracy. Officeholders are assumed to be more likely to act in the public interest when they are accountable to the governed (Pitkin 1967), that is, when they have to explain and justify their behavior and performance in public and face sanctions for misbehavior and power abuse (Tetlock 1992, Lerner and Tetlock 1999, March and Olsen 1995, Philp 2009). There is less agreement regarding how effective accountability is best achieved and what institutional arrangements are, can, and should be used to hold officeholders to account—that is, to what extent, and in what ways, accountability depends on the institutional settings within which accountability processes take place.

Over the last few decades many European (and other) democracies have faced declining trust in and deference to institutions of government. Accountability has (again) become a core democratic concern (Fisher 2004, Borowiak 2011, Dubnick 2011, Pollitt and Hupe 2011, Bovens et al. 2014, Peters and Pierre 2012: Part 13). Existing accountability arrangements have been challenged and new ones proposed. A resulting challenge for accountability theory is to explore how representative democracies cope with tensions between multiple, contested, and dynamic conceptions and standards of accountability. And here an institutional approach differs from mainstream approaches.

Agency theory and formal principal–agent approaches involve a family of models rather than a coherent, overarching theory of what fosters or inhibits effective accountability (Gailmard 2014). Among the core assumptions is that the unit of analysis is the individual, self-interested autonomous actor calculating costs and benefits of alternative actions. The identity of principals and agents is assumed and usually based upon formal legal institutions and normative theories of sovereignty, superiority, and subordination, prescribing chains of delegation/authorization and representation/accountability. Principals and agents have diverging interests that are often difficult to align. The principal's welfare is given normative priority. The task is to explain the agent's behavior and how different opportunity and incentive structures induce the agent to act in the principal's interest, and help to detect and sanction deviations from predetermined mandates, rules, goals, or contracts. Information is a strategic resource, with an asymmetry to the advantage of agents. Principals control incentives, and institutions are their instruments. Most often, principal–agent models are applied to the relationship between the people as voters and elected representatives, elected representatives and administrative agencies, or to autonomous institutions insulated from direct political control as guardians of credible commitments. More rarely, court systems are also studied (Waterman and Meier 1998, Strøm et al. 2003, Miller 2005, Carrubba and Clark 2012, Gailmard 2014). Institutions work through incentives. They affect the utility calculations of self-interested actors, and not the identity or behavioral logic of actors themselves.

In contrast, an institutional approach assumes that political orders and politics matter beyond compliance and control and that it is not fruitful to (always) assume that *the politics of political order* are not part of accountability processes. Public debate and political contestation are the primary processes involved in achieving democratic accountability and part of defining good government and the good society. Rather than assuming equilibrium, the starting points of this approach are the fluidity, ambiguities, inconsistencies, and tensions of democratic politics and the evolving nature of who is accountable to whom for what under different contingencies and with what implications. Accountability processes may involve political mobilization and struggles over who deserves to be accepted as principals and trustworthy agents or over how information is distributed, what are democratically desirable power relations, and what are legitimate identities and roles. It is also assumed that it may be useful to attend to how institutions affect accountability through socialization, internalization, and habitualization, as well as through incentives.

A narrow, rather than an ever expanding concept of accountability (Mulgan 2000), simplifies empirical research. However, the content of public accountability and the assumed best ways to ensure accountability vary across polities, policy areas, and groups, as well as over time. The historical-spatial context of this study is contemporary democracies, in particular European parliamentary systems committed to the idea that rulers should be accountable to the ruled. A reason for this choice is that whereas most theoretical approaches to principal–agent relations have been developed in an American context in a period of relatively stable institutional arrangements, Europe is currently involved in a grand-scale experiment in political integration and organization. Europe is in the process of transforming and thus in search of a political order and a unifying narrative. Political, economic, and social crises have generated a perceived need to reconsider and strengthen democratic legitimacy and accountability (Costa et al. 2003, Bovens 2007, Olsen 2007, Bovens et al. 2010, Curtin et al. 2010).

Theorizing accountability, then, requires examining unsettled polities and situations characterized by competing and contested accountability demands, ambiguity, and uncertainty, appeals to different audiences and normative standards, and multiple channels of accountability, as well as settled polities and routine situations with considerable agreement regarding appropriate accountability relations and processes. Therefore, in order to capture the complexity and dynamics of current developments, core principal–agent assumptions are relaxed and more aspects of accountability are treated as endogenous to politics and accountability processes. However, the aim is to outline an institutional approach, not to critique principal–agent approaches, and to take a modest step towards understanding areas of application for competing approaches to democratic accountability.

Accountability in Settled and Unsettled Orders

"Accountability" is a way of thinking about political order and a principle for organizing the relations between governed and governors. There are huge variations in what is meant and implied by "accountability," and in when the demand for compliance is considered to have been met (Verhey et al. 2008). Usually, however, the term refers to being answerable to somebody else, being obliged to explain and justify (in)action—for example, how mandates and contracts have been dealt with, how authority and resources have been applied, and with what results. Accountability and control are embedded in institutions, and the focus here is on the political order and accountability regime level, namely, how arrangements of political institutions affect conceptions and practices of accountability, and how accounts are influenced by a political order and also influence it.

Whereas "institution" in everyday language refers to parliaments, ministries, universities, hospitals, and so on, *institutionalism* is an analytical framework for understanding political life. An institutional approach, as understood here, goes beyond formal legal conceptions. A political order is an arrangement of "living" institutions and an institution is a set of behavioral rules and practices embedded in structures of meaning and resources (Chapter 1, Note 1). Institutions prescribe appropriate behavior for different actors in different situations. They provide rules and practices and mutual expectations regarding the exercise and control of authority, power, rights, and duties. Organizing ideas explain and justify rules and practices, while resources make it (more or less) possible to act in accordance with rule prescriptions. Institutions constitute and influence actors, identities and affective ties, conceptions of reality, and norms of assessment, endowments, and capacities. Institutions have some autonomy and dynamics of their own and some robustness in the face of environmental change and deliberate reform efforts, generating "historical inefficiency" rather than easy equilibrium (March and Olsen 1989, Olsen 2009a, 2010).

Any theory of accountability has to take into account that contemporary democracies combine a variety of institutional arrangements, prescribing who can legitimately talk and act on behalf of the community and who is accountable to whom. Over time, the distribution of tasks, power, and responsibility among institutions and actors has changed. A multitude of institutions, organizations, networks, and communities of account formation, authorization, legitimation, dissemination, and assessment have emerged. There is control *of* representatives and *through* representatives who are specialized and skilled in bringing other power holders to account (Lord and Pollak 2010: 969).

Some organizations have specialized in providing normative standards, certifying institutions and actors, or monitoring, analyzing, and assessing performance without authority or resources to sanction misconduct. Others debate and sanction but depend on relevant and reliable information and analysis from the outside. In addition to legislative and judicial scrutiny, there are independent auditors, ombudsmen, and other complaint mechanisms, epistemic communities, think tanks, credit-rating and standard-setting agencies, tribunals, and committees of inquiry operating at arm's length of popular control. New accountability relationships have been added to old ones, creating complex layers and combinations of co-existing institutions (Romzek 2000, Lægreid and Verhoest 2010). Democratic accountability regimes create elements of order, stability, and predictability as well as of change. Democracies institutionalize and legitimize political debate and contestation that support learning and adaptability. They provide opportunities for rethinking, challenging, and overturning authorities and institutions and changing what principal–agent/compliance–control approaches assume to be pre-political and exogenous.

An implication is that theory builders have to attend to the complexity and dynamics of accountability relations rather than assuming static, dyadic principal–agent relations. Institutions and actors are required to satisfy multiple demands of accountability. They have to report to a multitude of forums, through different channels, and in relation to different types of information and normative standards (Bovens et al. 2010: 40). They are held to account for both the consequences and the appropriateness of their actions, which can create a dilemma because it is difficult to get them right simultaneously (Thompson 1987: 11).

Settled and Unsettled Polities

Institutionalized routines are usually developed for fairly well-structured and recurring problems and situations. They are less likely to fit ill-structured and non-recurring issues. Repeated encounters in standardized situations routinize accountability, and in settled polities there is likely to be widespread agreement regarding who is accountable to whom, for what, under what circumstances, and according to which criteria. Attribution of accountability is guided by institutionalized, socially validated, publicly known, and relatively clear and stable doctrines, expectations, procedures, roles, rules, and routines. It is clear who should be blamed if things go wrong. Those authorized to call someone to account do so with reference to shared norms, commitments, purposes, and expectations. Those who have an obligation to render accounts to some legitimate authority tend to do what they are supposed to do. Activities are recorded in routinized reports, but there is little perceived need to explain and justify what is done. Although individual cases and situations often require interpretation, deliberation, and bargaining regarding what accountability means and implies, these processes take place within institutional constraints and with modest controversy (Olsen 2013, 2014b). Rule following (March and Olsen 1989), anticipation of others' reactions (Friedrich 1950), and incremental, mutual adjustments and "muddling through" (Lindblom 1965) are standard processes.

In unsettled polities, characterized by weak or contested institutions, accountability relations and processes are likely to be more controversial, politicized, and dynamic. Events and results are the product of "many hands" (Thompson 1987: 40). Multiple actors and accountability demands are activated. There are competing interpretations of proper representation (Saward 2006), ambiguous or controversial normative standards and role conceptions, and disagreement about what happened, how, and why, making it difficult to establish how well actors or institutions have performed (March and Olsen 1995: 157–8). Problems of attributing causal relations and accountability generate degrees of freedom regarding how blame and praise should be attributed and assessed and thus room for politicization (Rudolph 2003). Accountability relations and processes evolve through political debate and struggle in response to events, particularly to exceptional, unexpected, and undesired events such as scandals, accidents, and performance crises.

Indeed, democracies have an "anarchic" element. All citizens have the right to raise any issue in public and mobilize support for their view, making accountability processes open-ended. Rates of attention and participation vary. Political activists or whistle blowers may raise issues that fall on deaf ears. Or they may trigger a chain of unplanned events through media attention, political debate, and action so that many audiences and criteria are mobilized in uncoordinated ways. Politics is sometimes event-driven, involving improvisation in settings characterized by unclear causal understanding, ambiguous preferences, contested authority, fluid participation, and varying centrality of policy outcomes. There are chance combinations of decision opportunities, problems, solutions, and participants and accountability processes are overloaded or simplified depending on what else potential participants have to do (Cohen et al. 1972).

Theorizing accountability, therefore, involves understanding complex, multiple, and dynamic relations and processes in unsettled polities and unexpected situations, as well as dyadic, static relationships in settled polities with well-entrenched institutions and business-as-usual routines. Changing political realities have made it increasingly important to attend to the unsettled and unexpected. In particular, the role of the state has changed in ways that require reconsideration of conceptions of accountability developed in state-centered political orders.

A Changing Study Object

For centuries the sovereign state has been the basic unit of political organization in Europe and conceptions of accountability have developed in the context of the emerging state. However, over the last decades, the institutional foundations of the Westphalian state, as identified in the literature on state building and nation building (Eisenstadt and Rokkan 1973/1974), have been challenged. Challenges have been located in Europeanization and internationalization, together with a new zeitgeist and an international wave of public-sector reforms (Costa et al. 2003, Bartolini 2005, Olsen 2007, 2010).

The significance of *territorial boundaries*, which delimit a self-governing people, has become more amorphous. The *capability* to control territory and population has been reduced by increasing international interdependency, privatization, downsizing, devolution, and delegation to partly autonomous agencies and non-governmental actors. The *nation-state*, as an expression of a common identity and shared conceptions of public virtue, moral obligations, and worldviews has been undermined by cultural and religious pluralism, making appeals to appropriateness, reason, and justice more problematic. The *Rechtsstaat*, a legally constituted order based on the rule of law and a bureaucracy with authority embedded in impersonal offices, has been challenged by soft methods, governance networks, and a new emphasis on results, economy, and efficiency rather than on correct procedures. *Democratization* involves mass participation and reduced political inequality. Yet, the traditional model of the democratic state and representative democracy has been weakened through a declining trust in and support for conventional forms of political participation, political parties, elections, and institutions. Parliament is not a privileged center of power (Dogan 2005, Mair 2007). Agencification reduces the importance of political signals and controls (Egeberg and Trondal 2011), making it more difficult to balance institutional autonomy and accountability (Christensen and Lægreid 2005). The *welfare state*, which aims to reduce socio-economic inequality and is anchored in arrangements of interest-group representation, has been attacked by efforts to scale back welfare services and anti-corporatism. In an ideological climate of individualism, primacy has been given to individual choice, markets, and accountability to customers. "Reinvented government" implies a public sector working more like a results-oriented private enterprise (Osborne and Gaebler 1992), but public enterprises mimicking private enterprises have created new accountability problems (Leazes 1987).

These processes have been uneven across polities and there have been countervailing forces. The main development has, nevertheless, been that political order based on the sovereign state and conventional conceptions of accountability have been challenged. The EU has generated demands for new accountability institutions, and there is a perceived need to develop ways to think about cosmopolitan accountability and explore new mechanisms that improve accountability and limit abuse of power in world politics (Held 2004, Grant and Keohane 2005). As the distinctions between levels of government, between the public and the private realm—governments, civil society, and the market—have become less distinct, old accountability relations and processes have been challenged and new ones have evolved (Benz et al. 2007, Harlow and Rawlings 2007, Kohler-Koch and Rittberger 2007, Bovens et al. 2010). This raises questions regarding what accountability means and implies: What is involved in demanding, rendering, assessing, and responding to accounts and assigning accountability, and what is at stake in accountability processes beyond disciplining unruly agents?

What Democratic Accountability is All About

Democracies are communities of policymaking, implementation, and enforcement and the principal–agent/compliance–control literature focuses on the instruments principals have for ensuring that agents do what they are supposed to do. Following the Machiavellian tradition of "mirrors for princes" political advice, the literature addresses how rules are applied and enforced, sanctioning deviance from predetermined standards. Facing asymmetry of information, incomplete contracts, and goal conflict, it is usually assumed that legal sovereigns (the people, parliament, minister, or manager) have incentive control and can make deliberate institutional choices. When the distribution of information, purposes, ends, authority, power, and identities are treated as exogenous, the task is to identify the technically most efficient means to reach predetermined ends within existing constraints.

Principal–agent approaches are consistent with the idea that public accounts are vehicles for popular sovereignty and instruments for attaining goals. Those acting on behalf of the community and on the authority and resources embedded in public office are accountable to citizens informed by such accounts. All the same, those calling others to account face a dilemma. They have to reconcile the need for autonomy and discretion on the part of agents, so that they can do their work well, with the desire to keep them accountable and maintain democratic control (Dahl and Lindblom 1963: 273, March and Olsen 1989: 134, Barth 1993). Political ideologies, however, give different answers to the question of what is a proper balance between preventing abuse of public office and securing collective problem-solving capabilities.

Democracy is also an arrangement for developing and transmitting democratic beliefs and identities (March and Olsen 1995, Dahl 1998). A critical attitude is at the core of democratic will and opinion formation, and accountability processes provide occasions for interpreting, debating, and changing worldviews, normative criteria, distributions of authority, power, responsibility, accountability, and conceptions of legitimate roles and identities. Accountability processes invite the testing and validating of truth and moral claims by providing arguments, explanations, and justifications, as well as political struggle, with the potential to affect citizens' confidence in existing institutional arrangements. Accountability processes have a positive democratic effect when they contribute to improved communication and epistemic quality, support democratic standards and criteria of assessment, contribute to political equality, and help citizens find meaning in life through reflection and reasoning together, possibly internalizing a democratic civic ethos.

An implication of this perspective is that there is a need to go beyond the dominant concern in the principal–agent literature, namely how political orders and accountability regimes discipline unruly agents and solve the problems of predetermined principals. As will be elaborated in Chapter 4, shortcomings sometimes originate in principals rather than agents. Accountability deficits are located in institutions and actors who are supposed to call others to account and assess and sanction accounts but who are not motivated or capable of doing so and for improving the accountability system at large (Considine 2002, Shapiro 2005, Busuioc 2010: 220–23). Expectations, criteria, and signals to agents are often ambiguous, contradictory, or unrealistic. Rulers can be mistaken, and reforms driven by political ideology rather than evidence and analysis produce perverse effects, including loss of efficiency and service quality and unclear accountability relations. Trust is weakened or destroyed through intense monitoring. Efforts to retain democratic authority and claim credit while avoiding responsibility and blame often have the opposite effect (Gilmour and Jensen 1998, Klinger et al. 2001: 134). Trying to make sense of such situations, an institutional approach challenges many of the premises that mainstream approaches take for granted.

Information Asymmetry and Epistemic Quality

Principal–agent/compliance–control approaches assume information asymmetry and see information as an individual strategic resource. Agents are information-rich while principals are information-poor, and the two are in conflict. For example, echoing Weber's claim that every bureaucracy seeks to increase its powers through hiding its action and knowledge from public criticism (Weber 1978: 992–3), it is held that bureaucrats use their expertise to "systematically mislead legislators" (Lupia and McCubbins 1994: 96). A core concern of this approach is to reduce information asymmetry.

Democratic ideals assume a sincere search for understanding as a basis for enlightened government. Democracies are committed to the pursuit of intelligence through accurate information, careful analysis, and enlightening communication. Knowledge is a collective property and the quality of government is measured by the quality of the discourses an order allows or initiates (March and Olsen 1995: 174–5, Orbuch 1997). Officeholders are assumed to act honestly in accordance with relevant facts and the best reasoning available. A core belief is that democracies have a unique ability to learn from experience, and constitutional history is seen as a learning process (Habermas 2001: 775). The vision reflects the Enlightenment trust in human ability to use reason and experience to improve the human condition. It is also reflected in contemporary reformers' belief in auditing and account giving as vital instruments for collective intelligence and progress (Pollitt and Summa 1997: 331, Aucoin and Heintzman 2000).

An institutional approach assumes that different forms of political order generate variable information distribution and epistemic quality, and that accountability processes provide an occasion for common problem solving and consensus building. Such processes (a) offer an occasion for explaining and justifying institutions, behavior, and results, (b) for mutual learning from experience, through argumentation and deliberation, as well as (c) an occasion for control, blaming, and power struggles over the distribution of advantages and disadvantages. The influence of citizens depends on competing accounts and sources of information, and thus on the distribution of access opportunities and resources that affect which interpretative frameworks and what vocabulary, facts, and normative standards gain acceptance (March and Olsen 1995: 162–3, 180).

Whereas democracies in a comparative perspective seem to be able to learn on the basis of accounts, experience is an unreliable teacher and improvement is not guaranteed (March and Olsen 1975, March 2010). The Enlightenment-inspired belief in emancipation and improvement through human agency, science, technology, and organization working for the common good has not prevented things from going terribly wrong from time to time. Sometimes events are too obscure for accountability to be established validly in the sense to correctly assign causal responsibilities, making it difficult to give precise and valid accounts of what has happened, what could have happened, and conclude precisely what lessons to extract. New routines for information collection are not automatically followed by routines of analysis, debate, and sanctioning.

The assumption that identifiable institutions and individuals can be made accountable by disentangling their contribution to fiascos and successes is particularly problematic in unsettled polities, characterized by complex and dynamic interdependencies where the performance of one actor is highly dependent on the performance of other actors. In a world of interdependence, chance events, and long and uncertain causal chains, with significant effects sometimes surfacing only after years, the assignment of accountability may be capricious (March and Olsen 1995). Explanations of politics, nevertheless, are related to intentions, and the democratic faith in human will, understanding, and control makes it important to find or construct an "adequately blameworthy agent" (Shklar 1990: 62). Limited causal understanding and problems of assigning accountability create possibilities for political contestation, blaming and shaming, and for identifying scapegoats—issues that will be developed further in Chapter 4.

Institutionalized transparency is no panacea in a world of boundedly rational actors where attention, time, and energy are scarce resources and the ability to gather relevant, accurate, and timely information and to analyze, retrieve, and act upon information is limited and unevenly distributed. Citizens are usually unable to analyze and assess available information by themselves and democracies face potential threats to improved epistemic quality. Resourceful actors are likely to try to manage images of accountability, possibly perverting interpretations of what has happened, why it happened, whether it could have been avoided, and according to what normative standards events and accounts are to be assessed.

Democratic Standards of Assessment

Principal–agent approaches usually assume self-interested actors driven by a logic of consequentiality and rational calculation of expected utility.

The political order regulates self-interested actors through a nexus of contracts to their mutual advantage. In some instances there is voluntary exchange and aggregation of predetermined and arbitrary individual preferences while in others there is conflict and predetermined principals decide what normative criteria have priority.

In contrast, an institutional approach holds that accountability processes provide opportunities for exploring and changing normative standards (Mill 1962, March and Olsen 1995). Democracy assumes the moral autonomy and equality of citizens, and democrats are imagined to reason about principles and purposes and what splits or ties a community together. Will formation involves debates and judgment about collective principles, standards, and purposes, and democracies are committed to a variety of values and norms defining "good government." A democratic article of faith is that "the public is ultimately the sole source of sovereign authority, and it is the public to whom all public officials ought ultimately to be accountable" (Goodin 2008: 164). There are, however, different conceptions of what a sovereign popular will means and implies and how it is formed, expressed, implemented, and enforced. An example is democracy understood in terms of participation and procedure, or in terms of efficient services. There are also varying and changing views of the relative importance of (majority) democracy as a normative ideal as opposed to divine law, ethics, reason, science, rule of law, constitutional rights and freedoms, civility, duties of office, traditions, economic efficiency, or the perceived necessities of financial markets.

In settled democracies different normative concerns are embedded in traditions, morals, and institutional spheres with some autonomy and resources of their own. In unsettled polities there is less guidance due to contested or unclear normative standards. In contemporary democracies embedded in dynamic, multicultural societies committed to diversity, it cannot be taken for granted that actors share a conception of what democratic accountability means and implies and what are normatively valid arguments. Key issues include how political orders and accountability processes contribute to collective reflection and deliberation over normative ideals and how they possibly support democratic civic standards of assessment in different institutional settings.

Authority and Power Equalization

Accountability demands involve competing assumptions about political agency and action capabilities, including about what is malleable and what is foreordained or random. Within a principal–agent approach institutions are often seen as instruments for solving problems of accountability induced by representation, and democracies are understood to resolve issues over time, with agreed-upon results encoded into trustworthy institutions (Warren 2011: 523, 526). The power and accountability relations of a political order are in equilibrium, as no relevant actor has a better alternative and is motivated and capable to rebel against the existing order. Delegating discretion is a necessity, but democratic abdication is not. Agency loss is mitigated and citizens and legislators cope with conflicting preferences and information asymmetry through a variety of institutional devices, providing information about what agents are doing and why, as well as capacities for holding them to account. Control is embedded in the design of electoral, legislative, and bureaucratic arrangements, in processes of selecting agents, monitoring structures, reports from agents and from third parties, penalties for lying and misrepresenting facts, and overturning and reversing agents' decisions (Waterman and Meier 1998, Lupia and McCubbins 1994, 2000).

An institutional approach sees the political agency of citizens and elected representatives as more limited and variable. Visions of political equality, majority government, and non-elected officials subordinated to elected officials are difficult to realize. Equality of control is a constant battle "always on the verge of being lost" (Dahl and Lindblom 1963: 282), not a stable equilibrium. Political authority and power are constrained by unequal distributions of private resources and skills, and it is unclear what power follows from winning public office (Rokkan 1966). There is the suspicion that powerful actors are not properly held to account—that powerful actors fail to live up to their obligations to actors who lack the capacities to call them to account. If accountability holders are weak, the accountability mechanisms that rely on them are severely compromised (Rubenstein 2007).

It is problematic to assume that accountability regimes emerge and develop through institutional engineering and choice, and that formal legal institutions are translated into living institutions and routines that ensure accountability. Because accountability in Western culture is linked to what can be possibly controlled by the one called to account, to design accountability systems implies the ability to design a system of authority and power. However, key institutions such as parliament have developed through historically evolving processes rather than deliberate design. In Westminster democracies the principle of ministerial responsibility has been adapted to shifting circumstances and practice has come to reflect that no minister can know everything that they are formally responsible for (Stone 1995). The European Parliament (EP) has only recently succeeded in moving closer to a traditional parliament–executive relationship with the European Commission (EC), the latter being accountable to the EP, a position the EP for a long time did not have according to the treaties.

Rather than assuming a world divided into predetermined principals and agents, there is a need to examine how authority and power are actually organized, exercised, and controlled. Accountability processes provide an opportunity for explaining, justifying, challenging, and changing the existing order and for debating why its foundational normative and organizational principles deserve the allegiance of citizens. Contestations involve what are and should be the role of the represented and those whose life chances are affected. Answers to such questions have varied across polities and they have changed over time. At issue are what resources and skills different institutions require from citizens for effective participation in accountability processes, and the possible role of these processes in reducing rather than reinforcing the effects of skewed distributions of private resources.

Sense Making and Identity Building

Principal–agent approaches assume that control over behavior and policy outcomes are at the heart of accountability processes and that manipulating incentives is the main instrument used. Without denying the importance of democratic policy control and who-gets-what-when-how, an institutional approach observes that a democratic polity is more than an arrangement for making, implementing, and enforcing policies. It is also a collection of interlocking communities of explanation, justification, and criticism. Making the world intelligible in normative and causal terms is central to political and organizational life, and the search for identity, understanding, meaning, purpose, direction, and belonging can be as important an aspect of accountability processes as compliance and control (March and Olsen 1976, 1995).

Reason, then, implies institutionalized collective wisdom, virtues, and reflection on the good community, and not solely means–end rationality. Collective identity and individual character are acquired, not innate, and self-regarding maximization of expected utility is just one among several behavioral logics accepted as legitimate in different institutional contexts. The ordering effects of institutions do not come only through external opportunity and incentive structures. Accountability processes provide an opportunity for intellectual and moral self-development as well as self-governance (Mill 1962: 30–5).

In settled polities there are repertoires of socially constructed and validated accounts and responses to accounts, influenced by what is intelligible, expected, anticipated, appropriate, and legitimate in specific political-cultural contexts. Favored stories are embedded in ideologies and traditions and there are continuous attempts to fit events to those stories. Routinized accounts focus on deviances from shared rules and expectations and provide reassurance that events are controllable or have the appearance of being so (Thompson 1987: 44, March and Olsen 1995: 149, 161).

In unsettled polities, where the correct allocation of causal responsibility for events is problematic, participants may use the pursuit of accountability to make sense of political structures and practices. Under some conditions, accountability processes have an integrative community-building effect, promoting a culture of cooperation, compromise, and rule following. An important aspect of demanding, giving, and assessing accounts is also the construction of an agreed language of discourse (Day and Klein 1987: 2). Change in vocabulary and the meaning of terms is usually an indicator of change in political order, including perceptions and assessments of accountability relations. Under other conditions, accountability processes provide a rhetorical arena for the struggle over minds and purpose, generating suspicion, confrontation, and disintegration, and splitting a population in ways that do not follow simple principal versus agent dividing lines.

Treating epistemic quality, normative criteria, power distributions, sense making, and identity formation as endogenous to politics and accountability processes complicates the examination of how political orders affect accountability processes and how effective accountability is achieved in practice. The challenge includes determining which accountability institutions allow democracies to cope with multiple, contested, and dynamic accountability demands and which ones render them toothless. How then do political orders affect how accountability institutions work and change, and why are there varying perceived needs to call actors to account?

Accountability Institutions in Action

Principal–agent approaches assume that principals know which institutions are likely to enhance and hamper accountability and that they are able to choose desired institutions. An institutional approach holds that, under some conditions, institutions have expected and desired effects and they are deliberately designed and reformed. Institutions are, however, imperfect instruments. They affect but do not determine behavior and outcomes. They are human constructs but cannot easily be designed and reformed at will. *If* institutions always determined performance perfectly and in understood ways, and *if* they could be deliberately fashioned, calling to account and rendering, assessing, and sanctioning accounts would have less political importance. Imperfect institutions, however, affect accountability by influencing the discretion agents have. They make it more or less likely that mandates are overstepped and power misused and thereby affect the need to monitor, assess, and sanction account givers. They also help democracies develop practices that make it possible to cope with ambiguity and unresolved conflict.

The Varying Importance of Accountability

To call someone to account requires that the actor has some discretion that can be used or misused, judged by some predetermined normative standard. Misuse of power is less likely when institutions work thus:

- Compliance is secured through external controls of opportunity and incentive structures, so that the expected utility of complying is always greater than not complying.
- Reciprocal control is established through vertical or horizontal separation of power and expertise, checks, and balances.
- Congruence in norms, understandings, and role expectations is achieved through recruitment. Reliable and competent behavior is guaranteed by selecting and removing actors with certain characteristics (e.g. members of a specific party or profession) to/from office.
- Agreement is reached through communicative action and reciprocal discovery of normative validity and the best argument through deliberation among initially conflicting parties.
- Self-control is achieved through socialization, internalization, habitualization, and character formation, making the appropriate norms and codes of conduct understood and respected.
- Available resources make it possible to follow behavioral prescriptions and proscriptions.

If these processes were perfect, there would be no discretion and no reason for studying accountability relations. Accountability would be limited to detecting misunderstandings, incompetence, and criminal acts. However, claims about accountability deficits and disillusionment with traditional forms of representative democracy suggest that practice is less than perfect.

Imperfect and Contested Processes

The favorite narrative of representative democracy gives priority to accountability through electoral mechanisms. Debates in civil society and the public space are vehicles for will formation and sense making. Actors are discursively accountable to one another in an open forum and are supposed to comply with the force of the better argument. Popular rule and the authentic, sovereign will of the people are expressed, implemented, and enforced through free and competitive elections (Przeworski et al. 1999, Goodin 2008: 178). An example is parliamentarianism, which is portrayed as a chain of dyadic relations (Strøm 2000, Strøm et al. 2003). Competitive and free elections legitimize hierarchical accountability to the sovereign people, parliament, law, and leaders. Political parties structure agendas and conflicts. Campaigns inform about alternatives and invite discussions about causal understanding and normative standards. A representative assembly enacts laws, delegates authority to a hierarchy of non-elected public officials, and holds them accountable. Laws are prepared and implemented by an executive accountable to the legislature that can dismiss governments and individual ministers. Public administration is held accountable through a political and administrative hierarchy and (Weberian) bureaucracies provide incentives in terms of lifelong careers and socialization into the duties of office. Independent courts enforce the laws and there is legal accountability to constitutions and courts. A variety of auxiliary entities perform inquiries and provide information. The public sector is held accountable in the name of institutional and professional codes of conduct, through corporatist arrangements, market mechanisms, and competition.

The problems of this story are well known. Unenlightened and unmotivated citizens without clear, consistent, and stable preferences are unable to attribute responsibility and call power holders to account. Political communication through traditional mass media and the new social media misinform public opinion and inhibit rational reasoning and collective intelligence by giving priority to scandals and "celebrities." Leaders send ambiguous and inconsistent signals and the tasks and resources of agents do not match. Unclear lines between incumbents and opposition and a culture of compromise make responsibility ambiguous and uncertain. Powerful bureaucrats, technocrats, and organized interests are more concerned with their own interests than with the common good.

Over the last decades representative democracies have faced massive criticism and demands for improved accountability and control. A culture of suspicion has generated an "audit explosion" (Power 1994) and depoliticization reforms have devalued the role of electoral accountability, popular control, and political equality. A result is that electoral and legislative processes and ministerial and hierarchical-administrative accountability are no longer dominant (Mair 2007). Non-hierarchical forms of governance are important, even if they have not replaced electoral–legislative–ministerial accountability (Schillemans 2008). There are tensions between representation and accountability, making it difficult to optimize both simultaneously through the same institutions (Lord and Pollak 2010: 978–9). Public-sector performance is conceived in terms of efficient service production and consumer choice and quantifiable report cards are claimed to improve performance and control (Gormley and Weimer 1999). The plethora of horizontal accountability relations are, however, generating problems of their own (Michels and Meijer 2008) and the empirical evidence for improved performance is inconclusive (Lægreid and Verhoest 2010). Rendering accounts has, nevertheless, produced an increasing number of controllers. More resources are used for reporting than for getting the job done, generating complaints of accountability overload and reports not being read or followed up (Dubnick 2005).

Some lessons can be learned from unsettled, multilevel, and multicentered polities such as the EU, a polity with no unitary and stable "people"; competing claims regarding citizens' wants, interests, and needs; contested normative doctrines; and interdependent but partly autonomous institutions, loosely coupled to public opinion, elected representatives, and hierarchical superiors. There is criticism of weak links between the EP and citizens, and of the modest position of the EP and member state parliaments, as well as of the lack of transparency and accountability of the European Council. Bargaining in networks creates an accountability problem by making it difficult to identify who has been influential and who should be held accountable. Powerful "guardian" institutions such as the EC, the Court of Justice of the European Union, and the European Central Bank are shielded from direct popular control, making it difficult to hold them to account. What jurisdiction different levels of government, institutions, and actors are supposed to have is contested. It is not clear who can legitimately call whom to account for what, who controls relevant incentives and information, and what normative criteria and causal understandings should have priority. Calling someone to account and rendering, assessing, and sanctioning accounts requires pooling resources from several institutions and actors (Magnette 2000, Busuioc 2010). Furthermore, there are simultaneous perceived accountability deficits and overloads.

For example, the EC has become more accountable horizontally to other EU institutions, but less so to EU citizens. As a result, the EC perceives itself to be overloaded with accountability demands while in the eyes of the public it is unaccountable and deserves closer public scrutiny (Wille 2010: 83–5). Whether the EU is seen to have an accountability deficit depends on the standards used and polity advocated (Majone 1998). Proposals for making the EU accountable have been based upon different conceptions of its nature, purpose, and desired future and have varied among those who see the EU alternately as an intergovernmental, supranational, or regulatory entity (Fisher 2004, Bovens 2007, Harlow and Rawlings 2007, Bovens et al. 2010: 180, 189).

One interpretation is that the EU is constructed to be safeguarded against representative democracy, evading the constraints of voters, elections, parties, and majority government, and a consequence is that its system of government lacks conventional forms of democratic accountability. The EU is seen as a solution to the incapacities of popular democracy in the member states and democracy in the Union cannot be obtained by modeling it on the institutions of the nation-state. Alternatives are either to change European institutions or traditional conceptions of democracy, legitimacy, and accountability. The EU may be generating a new convention, with a lesser role for citizens' participation and partisan politics, so that popular disengagement and technocracy is part of a trend where democracy mutates (Mair 2007).

A new kind of accountability and legitimacy is then developing, balancing autonomy and accountability differently from classical parliamentarianism and hierarchies and thus requiring new models. For example, the European Central Bank has unprecedented autonomy. Still, there are emerging arrangements of parliamentary control through a variety of institutional links, practices, and forms of cooperation between the bank and political authorities (Magnette 2000). Similar observations have been made in studies of European agencies (Busuioc 2010) and "directly deliberative polyarchy" assumes that accounts are not validated by standard processes of representative democracy, rule following, and compliance with a clear mandate. There is no single authoritative center; instead accountability is dynamic and reciprocal, and arguments are deliberately used to destabilize settled practices (Sabel and Zeitlin 2010).

In sum, the EU illustrates that democracies can use a variety of imperfect accountability processes that do not ensure efficient adaptation to popular opinion. Processes appear in many and shifting combinations and how they work, interact, and change is not well understood. One challenge for future studies is to explore frictions in accountability processes, but it is beyond the scope of this chapter to identify relevant frictions in the many mechanisms and to spell out how different accountability regimes are likely to affect the character and quality of accountability. Another challenge is to explore processes through which democracies may cope with enduring unresolved conflicts over accountability demands.

Unresolved Conflict

In democracies accounts are often constructed when contending accounts collide. Democracies face inconsistent normative standards and causal understandings and there are warnings against trying to accommodate accountability demands that may be irreconcilable. "Multiple accountability disorder" refers to malfunctioning resulting from attempts to meet too many conflicting expectations (Koppell 2005).

An alternative to assuming authoritative conflict resolution is to consider how democracies live in practice with unresolved conflict, including competing conceptions of accountability.

An institutional approach holds that boundedly rational actors are looking for satisfactory, not optimal, solutions based upon coherent and stable preference orders. In a democracy partly autonomous institutions are organized around a variety of concerns and there are institutions that are supposed to guard the freedom of expression, legitimate opposition, independent courts and auditors, an active civil society, free press, and academic research, providing competing mechanisms for testing, gathering support for, authorizing, and rejecting accounts. Under some conditions accountability processes are likely to be institution-specific. Under other conditions they are likely to involve the interaction of a variety of institutions.

In settled polities and well-understood situations confronted repeatedly, accountability processes are likely to take place in parallel, relatively autonomous institutional settings. Processes are incremental and institution-specific. They are strongly influenced by the history, organization, and dynamics of the institution, yet they operate in the shadow of some basic understanding of political order. There are co-existing dyadic accountability relations, routines, standard operating procedures, self-restraint, and depoliticization. There is local rationality, where different institutions define accountability and hold different types of actors to account for different things and in accordance with different normative standards. There is also sequential attention to claims, and demands for coordination are buffered by limited attention and slack resources. Interpretations and responses are initially based on existing routines, but reduced slack and performance crises may initiate a search for new alternatives and aspiration-level adaptation may occur (Cyert and March 1963).

In unsettled polities and unprecedented situations, there are likely to be more demands for coordinated behavior, and accountability processes develop in a dynamic interplay between levels of governance and between institutional spheres. As will be discussed in more detail in Chapter 4, when experience offers little guidance causal, understanding is low, normative criteria are in conflict, and control is uncertain—there may be image management and shame-and-blame behavior. But there can also be unifying symbolic behavior and sense making. Over time institutions can learn their place in the larger order.

Theorizing accountability also requires a re-examination of *where* coping with unresolved conflict takes place. Conflict resolution is usually assumed to be located in electoral politics, with elected representatives as key actors. Empirical studies, however, call renewed attention to a large-scale, formally organized, professionalized, and partly autonomous public sector. A theory of public administration means a theory of politics (Gaus 1950: 168), making dichotomies such as ends–means and politics–administration problematic. Public administration and other non-elected officeholders are involved in policy advice, interpretation, implementation, and enforcement. They have discretion and multiple relations to constituencies (Egeberg 2006, Lægreid and Verhoest 2010, Peters and Pierre 2012) and the challenge is to examine the complementarity of distinct administrative roles and the possibility of usurpation of power (Svara 1999).

Most issues and the premises that guide administrative behavior never reach the attention of elected politicians and citizens, and political rhetoric fit for mobilizing support is not always fit for making programs work well (Barth 1993: 176–7, Klinger et al. 2001: 136–7). Administrators have to decipher political decisions and legal documents and develop practical, viable solutions. They are not held to account solely as a tool for elected leaders. They are exposed to a variety of pressures and the legitimacy of public administration depends on their ability to reconcile contradictory premises and competing accountabilities to multiple principals on specific issues in specific situations. Attending to political and administrative premises has always been the responsibility of administrators. Adding market thinking and control by individual consumers has, however, made things more complicated. The preconditions for perfect market competition are rarely found in the public sector and tripartite accountability relations among logics of politics, administration, and markets have turned out to be difficult to reconcile (Klinger et al. 2001).

Emerging Institutions, Shifting Balances

The EU, as an unsettled polity with co-existing orders and no shared vision of how accountability is to be organized and legitimized, provides several examples of evolving practice being explained, justified, and theorized post hoc. The Union *has* been concerned with how codes of conduct may nurture accountability, responsibility, and integrity. Still, there is no regime or culture that ensures accountability of officeholders to a European constituency. A standard claim is that functional efficiency and economy are prioritized over democratic accountability. Consistent with continental traditions, the EU has great confidence in formal legal institutions. However, after having been formally established, living institutions and their practices have evolved gradually through a more or less coordinated struggle for attention, resources, and support, and ahead of political visions and academic theories. Processes of delegation and accountability have developed in parallel and partly informally and independent of each other during "normal times." Performance crises have generated demands for coordination and improved accountability.

For example, judicial institutions, networks, and culture have emerged through interaction between the European Union Court of Justice, national courts, and the legal profession. Similar processes have taken place among European agencies (Busuioc 2010, Busuioc et al. 2011) and among ombudsmen, as part of building an institutional identity, winning acceptance for the office, and building a European-wide professional network (Curtin 2007, Harlow and Rawlings 2007, Bovens et al. 2010). The European Court of Auditors, from its establishment in 1977 until it became "a full institution" in 1993, had difficulties developing an institutional identity as the guardian of sound financial management and gaining the attention of the EU's executive powers. Contestation and resistance arose before an institutional action capacity was built and the court was able to assert its role as a central node in a matrix of financial accountability. As part of wider processes of institution building in the EU, the court gradually gained confidence and was accepted in the political-administrative milieu. It was helped by the growing power of the Union, bigger budgets, more net contributors to the EU budget, broad media coverage of fraud and scandals, and support from the EP. The reconfiguration of accountability involved institution building, shifts in interinstitutional relations, and change in the culture of sound financial management (Laffan 2003).

The EU cohesion policy saw an audit explosion as a result of the EC's 2000 administrative reform program, triggered by financial management scandals and a loss of legitimacy. However, whereas the aim was to achieve better policy performance, attention became focused on compliance and traditional financial accounting practice related to legality, regularity, and detecting errors, fraud, and corruption more than on learning and discovering how performance could be improved. There were complaints regarding the scale, intensity, redundancy, inefficiency, and overlapping of audits, diverting attention from results, strangling risk taking and innovation, and generating disappointment and distrust. Resources and power were redistributed in favor of the watchdogs rather than those implementing cohesion policies. New auditing practices and regimes were layered on top of old ones (Mendez and Bachtler 2011).

Preliminary Conclusions and Undecided Issues

This chapter has explored the organizational basis of democratic accountability and how the properties of a political order affect accountability processes. Democratic theory requires a theory of accountability, but no such theory is available. An institutional approach to accountability has been offered as a starting point for understanding accountability regimes with multiple institutions, actors, relations, processes, criteria, and demands and how they are affected by, and in turn affect, political order and orderly change. One aim of this chapter has been to take a modest step towards understanding areas of application for competing approaches.

Much is known about specific accountability relations and processes in settled polities and well-known situations. Less is known about the interaction among multiple accountability claims in unsettled polities and unfamiliar situations. The complex combinations of accountability institutions in contemporary democracies are difficult to capture in a few stylized categories, and in empirical studies, complexity is often reduced by studying a single polity, policy area, institution, or mechanism rather than attempting to theorize the interdependence, interaction, and dynamics of multiple accountabilities. Complexity is also reduced by privileging the electoral channel—a single, dominant formal legal chain of dyadic relationships, or a checks-and-balances system in equilibrium—as a mechanism for ensuring accountability. Theorizing accountability, however, requires addressing mixed orders characterized by complex combinations of multiple, co-existing, contested, and dynamic accountability relationships and processes, making compliance and control, epistemic quality, normative standards, the distribution of power, sense making, and identity formation endogenous to politics and accountability processes.

Democratic accountability is a continuous, open-ended process. Accountability is never perfectly institutionalized, fulfilled, or static, and ahistorical and non-contextual conceptions of accountability are unlikely to be fruitful. However, attempts to theorize how democracies cope with contested and dynamic accountability demands involve a dilemma. Making most aspects of accountability exogenous to politics and accountability processes is likely to lead to gains in formal elegance and losses in relevance. Making most aspects endogenous is likely to have the opposite effect. Whereas all approaches have to take something as given, I hold that principal–agent/-compliance–control approaches are based on an unacceptable number of unexamined assumptions that reduce their area of application. Yet I also argue that approaches based on different assumptions are likely to be complementary rather than mutually exclusive. Theory builders need to reconcile competing ideas and consider what their strengths and weaknesses are and specify circumstances under which different institutional structures and processes are likely to foster or hinder effective accountability.

For example, mainstream principal–agent approaches are most likely to be applicable (a) in settled polities, routine situations, and in a short-term perspective; (b) in polities with a sovereign center of authority and power, controlling recruitment and reorganization, or a single dominant set of normative and organizational principles; (c) in polities where compliance and control dominate other concerns and formal legal authority is more important than living institutions and practices; or (d) in settings where external controls of actors are dominant. Principal–agent approaches are less applicable in unsettled polities, unfamiliar situations, and in a long-term perspective and in mixed, multi-level, and multi-centered orders characterized by partly autonomous living institutions and networks embedded in heterogeneous and pluralistic societies. In such contexts, no single process is sufficient to guarantee accountability and their combinations and interrelations are hard to understand and assess for both citizens and theory builders.

Aspiring theory builders, therefore, have some way to go before accountability relations and processes are well understood. There are many unsolved issues, and theorizing requires a repertoire of conceptions of accountability institutions: How they are organized, how they work, what effects they have, and how they change. Theorizing also requires a repertoire of ideas about actors and how institutions work on actors. Principal–agent approaches usually assume that effective accountability is secured by incentive structures, regulating and aggregating competing individual preferences. If incentives are right, accountability is achieved independently of the motives of individuals.

An institutional approach holds that external controls and incentives are not enough in complex and dynamic settings and calls attention to processes of socialization, internalization, identification, and habituation that make actors accept codes of conduct specifying appropriate behavior of different roles in different situations as legitimate. A complication is that whereas the ancient *zoon politikon* was assumed to identify with the city-state and feel obligations to his political community, seeing authority and the duty to obey as the natural moral state of affairs (Klosko 2011), contemporary democracies are characterized by a multitude of allegiance claims and a possible loss of shared conceptions of appropriate behavior and duty. At issue is whether effective accountability requires democrats, citizens, and officeholders that have internalized and habitualized a democratic civic ethos. If so, in which institutional settings are such civic dispositions acquired and what is the contribution of accountability processes? The democratic principle that anyone who exercises power shall ultimately be accountable to the people for how power is used has not been implemented consistently (March and Olsen 1995: 150–3). Therefore, the conventional emphasis on the electoral channel has to be supplemented by a renewed examination of the democratic roles of guardians and citizens.

The Role of Guardians

Whereas conceptions of accountability have come to rely more on non-majoritarian, guardian institutions (Thatcher and Stone Sweet 2002), delegation to non-majoritarian entities has posed problems. Autonomy does not imply complete individual freedom, but rather acting in accordance with an institutional identity and ethos. A professional is supposed to act on the basis of what is accepted as best professional judgment. However, self-control and checks and balances among guardians have been assessed as democratically inadequate, and without a reinvention of accountability, the current wave of delegation has for some time been expected to generate new reform demands from citizens and their representatives (Gilmour and Jensen 1998). Again, democracies face issues regarding what kind of guardians democratic accountability requires. Who and what shall be insulated from political accountability and for what reasons? What are proper accountability relations between majoritarian and non-majoritarian institutions and citizens, under which conditions can technocratic institutions and actors be trusted to act selflessly, and who watches the watchmen?

For example, courts, usually seen as the least dangerous branch of government, are often portrayed as guardians of democracy and individual rights. Still, the power and accountability of courts and judges has been reproblematized because judicial activism has strengthened their position vis-à-vis legislatures and executives. Arguably, there has been a juridical coup d'état in the EU, where courts have transformed the normative foundations of the legal system in fundamental ways through constitutional law making (Stone Sweet 2007: 915). Supreme audit institutions see independence as key to performing their tasks well. They portray themselves as working according to customary audit practice, as guardians of sound financial management and the public interest, and not as agents of a specific principal. However, a study of supreme audit institutions in Finland, France, Sweden, the United Kingdom, and the EU shows that they perceive their roles differently. They use different strategies for explaining themselves. Some use managerial language, others constitutional language. They do not use the same instruments and standards to explain and justify their own performance, nor do they provide the same information about their own quality and effectiveness as they and demand from and use to evaluate the institutions they audit (Pollitt and Summa 1997).

The Role of Citizens

The questionable ability of citizens to hold rulers to account is a major theme in democratic theory. Currently there are demands for more transparency and direct participation of citizens, and the erosion of confidence in authorities has been interpreted as a sign of democratic political maturity (Dogan 2005: 46). An institutional agenda attends to citizens' capabilities and also poses questions regarding citizens' responsibilities toward the community at large as the ultimate source of power and foundation of representative democracy. The ancient idea that a citizen is accountable to the citizenry for his performance as citizen is alien to modern democracies (Borowiak 2011: 93, 97). Yet a people claiming a sovereign's right to be accountable to no one, the combination of citizen power with citizen exemption from accountability, masks the contribution of ordinary citizens to democratic successes and failures and introduces unacceptable irresponsibility into democratic government (March and Olsen 1995: 153).

For normative theory the issue is what responsibilities moral agents should have to their community (Goodin 2008: 58). An institutional agenda calls attention to what normative ideals citizens actually prioritize and how democratic ideals are eventually internalized and practiced in different institutional settings. At stake is whether citizenship is primarily seen as carrying rights and consuming public services, or implying adherence to socially validated and individually internalized behavioral codes, like membership in a profession assumes loyalty to professional codes. That is, whether citizens see themselves as responsible members of a political community, accountable to each other for participating in political and civic life, keeping informed, not making unattainable demands, and accepting duties towards the welfare of other citizens, including the vulnerable who cannot protect themselves.

In sum, accountability theory has to examine how settled and unsettled orders, and orders integrated in different ways, provide different access structures and roles for citizens and affect what accountability processes are all about. Likewise, accountability theory has to examine how accountability processes, in turn, affect political order and orderly change—how they may take the form of order-maintaining institutionalized routines or order-transforming politics.

3

Order-Maintaining and Order-Transforming Accountability Processes

Accountability and Orderly Change

Accountability regimes are part of a democracy's institutional arrangement for preserving order and securing continuity, as well as for creating dynamics and securing orderly change. Accountability processes can involve order-maintaining and order-transforming processes (Eisenstadt 1995: 306). They can be governed by order-maintaining routines and order-transforming politics (Chapter 1). Some polities, policy sectors, and time periods are characterized by accountability routines and a "business as usual" culture, and accountability is presented in a neutral technical language of efficiency and improved performance. Other polities, policy sectors, and time periods are characterized by accountability processes involving reassessment, political contestations, and reforms of the terms of political order.

This chapter, then, explores how accountability processes, conditioned by varying and shifting political orders and accountability regimes, affect the future terms of political order and orderly change. I am especially interested in the conditions under which accountability demands with an order-transforming potential are activated and how different political orders and accountability regimes open the way for different forms of popular participation, problems, and solutions, making order-maintaining and order-transforming accountability processes more or less likely.

Conceptions of order-maintaining and order-transforming processes differ when it comes to assumptions about what is exogenous and endogenous to democratic politics and accountability processes. There are competing claims about what is involved in demanding, rendering, assessing, and responding to accounts, what are effective accountability institutions, how accountability regimes emerge and change, and what effects they have. According to one view, accountability processes are part of policing, sustaining, or strengthening an established political order. The main challenges are to understand the processes through which accountability is, or can be, brought about, to discover mistakes, sanction unruly agents, and restore order. Examples include investigations into whether public funds have been spent as intended, laws have been followed, and powers have been misused. According to another view, accountability processes contribute to the reassessment and reconstruction of political orders and accountability regimes. Accountability processes are part of establishing order where none exists or challenging, reforming, or replacing an existing order and its causal beliefs, institutionalized ethical–moral standards, and power relations.

These two ways of understanding accountability processes are not mutually exclusive. Both are relevant for making sense of democratic accountability. At issue are their scope conditions and how one approach may be more or less important in specific polities, policy sectors, and time periods. The first is, for example, likely to be most helpful during normal times and in stable political orders with well-entrenched institutions. The second is more likely to be useful for understanding unsettled and emerging polities and exceptional times.

As observed in Chapter 1, there is a huge literature on order-maintaining accountability processes: The effectiveness or shortcomings of accountability regimes when it comes to monitoring and controlling agents, detecting and preventing non-compliance, achieving predetermined purposes, and maintaining order. Less attention has been paid to order-transforming accountability processes, beyond the idea that some predetermined authority or principal learns from experience and deliberately redesigns institutional arrangements in order to improve accountability and achieve better substantive results, as defined by the principal. Mainstream accountability literature has shown only a modest interest in how accountability processes in modern democracies involve a search for, and struggle over, definitions of legitimate political orders and accountability regimes, that is, how accountability processes might contribute to delegitimizing and deinstitutionalizing existing institutional arrangements and political identities, and to legitimizing and institutionalizing new ones.

In short, little has been written about what effects accountability processes have upon the dynamics of political orders and the conditions for orderly change. There has been limited interest in how accountability processes might be part of the mechanisms through which political communities develop, accept, apply, and change normative principles for the appropriate allocation, use, and control of powers and action capabilities. Likewise, there has been little attention to how accountability processes affect how political communities develop, accept, apply, and change normative criteria for assessing what are legitimate identities, roles, behavior, and results, and how they develop ideas about what are effective institutions for achieving desired substantive outcomes.

Over the last several decades, however, there have been increasing demands for making elected representatives, governments, and public officials accountable for political order and developments, and radical reforms have been advocated (Lerner and Tetlock 1999, Borowiak 2011, Dubnick 2011, Flinders 2011, Pollitt and Hupe 2011, Bovens et al. 2014, Wright 2015). An example is recent ideological disputes in Europe and elsewhere over what a legitimate political order is and how best to balance government's capacity to act on common problems and a political order's ability to protect citizens' freedom from government intervention.

Since accountability and consent by the governed are usually conceived of as a precondition for legitimate democratic government, popular discontent and heavy criticism of institutions and leadership in contemporary representative democracies suggest that current accountability regimes do not work satisfactorily. Rulers seem to be unable or unwilling to anticipate what the ruled are willing to accept. Or they are unwilling or unable to give explanations and justifications for what they have done and achieved that citizens find satisfactory. The situation in Europe (and elsewhere) therefore invites a re-examination of how democratic accountability works, the varying and shifting roles of citizens, elected representatives, and non-elected officials, and the effects accountability processes have on political order and orderly change.

A Possible Frame

The aim of this chapter is to provide a framework for thinking about the order-maintaining and order-transforming aspects of accountability processes as part of the broader question of where political orders and accountability regimes come from, how they are maintained, and how they change. Making sense of democratic accountability's effects on political order and orderly change presents two challenges. The *first* is to analyze how accountability processes work, and with what effects, when they are governed by well-entrenched institutionalized routines. The *second* is to analyze how accountability processes feed back into political orders and accountability regimes when they are governed by accountability politics.

Democratic accountability involves (a) establishing facts and assigning causality and responsibility; (b) formulating and applying normative standards for assessing conduct and the reasons given for behavior and outcomes; and (c) building and applying capabilities for demanding, rendering, and assessing accounts and for sanctioning inappropriate conduct and accounts.

The institution-centered approach used here assumes that perceived performance failure, discontent, and political contestation are drivers of non-routinized change. Uncertainty about facts and causality, ambiguous and contested normative standards, and unclear power relations create a space for competing interpretations and accountability politics.

Accountability processes provide opportunities for naming, shaming, and delegitimizing, as well as for praising, justifying, and legitimizing institutions and actors. Controversies are sometimes linked to single events, decisions, actors, or institutions and they do not involve demands for radical change in the terms of order. At other times, there is mobilization around crises of confidence in political orders or accountability regimes. The democratic legitimacy of the existing order is threatened, and accountability processes have potentially order-transforming effects. At stake are how powers and responsibilities are to be organized and exercised and how peaceful succession of power and civilized coexistence are to be secured.

A distinction can be made between two types of accountability politics (Chapter 1). On the one hand, there is accountability politics *within* an established order and an accountability regime with fairly stable power relations and role expectations, specifying what different actors are expected to do and standards of good conduct. On the other hand, accountability politics can be conceived of as structuring and restructuring processes in less institutionalized contexts and in periods of transformation. They contribute to shaping and reshaping political order and accountability regimes as part of constituting and re-constituting a political community and its borders, membership and identities, and form of government. According to the latter view, accountability politics is conceived of as an inherent part of democratic debate and struggle over political order and its cognitive, normative, and power basis. Ideas about what accountability arrangements are for, who is entitled to hold whom to account, and what counts as good reasons and reasoning are challenged. Political orders, institutions, and actors can gain or lose legitimacy and support.

As argued in Chapters 1 and 2, an institutional approach holds that understanding order-transforming accountability processes requires us to relax several assumptions made by mainstream rational actor principal–agent approaches regarding political institutions, actors, and change. This literature usually takes for granted predetermined principals and agents, their relations, interests, resources, logics of behavior, and dividing lines. It is clear who can (and shall) call whom to account for what, according to which normative standards, and why. The literature is concerned with whether predetermined agents comply with mandates and authorized behavior and with the effectiveness of accountability regimes when it comes to monitoring and controlling agents, detecting and preventing non-compliance, and achieving public purpose. As a result, the main concern of this order-maintaining literature is the knowledge basis and epistemic quality of accountability: How principals figure out what has happened and why; how they make sense of and learn from experience; how they construct and legitimize interpretations of truth and causal links between behavior and events; how they attribute responsibility, blame, and praise; how they figure out whether things could have been done differently and possibly impose sanctions; and how they redesign accountability regimes.

An institution-centered approach assumes fewer things as predetermined. Cognitive beliefs, normative standards, and actors and their relations, interests, dividing lines, and resources are seen as endogenous to democratic politics and accountability processes. Modern democracies are compound polities with complicated and dynamic lines of authority, power, responsibility, and accountability. The degree and form of political integration and the institutionalization of accountability regimes are variable and changing, and deliberate institutional design and reform is just one of a variety of change processes. Actors may be principals in some institutional settings and agents in others. They face, and have to accommodate, multiple and inconsistent demands from a variety of forums embedded in increasingly heterogeneous societies with powerful special interests. Understanding the effects of accountability processes makes it necessary to go beyond who makes formal decisions. Decision making is less an individual choice and more a social process. It involves drawing conclusions from complex streams of premises (Simon 1957: XII). Attributing responsibility and accountability, and sanctioning unauthorized behavior, requires knowledge about who has supplied the premises, something that is often difficult to disentangle.

The nature of accountability demands, and whether they are primarily order maintaining or order transforming, is affected by shifting trust in majority government, hierarchical command, the rule of law, corporatist bargaining arrangements, meritocracy and expert decisions, and markets and price systems. Likewise, the nature of accountability demands and the relative importance of order-maintaining and order-transforming aspects of accountability processes are also affected by the varying and shifting trust in, and conceptions of, the legitimate role and autonomy of citizens, elected representatives, and non-elected officials. Exploring the effects of accountability processes requires an understanding of how democracies organize ordinary citizens (and other actors) in and out of accountability processes in different institutional settings and give them different roles in accountability processes.

Organizing Orderly Change

Accountability is a principle for organizing the relations between rulers and ruled and constituting, maintaining, and changing a democratic political community and government. Democracy, rule by the people, is the dominant normative principle for organizing the distribution, exercise, control, and legitimization of power in what are called "democracies" in everyday language. There is fairly broad consensus that the people are the ultimate source of power and legitimacy—in Madison's words, "the only legitimate fountain of power" (Hamilton et al. 1964: 117). Citizenship is the key institution of democratic government, and the people, as a collection of free and equal citizens, are entitled to hold their rulers to account. Making government and public officials accountable is a democratic ideal and to some degree an achievement. Officials are obliged to describe, explain, and justify what happens and why to an authoritative forum. A legitimate democratic order requires strong accountability institutions and control with both actors exercising powers on behalf of the public and actors affecting the public good in important ways.

However, democracy, power, and accountability are slippery and contested concepts. They offer some guidance, but they are open to competing interpretations of their meaning and implications. There are also disputes regarding what institutions are most likely to secure effective accountability and what the proper role of citizens, elected representatives, and non-elected officials are. For example, whereas (nearly) everyone embraces democracy as an ideal, it is argued that the term has lost its meaning "in a cacophony of competing interpretations", and that there is a need to reconsider what citizens expect from each other and what it means to conduct oneself democratically (Hanson 1987: 86). Polities called democracies also differ considerably when it comes to organizational structures prescribing where powers, autonomy, responsibility, and accountability are to be located. Hierarchical, specialized, and open-access structures (Cohen et al. 1972) include and exclude participants and issues differently. They give rank-and-file citizens different roles and affect the likelihood of order-transforming demands.

Hierarchical Structure and Citizens as Voters

A hierarchical structure implies that decision makers, issues, and decision opportunities are ranked according to importance, and that high-ranking actors and issues have access to high-ranking decisions. A favorite narrative portrays parliamentary government as a chain of dyadic hierarchical relations of delegation and accountability. Voting in free, competitive elections is the core mechanism for authorizing representatives to act on behalf of the community and for holding them accountable to citizens. Citizens delegate power to a representative assembly. Elected representatives make authoritative decisions backed by coercion, also with regard to the terms of political order. Majority rule is a key principle. Accountability to the sovereign parliament is provided through a chain of top-down command and control from elected representatives to government, ministerial hierarchies, and public administration.

For example, principal–agent approaches to parliamentary government make assumptions about who is accountable to whom and for what (Strøm 2000, Strøm et al. 2003, Gailmard 2014). Accountability is about facts and causality and compliance with orders, rules, and purposes. Predetermined superiors and subordinates—principals and agents—have different preferences. There is information asymmetry, and the agent is the expert. Principals formulate mandates, set normative standards, and administer incentives and coercion to induce desirable behavior by agents. They delegate powers to agents and monitor and assess their performance. They also have the capability to sanction, discipline, and correct misconduct.

The idea that humans are not angels, and therefore have to be monitored, controlled, and called to account (Hamilton et al. 1964: 122–3), and that the power of the state is a threat to the welfare of citizens (Gailmard 2014: 93) and therefore requires institutional checks and balances, where ambition counteracts ambition, has deep historical roots. All actors are self-interested. The political community is held together by individual utility calculations embedded in a contract. Yet, there is a culture of mistrust, concerned with agents shirking their responsibilities and moral hazard, and institutions are instruments for making rational, self-regarding agents find it worthwhile to serve the interests of the principal. A key question is how to organize effective accountability regimes and what degree of agent autonomy will be helpful to fulfill the principal's preferences. Institutional change is the result of structural (constitutional) choice by principals. Order-transforming accountability demands are less likely the more electoral mechanisms and hierarchies work according to democratic ideals. Hierarchies, however, have limited capacity and legitimacy in modern democracies and orderly change depends on the working of a variety of specialized structures prescribing different roles to citizens.

Specialized Structure and Citizens in Multiple Roles

A specialized structure implies that participants, issues, and decision opportunities with specific characteristics are linked to each other. Citizens do not place all their eggs in one basket (the parliament). Polities are composite orders with a complicated ecology of interconnected and overlapping rules and accountabilities. There is institutional specialization, with different missions, mandates, identities, legitimacy bases, and powers. Several interdependent yet relatively autonomous, partly self-organizing, and resourceful institutions and professions are validated as the legitimate guardians of reason, truth, justice, and equity (March and Olsen 1989: 170, Olsen 2009b). A majority cannot claim sovereignty and ultimate authority. There are a variety of relationships between specialized agents and forums applying different normative criteria (Bovens et al. 2010). Citizens are voters as well as direct participants in public policymaking, carriers of rights, jury members, soldiers, members of political parties and organizations, customers, and clients.

This narrative has affinity with liberal–constitutional democracy. Liberalism is "the art of separation" (Walzer 1984) and a story about life spheres governed by different laws (Weber 1970: 123). Institutions have emerged gradually with separate origins and histories. Over time, compromises and struggles have been encoded into configurations of institutions working according to different normative and organizational principles and behavioral logics. Experiences with how powers have been exercised have caused popular trust in the competence and integrity of institutions and actors to shift. The reputations and legitimacy of legislatures, executives, courts, public administrations, central banks, experts, political parties, organized interests, mass media, private enterprises, and markets vary across polities and change over time. The same is true for public trust in ordinary citizens and their ability to govern themselves (Friedrich 1942). Autonomy can be embedded in shared normative and causal beliefs or in the support of powerful groups in society. Political community can be based upon a calculated contract or on a shared identity and loyalty to a community of history and fate, embedded in an enduring pact and shared traditions. In some institutional spheres, actors are expected to be self-serving utility maximizers; in others, to follow institutionalized codes of conduct and act with competence, integrity, and impartiality. There are several processes of institutional change, and they are not necessarily synchronized and coordinated.

An implication is that studies of orderly change and the institutional foundations of autonomy and accountability have to go beyond questions of what discretion legislators grant, for example, bureaucrats (Huber and Shipan 2002). It is not enough to study the legislative act that establishes an agency. Students of democratic accountability must pay attention to how agencies are transformed after they are formally founded through a variety of processes (Simon 1953, Laffan 2003).

Democratic government and politics have been, and still are, in competition with other resources than the ballot (Schattschneider 1960) and with other identities and loyalties than national citizenship. Authority and power founded on competitive elections are not necessarily dominant. Their importance is modified by other, unevenly distributed resources (Rokkan 1966) and by institutionalized rights that limit public intervention. Agencies build reputations and support, making it difficult for political authorities to intervene, and giving voluntary accounts can be part of documenting expertise and protecting or enhancing their legitimacy and autonomy. Agencies can be captured by a single constituency or develop several sources of support and thereby relative independence from each of them (Carpenter 2001, Schillemans and Busuioc 2014, Karsten 2015). Order-transforming accountability demands are likely to be related to interdependencies and interactions between institutions, for example when one or more institutions malfunction in ways that seriously hurt other institutions, or they try to radically redefine their place in the larger political and social order. Such demands are also more likely if there are open structures that invite participation of rank-and-file citizens.

Open Structure and Citizens as a "Sleeping Bear"

An open structure allows any combination of participants, issues, and decision-making opportunities. It gives access to all citizens and their concerns. There are no predetermined principals and agents. Citizens determine the rules for living together, and they can at any time call any official and each other to account. There can be citizens' initiatives, referenda, popular movements, direct contact with public administration, issues taken to court, and social protests that mobilize mass media and institutions with formal powers. Reason giving is the foundation of political community. Accountability regimes and political orders arise, are maintained, and change as a result of which participants and issues are activated at different points in time.

Open structures and transparency are, however, no guarantee for equal participation. Whereas citizens, in principle, can demand participation and representation in all institutions affecting their lives, their motivation and capabilities are limited in practice. The ideal of a responsible citizen participating in the collective life of the community is difficult to achieve. Citizenship—being a member of a political community—is not the dominant identity in modern democracies, except under special circumstances (Wolin 1960). Available access and information are not necessarily used (Pollitt 2006: 38). Attention is a scarce resource. Most public issues, handled within specialized or hierarchical structures, never reach the attention of the public, and most citizens are most of the time unlikely to be activated. Elected leaders' attention to reforms also varies over time as issues and participants appear or disappear (March and Olsen 1983). This is a narrative about a rather anarchic polity. Open, undifferentiated access structures have some affinity with both ideal participatory and deliberative democracy and free-exchange (market) systems. Such structures are particularly relevant in unsettled polities, polities in transformation, and situations where established institutions are set aside due to exceptional circumstances (Olsen 2014b). Order-transforming accountability demands and mass mobilization in open structures are most likely when there are major frictions and inefficiencies in hierarchical and specialized structures.

Modern democratic orders are more or less integrated and institutionalized. They have elements of hierarchical, specialized, and open-access structures. Accountability processes include both institutionalized routines and spontaneous demands for accounts. Routine processes often take place among elites within hierarchical or specialized structures. However, in Europe today, hierarchical and specialized institutions of democratic government are under attack. Political borders and the hegemonic role of the territorial state are being challenged. Representative institutions and their leaders are contested and so are the roles of citizens. Theorizing the effects of democratic accountability upon the terms of political order, then, will require us to comprehend conditions for citizens' mobilization and their use of different structures and how such mobilization influences the likelihood that accountability processes will take the form of order-maintaining institutional routines or order-transforming accountability politics (Chapter 1).

Order-Maintaining Institutional Routines

Within settled, highly institutionalized regimes, accountability and orderly change are routine. Good government implies exercising authority and power in accordance with fairly stable principles, approved procedures, and recognized authority and autonomy. Accountability and change are organized by hierarchical and specialized structures rather than open structures. Power relations and expectations of how accountability and orderly change can be achieved are taken for granted. The "sleeping bear" is sleeping most of the time. In such contexts there is, as observed in Chapter 2, widespread agreement about what different institutions are for and who is accountable to whom, for what, under what circumstances, and according to which normative criteria. It is clear who should be blamed if things go wrong and attribution of accountability is guided by clear, well-known, stable, and socially validated doctrines, roles, rules, routines, procedures, and resources. Accounts focus on deviances from shared rules and expectations. Actors are evaluated in terms of whether they perform the duties of their roles with dedication, integrity, competence, and conformity to proper procedures and purposes.

Attention is upon how effectively an institutional accountability regime governs behavior and achieves desired performance and orderly change. Accountability is usually claimed to be linked to improving the quality of democratic governance. Accountability processes largely take place within institutional constraints and with modest controversy and they have order-maintaining more than order-transforming effects (Olsen 2013, 2014b).

In settled polities and highly institutionalized (hierarchical or specialized) contexts, it is not unreasonable to treat mandates, normative standards, expectations, authority, and power as predetermined and exogenous to accountability processes. The challenge is to monitor behavior and results, make sense of facts and causality, develop performance measures and score cards, detect non-compliance and undesirable behavior, pin down responsibility, and assign blame and culpability. Key issues are linked to experiential learning and rational adaptation to shifting circumstances, namely how effective institutions are in detecting fraud, waste, incompetence, and corruption; whether mandates and jurisdictions have been exceeded and powers usurped or misused; and whether powers have been used to prevent undesired behavior and outcomes.

Arguably, mainstream principal–agent approaches assuming settled, highly institutionalized political orders and accountability regimes capture routine situations better than they capture accountability processes in unsettled polities and complex, conflict-ridden, and dynamic situations. They are more likely to be useful when accountability processes are concerned with single actors, events, and operational responsibility. They become more problematic when order and system responsibility is at issue: Who recruited and trained the operator, designed the system of rules and routines, monitored the operations, and so on? They are even less likely to be useful when the task is to disentangle the long-term effects of government actions upon the distribution of citizens' life chances and welfare compared to the effects of economic, technological, cultural, and demographic processes—situations where there are usually ideological disputes over the actual and desired role of politics and government. Even though the explanatory power of a principal–agent approach may be modest under such conditions, many public-sector reforms are based on and justified in terms of principal–agent thinking, and these models might also be evoked in unsettled periods or in the aftermath of a crisis as a means of criticizing behavior and events (Schillemans 2013). However, in such situations principal–agent approaches are likely to fit democratic rhetoric better than democratic practices.

Therefore, to make sense of the complexity and dynamics of accountability in modern democracies, it has to be recognized that accountability processes are about more than order maintenance and compliance with predetermined principals and their success criteria. Sometimes accountability demands are order transforming. They are part of debates and contestations over the terms of political order and accountability regimes. They challenge and possibly change the roles, powers, and responsibilities different institutions and actors have in the wider order. How, then, do accountability processes feed back into political orders and accountability regimes by challenging institutionalized causal beliefs, ethical–moral standards, and power relations, and possibly contribute to a reconstruction of the terms of political order and orderly change?

Order-Transforming Accountability Politics

An institution-centered approach goes beyond the assumption that accountability regimes emerge and change as a result of deliberate structural choices of predetermined principals. Attention is directed to accountability processes as part of the dynamics through which political orders and accountability regimes are constituted and reconstituted, integrated and disintegrated, institutionalized and deinstitutionalized (Olsen 2013, 2014b). Demanding, rendering, assessing, and responding to accounts are constitutive political processes. Interpretation of experience and creation of meaning; testing of causal beliefs, normative standards and power relationships; and distributing glory and blame are related to fundamental issues in political life (March and Olsen 1995, Borowiak 2011).

Accountability processes do not only provide an opportunity for the interpretation of experience and for exploring how accountability may be enhanced within an existing regime. They also provide an opportunity for challenging, delegitimizing, and transforming existing regimes and the codes of conduct, identities, normative standards, causal beliefs, and power relations upon which they are based (Chapter 1). Accountability regimes can change through reallocation of relevant resources, through modifications of opportunity and incentive structures, and through fashioning rulers and ruled through socialization, internalization, and habitualization. Identities are endogenous to accountability processes. Identification is a fundamental mechanism in group integration (March and Simon 1958), and behavioral logics, preferences, and commitments are changing and variable, not fixed and universal (March and Olsen 1989).

Ideally, democracies are self-reflecting communities, involving self-development (Mill 1962: 30–5). Citizens reason and deliberate about experience, critically re-examining ends, means, and power relations. Some of the key institutions of democracy are institutions of discourse, and the quality of democratic governance is measured by the quality of its discourses and what is accepted as public truth (March and Olsen 1995: 146, 174–5).

Civil society and a public space for free debate provide an open structure for sense making, will formation, and structural change (Goodin 2008). Freedom of expression, legitimate opposition, and a free press are institutions that help citizens and officials to construct a moral account of the good society, recognize appropriate tasks, ends, and forms of governance, and develop confidence in their mutual motivation and capacity for reason and justice.

An optimistic democratic interpretation of accountability processes is that communicative rationality and experience-based learning will generate mutual understanding, stepwise rational adaptation, and improvement through the exchange of reasons and arguments. Accountability is based on discretionary reasoning and argumentation. Actors comply with the force of the better argument (Habermas 1996a, Molander et al. 2012). In such a world, there will be honest reporting, free flow of information, and diagnoses. Mistakes and imperfections will be discovered. There will be willingness to modify rules and routines as a result of the lessons learnt. Equilibrium will be established and progress achieved. Order-transforming accountability demands are unlikely.

Empirical evidence, nevertheless, suggests that experience-based learning involves imperfect processes and that improvement is not guaranteed. Accountability regimes are not fully accepted by everyone. The people rarely speak with one voice in democracies. Accounts are often contested. There are competing narratives of what happened, why it happened, who and what caused it, what else could have been done, and whether what happened is good. Political actors struggle to solicit support for their understandings. Intrusive monitoring and lack of trust can reduce motivation to speak freely. Heavy blaming and punishment of mistakes ("throw the rascals out," "heads must roll") create defensiveness and formalistic rule following, rather than experimentation, learning, and improvement.

As held in Chapter 2, in a world of interdependence, chance events, and long and uncertain causal chains, with significant effects sometimes surfacing only after years, the assignment of accountability can seem largely arbitrary. Still, democracies seek to interpret history in ways that praise, justify, or condemn actions and establish responsibility. They foster demands for calling someone to account, even when experience offers little guidance (March and Olsen 1995: 158, 173–7). Deciding who to praise or blame does not depend only on hard evidence and correct causal understanding. Interpretations of experience compete for acceptance on the basis of both evidence and power (March 1987, 2010). The ability to gain acceptance for a type of discourse, an interpretative community, and a special vocabulary is a source and indication of power (March and Olsen 1995: 180).

Typically, the very meaning and implications of accountability are challenged when accountability regimes collide or principles confront practical situations, generating new cleavages. Then a polity may be turned into a conceptual battleground and institutional building site. There are debates over competing visions of political order; what legitimate public affairs and private realms are; which principles for organizing and governing common affairs deserve the consent and allegiance of citizens; what legitimate identities, roles, codes of behavior, and power relations are; and which institutions and actors deserve to be accepted as competent and trustworthy (Olsen 2010).

Accountability processes and change also depend in large part on post-event processes. The style of presentation of an account and how criticism of malperformance is met can be as important for responses as the act to be accounted for. That is, accountability processes are influenced by what explanations and justifications are given for an action or outcome: For example, whether actors humbly submit to criticism, express regret, and ask for forgiveness or excuse, justify, or reframe interpretations (Dubnick 2005). Some interpret what has happened as an unfortunate but unavoidable accident. Others claim that there was an error due to inadequate resources and skills, or that events were the result of purposeful acts, a criminal offense, or as a system failure. Behavior can be forgiven and justified, or disapproved and punished, and account giving can under some conditions develop into rituals, with no negative implications (Chapter 2). Accountability claims can also be met with talk rather than action (Brunsson 1989). For example, the 22 July tragedy in Norway—when the government's headquarters were blown up and a camp arranged by the governing Labor Party's youth organization was attacked, killing 77 people (NOU 2012: 14)—generated public manifestations and strong talk about democracy, openness, and community. Nevertheless, action was slow and cautious (Lango et al. 2014).

An implication is that the conception of accountability as a neutral technique and routine process involving truth finding, causal understanding, correct reporting, control and compliance has to be supplemented by accountability politics with an order-transforming potential. Problems of objectively assigning responsibility create possibilities for political contestation, image management, and naming and shaming, as well as collective sense making and integrative behavior. Accountability processes might involve debates and struggles over what are considered legitimate terms of political order, good government, and preferable appropriate accountability regimes (Costa et al. 2003, Bovens et al. 2010, Curtin et al. 2010). Accountability processes in unsettled and emerging political orders and in open structures are in particular likely to be related to political contestation and order-transforming accountability demands, with the possible rise and fall of political orders, institutions, actors, ideologies, cleavages, and coalitions as a result.

Accountability in an Era of Political–Administrative Transformation

The last several decades exemplify such an era of transformation. There has been an obsession with accountability (Dubnick 2011) and arguably as much attention has been focused on public-sector reforms as on reforms of electoral democracy. Accountability demands and claims have been based on a new understanding of the relations between levels of government, between institutional spheres, and the legitimate role of government and the public sector in society.

The main trend has been interpreted as a paradigm shift from collective responsibility to individual responsibility, from democratic government in sovereign states to borderless market exchange and competition. The major tendency has been a shift away from a social-democratic welfare state order emphasizing equality and holding that health, education, and social security should not be treated as commodities for sale in markets toward a liberal order emphasizing free market exchange, emancipation from over-regulation, a shorter social contract, and more freedom for the individual (Dahrendorf 1988, Sejersted 2005). The trend has also been interpreted as a shift from a hierarchical state and Weberian bureaucracy to a managerial state giving priority to performance and substantive outcomes rather than compliance with legal rules and procedures (Saint-Martin 2000).

Neo-liberal inspired New Public Management reforms, which have introduced corporate accountability principles, have been based upon mistrust in "big government" and "excessive bureaucracy." They have celebrated limited government, structural disaggregation, privatization, competitive markets, price systems, management autonomy, performance, public–private partnerships, and citizens as customers. Government has been disempowered, while private actors have been empowered. Non-majoritarian institutions have been given more autonomy. We are said to live in the age of the unelected (Vibert 2007), and conceptions of accountability have increasingly come to rely on watchdog agencies deliberately placed outside a unitary ministerial hierarchy and at arm's length from politics and direct electoral control (Thatcher and Stone Sweet 2002, Busuioc et al. 2012, Egeberg and Trondal 2011). "Autonomy" has meant detachment from the political center, often hiding a transfer from political dependencies to dependencies on markets, managers, stakeholders, and rating agencies. In addition, neo-constitutionalism has promoted juridification of political life and constraints on politics. Courts have been empowered to guard society against arbitrary use of majority power (Olsen 2009b, 2010, 2015a).

Reforms have also challenged the hegemonic role of the territorial state. For centuries, conceptions of democratic accountability have developed in the context of the sovereign state (Eisenstadt and Rokkan 1973/1974, Tilly 1975). But that role has been defied by increased international interdependence, globalization, and European integration. There has been a perceived need to develop new ways of thinking about global accountability, explore new mechanisms securing accountability and popular control beyond the state, and limit abuse of power in world politics (Grant and Keohane 2005). Europe is in search of political order (Olsen 2007, 2010) and a new type of order has emerged—one that is multi-leveled, multi-centered, hybrid, networked, and fluid (Hooghe and Marks 2009). Distinctions between levels of government and between the public and the private realm have become less clear. Old accountability relations have been challenged and new ones have evolved.

There are elements of "normalization" of government and public administration at the European level (Egeberg 2006, Curtin and Egeberg 2008, Trondal 2010, Wille 2013). However, proposals for making institutions and actors accountable have been based upon competing conceptions of the nature, purpose, and desired future of the EU. Visions have varied among those seeing the Union alternately as an intergovernmental, supranational, or regulatory entity (Bovens et al. 2008, 2010). The EU's financial and social crises have generated a perceived need to strengthen institutions of democratic accountability and restore popular confidence in the European project. Arguably, the result has been more accountability and less democracy (Curtin et al. 2010, Papadopoulos 2010).

Public-sector reforms have made it more difficult to pinpoint the loci of accountability and to balance political–administrative control and institutional and professional autonomy (Christensen and Lægreid 2006, Lægreid and Verhoest 2010, Lægreid 2014). Accountability to the EU, international human rights regimes, courts, and markets has constrained accountability to domestic voters and parliaments. It is far from obvious how democratic accountability and orderly change can be safeguarded when government is embedded in networks across levels of government, institutional spheres, and the public and private realms and when governance is based on informal partnership and dialogue, more than hierarchical command and formal control relationships (Michels and Meijer 2008: 168, Klijn and Koppenjan 2014: 246). Reforms have contributed to increased attention to the results achieved by the public sector, but functional superiority and efficiency gains have been difficult to prove (Verhoest et al. 2004). It has been wondered whether reinventing government implies reinventing democracy (Pierre 2009) and there have been efforts to reassert the political center and political leadership (Dahlström et al. 2011).

A narrative of order-transforming accountability processes has, however, to be held together with a narrative of inertia and "historical inefficiency" (March and Olsen 1989). The European nation-state and national identities have showed considerable resilience, in spite of discontent with their ability to deal with the expectations, needs, and interests of citizens. Observations about the difficulty of cutting back the public sector have been supplemented by observations about how neo-liberalism has survived the financial crises since 2007 (Crouch 2011). Like welfare-state ideology, market ideology is embedded in strong institutions and supported by powerful groups.

Theories of democratic accountability have to take into account that the political salience of accountability processes and their effects upon the terms of political order are not static. A key question is under what conditions, and through which processes, does accountability capture public attention (Chapter 6)? When is the "sleeping bear" sleeping because political–administrative processes and outcomes are perceived as satisfactory by most citizens? When is inactivity caused by alienation and absence of hope of making a difference? There is a need to understand when accountability processes go beyond hierarchical and specialized structures with predetermined principals and agents and who then gets into the political contestations (Schattschneider 1960, Cohen et al. 1972). There is also a need to understand under what conditions accountability processes are likely to involve the legitimacy of the established order and order-transforming demands and how public mass mobilization affects the likelihood of order-maintaining and order-transforming effects.

Some Suggestions

Although there is a long way to go before the intricacies of accountability processes and their effects are understood, we can identify some elementary hypotheses regarding the increasingly felt need for holding actors to account that are probably shared by most approaches. *Ceteris paribus*, the more autonomy and discretion actors have, the more likely there will be accountability demands. Demands will be linked to actors, issues, policy areas, and institutional spheres regulated by broad framework laws and open mandates allowing arbitrary judgments, rather than precise institutionalized standards, rules, and procedures. Accountability claims are likely to be triggered by indications that something is wrong, such as real or perceived performance crises and scandals and ideological confrontations over what constitutes proper political order and good government. Such claims are also more likely when there is reduced economic slack (Cyert and March 1963) than in resource-rich polities or periods, which allow more institutional autonomy and actor discretion.

An institution-centered approach holds that theorizing democratic accountability and the growing demand for accountability require studies of how accountability processes can be order transforming as well as order maintaining. Accountability processes are part of both complying with and challenging established political orders and accountability regimes, and the latter in particular is important in unsettled polities and periods of lack of trust in and discontent with institutions and leaders. Principal–agent approaches have, however, given more attention to how existing accountability regimes can be made more efficient and how order can be maintained than to regime dynamics. As a consequence, accountability has primarily been related to facts and causality relevant for predetermined principals' control and predetermined agents' compliance. Power relations between principals and agents and normative standards have been taken for granted. The political order has been assumed to be in equilibrium, or change has been seen as a result of deliberate structural choices made by principals.

While the limited feasibility of unambiguously establishing facts and causal responsibility creates a problem for academics, it creates a space for accountability politics related to the terms of political order. An institution-centered approach, therefore, attends to how accountability processes are part of the structuring and restructuring of political orders and accountability regimes, including the normative standards and the power relations in which they are embedded. Theorizing accountability, then, requires exploration of how competing approaches interpret political–democratic orders, actors, and institutional sources of accountability demands and responses.

Principal–agent approaches to parliamentary government portray democratic order, orderly change, and accountability regimes in terms of predetermined, dyadic principal–agent relations between the people, elected representatives, and non-elected public officials. Modern democracies are, however, compound and dynamic orders with a variety of specialized mechanisms for demanding, rendering, assessing, and sanctioning accounts. Responsibilities and powers are dispersed among partly autonomous levels of government, institutions of government, and private groups with a power base of their own. Furthermore, principal–agent approaches usually see problems of accountability as being caused by agents, not principals. Empirical studies, however, suggest that accountability problems may be caused by "forum drift" rather than "agency drift" (Schillemans and Busuioc 2014). Democratic politics often provide vague compromises and mandates that are difficult for agents to interpret, implement, and enforce. Agents are also often provided with resources that do not match their tasks and responsibilities.

Understanding accountability dynamics requires us to examine how democracies cope with and legitimize accountability at different levels of government and in different institutional spheres while remaining a community of organized cooperation. There are competing and contested accountability demands, appeals to different audiences and normative standards, and multiple channels of accountability. Hybrid regimes with mixes of self-governance and external control are, for example, tried to be captured by the term "accountable autonomy" (Fung 2001: 75), which implies a certain independence from central power, rules, and oversight combined with local initiative, dialogue between officials and citizens, transparency, horizontal account giving, and learning.

Principal–agent approaches see political orders, orderly change, and accountability regimes as being based on a constellation of interests and power and involving a calculated contract between rational, self-regarding individuals. Priority is given to *external* control through opportunity structures, incentives, and coercion. Elections, political administrative hierarchies, and institutional checks and balances are the dominant institutional mechanisms. Accountability is achieved by selecting and removing agents with certain characteristics for/from office, hierarchical command, or reciprocal control established through vertical or horizontal separation of power. If incentives are such that the agent's expected utility of complying is greater than of not complying, accountability is achieved independent of the motives of actors.

Arguably, principal–agent approaches to accountability overestimate the importance of external control, electoral mechanisms, the dichotomy between politics and administration, the hierarchical relation between elected representatives and non-elected officials, and the dominance of rational self-regarding actors. Democracies do not trust a single institution, mechanism, or behavioral logic. An institutional approach, therefore, calls attention to the possibility of authority, as well as power struggles. It attends to how *internalized* identities and role conceptions are formed in accountability processes and elsewhere, supplementing external controls. Accountability processes can facilitate the development of agreed-upon identities, roles, and self-restraint through communicative action. Congruence in norms, behavioral codes, and expectations can develop by means of reciprocal discovery of normative validity through deliberation among initially conflicting parties, or through socialization and habitualization.

Thus, we can (under some conditions) understand the political order to be founded on a belief in its legitimacy, voluntary consent, and a felt duty to follow rules and prescribed behaviors (Weber 1978: 31). An example is a public administration governed by public-service values, due process, fairness, impartiality, honesty, and democratic control. In this case, administrators see themselves as "stewards" of the public good. They share goals and principles with their elected political principals (Schillemans 2013). Generally, an institutional approach assumes that actors are governed by authority within a zone of acceptance (Simon 1957: 12, March and Simon 1958: 140–1) that defines acceptable purposes, methods, codes of appropriate behavior, and powers.

Public administration is perceived as something more than technicians implementing and enforcing goals and rules determined by elected representatives. Administrators take part in defining problems and shaping policies. Citizens have direct channels to public administration and under some conditions they trust administrators, experts, and judges more than elected representatives. The quality of citizens' lives, their subjective satisfaction, and the legitimacy of government depend on political–administrative institutions that work on the basis of integrity and impartiality (Rothstein 2011). It has been claimed that if Aristotle were writing today, he would be more of an administrative theorist than a political theorist (Harmon 1995: 206).

An institutionally differentiated and specialized order, however, legitimates competing identities, roles, behavioral logics, and resources. In doing so, the order opens up for interinstitutional tension and conflict. Actors do not act solely on predetermined personal preferences or the prescription of an institutional role. They are also influenced by their interactions with others, in dialogue and struggle, processes affecting how discretion and resources are used. Accountability politics involves interaction between external and internal controls, and because both are imperfect, it is likely to be useful to study frictions in all the mechanisms institutions work through to secure human cooperation, problem solving, and accountability (Olsen 2013: 460, 2014b: 110).

History matters. Demands for explanation and justification of the political order, and the possibility of order-transforming effects, will be less likely the more an institution historically has been seen to show competence, honesty, and integrity. As a corollary, there is a need to understand under what circumstances orders founded on authority are likely to break up. For example, the more obvious performance failures and the less trust there is in authorities and institutions, the more likely are order-transforming accountability demands, confrontations over definitions of legitimate political order and forms of governance, and possibly changes in the terms of order.

An institutional approach suggests that accountability regimes and orderly change are least likely to be dominated by self-serving actors calculating private expected utility in societies with strong civic identity and citizenship. The stronger shared ethical–moral standards, we-feelings, and solidarity a society has, the more likely that accountability processes will be governed by relatively autonomous institutions, and the less likely that there will be order-transforming accountability demands and radical changes in the existing order. Autonomy does not imply the right to arbitrarily exploit discretion for personal gain. It is a political trust, embedded in a mandate and general principles. Discretion is guided by an institutional identity that largely meets codes of appropriate behavior and criteria of reason and justice, as understood by the population. Citizens have their values, interests, and worldviews accommodated routinely without continuous participation. They are not obsessed with possible misuse of political and administrative powers. Consequently, demands for accountability increase under conditions of normative fragmentation, confusion, and contestation, where behavior is no longer guided by shared codes and a new order organized around another mobilizing narrative has not yet emerged.

An institution-centered agenda recognizes that democratic accountability is a difficult ideal to realize. Accountability as order-maintaining routines is fairly well understood. It is more challenging to understand order-transforming accountability processes as parts of ideological battles over political order and attempts to "reinvent" government. However, democratic orders and their institutional distribution of power and autonomy, and democratic actors and their attention, activity level, behavioral logics, and relationships are dynamic. They vary over space and change over time. An institutional agenda therefore explores the conditions under which accountability processes are likely to attract few or many participants and issues, and how public mobilization may affect the content of accountability demands and their effects (Chapter 6).

Making assumptions about citizens' participation, consent, and approval calls for realism regarding their motivation and capacity. There is no guarantee that citizens or their elected representatives will be motivated and capable of living up to the roles prescribed for them as principals in rational principal–agent approaches or democratic theories. The issue is relevant not least because it is unclear whether Europe is in a transition period or has reached a new normal with discontent and distrust in political institutions and leaders. It is not obvious whether the "sleeping bear" will remain sleeping in the decade to come, how angry he will be if he wakes up, and how he will relate to existing accountability institutions and their access structures. Competing answers to such questions are related to different conceptions of political agency and authorized and unauthorized action.

After challenging mainstream assumptions about political order and the effects of accountability processes it is therefore time to reconsider assumptions about the role of political agency, decision making, and rational adaptation in accountability processes. In Chapter 4, I argue that accountability theory has to take into account that whereas ambiguity is usually seen as an enemy of effective accountability, ambiguity is intrinsic to political and organizational decision making (March and Olsen 1976) and that ambiguity and uncertainty about the past—what has happened, why, and who is responsible and should be held to account—open the way for the politics of accountability, involving sense-making processes and coping with competing interpretations of accountability.

4

Ambiguity and the Politics of Accountability

Accountability, Agency, and Rational Adaptation

In a democracy, reasonable demands for explanations and justifications require identifiable actors with relevant autonomy, discretion, and powers that can be used or misused. Democratic normative theory, organization theory, and mainstream principal–agent theory usually link accountability to an instrumental vision and belief in human agency, rational choice, and history determined by human will, causal understanding, and control. There appears to be a strong link between rational decision making and accountability and there is a clear distinction between authorized and unauthorized behaviors and outcomes. Orderly change and improvement are secured through experiential learning and rational adaptation of ideas, behavior, and institutional arrangements.

Ideally, then, democratic actors are political agents involved in rational decision making and adaptation. Accountability and autonomy must be commensurate; there can be no power without accountability and no accountability without autonomy (March and Olsen 1995: 152, Chapter 1 of this book). Legitimate democratic government requires that elected representatives, appointed officials, and other power holders are accountable to a well-informed public for the exercise of their discretion and powers. They have to present arguments citizens can accept, and in modern democracies this implies rational decision making, goal achievement, and contract fulfillment. Formal organizations and formally organized institutions are portrayed as tools of effectiveness, efficiency, control, and compliance. They are characterized by clear and consistent goals, as well as formalized division of work, information, power, responsibility, and accountability. Accountability processes, then, link two fundamental processes of political intelligence. First, there is decision making based on rational calculation of the expected utility of available alternatives. Second, there is learning from experience providing the basis of rational adaptation, governance by feedback, and informed consent by the governed.

Such conditions are sometimes met in modern democracies. There are clear, consistent, stable, and agreed-upon answers to standard accountability questions: What happened? Is what happened good or bad? Why did it happen and could it have been avoided? Who made it happen? Who authorized, supported, or opposed it? Who is responsible and who is to blame or be praised for what? Who can be called to account and possibly sanctioned? What can be done or has to be done?

But often these conditions are *not* met, and this chapter considers the possibility that events are not necessarily a product of the deliberate choices of identifiable actors. It is not always easy to conclude who is responsible and should be held to account. It is not obvious that history is determined by human will, causal understanding, and control. Learning from experience and rational adaptation are not guaranteed. There are limitations, not only with regard to predicting the future and the consequences and expected utility of alternative choices, but also when it comes to making sense of the past. Facts, causality, normative standards, and powers can be ambiguous and contested (March and Olsen 1975, 1976: Chapter 4) and ambiguity and uncertainty can make it problematic to give correct answers to questions about what has happened and why. The causality of events is difficult to disentangle and it is uncertain whether what happened was avoidable. Purposes, mandates, intentions, roles, and rules are not clear and it is problematic to distinguish success from failure. Existing authority and power relations do not secure any identifiable group of actors' control over events or the capability to sanction undesirable behavior and unacceptable accounts.

Widespread ambiguity challenges mainstream accountability theory and creates a need to re-examine and reassess some key assumptions about the ways in which accountability processes work in practice when history is ambiguous, interpretations are not completely determined by events, and adaptive rationality cannot be guaranteed. Still, participants and onlookers also try to make sense of what has happened and why; when, for example, fundamentally ambiguous stimuli open for garbage can-like processes with the shifting activation of participants and definitions of problems and solutions, and non-intended outcomes (Cohen et al. 1972). Ambiguity and uncertainty extend the space for interpretation, argumentation, and accountability politics; and because events are not self-evident, what happens afterwards becomes important. Interpretations, assessments, and responses are constructed in accountability processes and they are affected by existing institutions, identities, belongings, loyalties, interactions, and trust relationships, and by what participants believe, expect to see, and want to see (March and Olsen 1975, 1976: Chapter 4).

Such situations are relevant because ambiguity and uncertainty are intrinsic to political life and not limited to the performance of agents. It is difficult for modern democracies to formulate clear, consistent, and stable goals and normative standards for success to which agents can be held accountable. Democracies also have difficulty with designing institutions, rules, mandates, and roles that unambiguously prescribe authorized action. Accountability theory, therefore, has to explore the role of ambiguity and what is really going on in accountability processes beyond rational decision making, control, and experience-based rational adaptation. Theorists have to address the fact that accountability processes sometimes take place under conditions of goal ambiguity, uncertain and competing understandings, and limited powers and action capabilities. We must avoid taking for granted the dominant explanatory power of human will, understanding, and control and try to understand how the ambiguity and unresolved conflicts of political life make it difficult to correctly assign causal responsibility and learn from experience. There is a need to explore institutional sources of ambiguity and how accountability processes under such conditions open the way for accountability politics related to the terms of political order—debates and struggles over what are legitimate terms of political order, how government is and should be organized, and where responsibility and accountability over different issues reside and should reside.

Accountability processes, then, involve sense making, competing narratives, argumentation, persuasion, image management, and blame games. Under some conditions, accountability processes involve efforts to discover or construct shared meaning and assessment. Under other conditions, they involve contestations over the terms of order. Accountability is often used as a rhetorical device in partisan battles (Hood 2014) or in attempts to create a sense of control and efficiency that strengthens the legitimacy of the political order. Account giving can develop into rituals, ceremonies, and myths providing illusions (Gustavsson et al. 2009) and accountability regimes can be understood as social constructions through which a political community affirms its myths about the pre-eminence of rationality, democracy, and intentional human control over history.

I hold that mainstream accountability approaches reduce their area of application by not taking ambiguity seriously enough. Assuming that compliance–control is only one aspect of accountability relations and processes, and that ambiguity is intrinsic to political life, an institutional approach suggests that it may be fruitful to relax mainstream assumptions regarding what accountability means and implies, including (a) what is involved in demanding, rendering, assessing, and responding to accounts; (b) what factors foster effective accountability; and (c) how accountability regimes emerge and how they change. It may be useful to examine *a priori* assumptions regarding purposes formulated by predetermined principals, mediated through competitive elections, laws, hierarchical arrangements, and dyadic relationships between the people, a representative assembly, government, and non-elected agents.

Theorizing accountability requires questioning the standard assumptions about authority, power, and success criteria embedded in normative representative democratic theories and in formal legal institutions prescribing chains of delegation of authorization and accountability of representation (Olsen 2014b, Chapter 2 of this book). Likewise, there is a need to relax *a priori* assumptions about dividing lines, information asymmetry, control through external mechanisms and opportunity and incentive structures, and principals deliberately designing and redesigning institutional arrangements to make accountability regimes more effective. Much depends on how the relation between ambiguity and accountability is conceived, whether ambiguity is seen as the enemy of accountability or as an inherent part of political life and accountability processes.

Ambiguity as the Enemy of Accountability

"Accountability" refers to being answerable to somebody else, being obligated to explain and justify action and inaction, for example, how mandates, authority, and resources have been applied, with what results, and whether outcomes meet relevant standards and principles. However, as observed in Chapter 2, the precise definition of and assumed conditions for ensuring effective accountability vary across European democracies committed to the idea that rulers should be accountable to the ruled (Verhey et al. 2008). There are also huge variations across policy areas and groups and over time (Stone 1995, Bovens 2007, Bovens et al. 2010).

"Ambiguity" implies a state of having more than one meaning. A situation can be interpreted in different ways and it is not always easy to distinguish between multiple interpretations (March and Olsen 1975, 1976, Weick et al. 2005). Accountability under ambiguity refers to calling for, rendering, assessing, and sanctioning accounts in situations where objectives, technology, and experience are unclear, participation is fluid, and the legitimacy of different participants, issues, and resources are contested. Here ambiguity refers to the perceptions of individual actors and not to a scientific–objective assessment of a specific situation.

It is commonplace to assert that accountability thrives on clear and consistent mandates, authority, responsibility, rules, normative standards, expectations, self-evident facts, and well-understood causality. The aim of accountability regimes is to reveal incompetence, fraud, malpractice, and abuse of power, and ambiguity is the enemy of effective accountability and should be eliminated. "Accountability abhors ambiguity," thus "clarity of accountability and contribution must be one of the attributes of every single role that makes up the system" (Porter-O'Grady et al. 1997: 54).

The idea that ambiguity is the enemy of accountability has its roots in democratic theory and organization theory. A democratic article of faith is that "the public is ultimately the sole source of sovereign authority, and it is the public to whom all public officials ought ultimately to be accountable" (Goodin 2008: 164). Democratic theories emphasize providing relevant and timely information as a necessary requirement for legitimate governance. Democracy requires well-informed citizens and officials, and public accounts are vehicles for popular sovereignty (March and Olsen 1995). Effective accountability requires constitutional and formal legal clarity regarding who is obligated to render an account, who can call whom to account for what under different circumstances, and who shall assess accounts and possibly sanction malpractice.

The idea is also central to conceptions of formal organizations as instruments for problem solving and conflict resolution. Organizations are tools of rationality, effectiveness, and efficiency, characterized by clear and consistent goals and formalized division of work, information, power, and responsibility. Organizations are deliberately structured and restructured and there is a constant need to provide mechanisms of control to check that orders are fulfilled and rules adhered to. Supervision is built into the hierarchy of authority and accountability. The role of those "higher in rank" includes the obligation to check on the performance of the "lower in rank" (Etzioni 1964: 25). In contrast, this chapter explores the implications of seeing ambiguity as essential to human agency, democratic politics, formal organizations, and human existence.

Ambiguity as Intrinsic to Life

Ambiguity is not necessarily transitory or pathological. According to existential philosophy, ambiguity is intrinsic to human existence (de Beauvoir 1972) and it is a core aspect of political and organizational decision making, leadership, and sense making (Cohen et al. 1972, March and Olsen 1976, Cohen and March 1986, March and Weissinger-Baylon 1986, Weick et al. 2005). Democracies cannot (and probably should not) completely eliminate ambiguity, and therefore have to find ways to cope with it as part of accountability processes. Comprehending such processes may contribute to an improved understanding of democratic accountability, political order, and change.

Under some conditions, concealing one's preferences rather than taking a clear stand may be an electoral strategy (Shepsle 1972, Page 1976, Alesina and Cukierman 1990). Ambiguity can also be seen as a political necessity. So that agreement can be reached, compromises are made sufficiently ambiguous to allow for competing interpretations. Generally, change is easier when it involves modifying the relations between coexisting, ambiguous principles rather than replacing one clear principle with another. Ambiguity can be embraced because detailed rules are likely to be counterproductive in terms of outcomes, adaptability, discovery, and innovation (Goodin 1982: 59–72, Hood 1999). A recent example is the incomplete and unclear rules for exiting the EU set out by Article 50 that are now to be applied following the Brexit vote in the United Kingdom. In this case, the difficulty of anticipating the implications of a member state exiting the Union has left room to cope with particular needs and unseen circumstances (Hillion 2015). Furthermore, ambiguity can involve blame avoidance. Superiors wanting to avoid association with torture, for example, may prefer ambiguous and obscure language regarding how to handle prisoners. By not defining precisely what it means to "apply pressure," they shift accountability onto the lowest ranking and least powerful (Manning 2004).

When theorizing accountability, it is necessary to take into account the ambiguous character of the foundational standards and principles of democracies (Connolly 1987). Demands for clarity and consistency are hard to meet because Western culture is incoherent. There are several competing interpretations of what democracy means and implies in different contexts (Hanson 1987: 69) and unresolved conflicts between rival traditions regarding how concepts such as rationality and justice should be interpreted (MacIntyre 1988). Normative theories and formal legal institutions give limited behavioral guidance. Democracies legitimize competing opinions and there is disagreement regarding what institutions make accountability effective (March and Olsen 1995: 59, 162). Because modern politics unfolds within and between large-scale and resourceful formal organizations and formally organized institutions, it is also worthwhile to note that organizations are sometimes "organized anarchies" characterized by unclear causal understanding, ambiguous preferences, contested authority, and fluid participation (Cohen et al. 1972, Lomi and Harrison 2012). Thus, accountability processes are not necessarily integrated by institutions or driven by human agency and intentions. Politics and accountability processes are also event-driven and involve improvisation and elements of chance, confluence of events, and temporal structures.

The relevance of ambiguity is illustrated by processes of political transformation such as those currently taking place in Europe. There is widespread discontent with and distrust in existing institutional arrangements and the "establishment." Things are seen as not functioning as expected and desired, but there are competing interpretations of what is going on and why. The hegemony of the sovereign state, as the basic unit of political organization, identification, and accountability and the governmental institutions of the Westphalian state are challenged by Europeanization, globalization, and an international wave of public-sector reforms. These are processes that have created both winners and losers and segments of the population feel that they have been left behind and that their welfare and life chances have been reduced. There is a demand for making political elites more accountable to the people and, for example, "monitoring democracy" is presented as a new historical type of democracy involving continuous public scrutiny and control over power holders across territorial boundaries and institutional settings (Keane 2009). An increase of scrutiny and multiplication of accounts may foster redundancy that generates waste and inefficiencies, which can be a problem for democracies. Yet redundancy may also make accountability arrangements more reliable and facilitate adaptation to shifting circumstances (Landau 1969).

Political developments in Europe invite reconsideration of conceptions of accountability and some remaining challenges for accountability theory include comprehending how political orders and their social, institutional, and behavioral bases affect the degree of ambiguity and how modern representative democracies in practice cope with ambiguity and multiple contested conceptions of accountability.

Sources of Ambiguity

Institutionalization refers to processes through which something diffuse, unstable, and unfixed turns into something that is settled and integrated (Selznick 1992). Institutions are social conventions that create elements of temporary and imperfect order and predictability. Rules and practices prescribe appropriate behavior and specify what is perceived as normal, reasonable, right, good, and true. They define what must be expected, what can be relied on, and what makes sense in a community. Institutionalized resources and action capabilities affect the degree to which actors are capable of complying with what rules prescribe and proscribe. Belief in a legitimate accountability regime simplifies political life and reduces the degree of ambiguity of a political order by ensuring that many things are taken as given (March and Olsen 1989, also Chapter 1, Note 1 in this book).

Institutionalization implies increasing clarity and agreement with regard to accountability practices. Standardization and formalization reduce ambiguity, uncertainty, and conflict concerning who is accountable for what, to whom, when, and how. Some ways of acting are perceived as natural and legitimate. They are internalized and habitualized. Thus there is less need to use incentives or coercion to make people follow prescribed accountability rules, to explain and justify, and to struggle for resources (Olsen 2008: 196). Attribution of accountability is guided by socially validated, relatively well-known, clear, and stable roles, rules, routines, procedures, doctrines, expectations, and resources.

Although institutions may limit ambiguity, they do not eliminate it. Institutions exist because people believe they exist. They require continued public recognition and acceptance (Searle 1995: 1, 45), and sometimes institutions face erosion, decay, and revolt. Deinstitutionalization generates ambiguity, uncertainty, disorientation, and conflict. The ordering effect is strongest in settled polities with well-entrenched institutions staffed by experienced, well-socialized people performing socially standardized activities. It is less strong in unsettled polities with weak or competing institutions staffed by inexperienced personnel doing novel things (March and Olsen 1976: 50).

As a supplement to formal legal interpretations of accountability institutions, an institutional approach offers ideas regarding how "living" institutions affect conceptions and practices of accountability and how accounts are influenced by, and in turn influence, a political order, including its accountability regimes. A living institution prescribes rules of appropriate behavior for different actors in different situations. Organizing ideas provide norms of assessment and conceptions of reality that explain and justify rules and practices, and institutionalized endowments make it (more or less) possible to act in accordance with prescriptions. Institutions constitute and influence actors, identities, and effective ties. They have some autonomy and dynamics of their own and robustness in the face of deliberate reform efforts and environmental change, generating structural inertia and "historical inefficiency," rather than simple equilibrium (March and Olsen 1989).

The organization of accountability in modern democracies is characterized by different degrees of institutionalization, specialization, and coordination. Theorizing accountability, therefore, requires attention to variations in the complexity, imperfections, and dynamics of accountability relations and processes. It implies exploring how accountability regimes work and change in more or less settled orders and institutionalized settings and in more or less well-structured, recurring, and consensual situations (Chapter 2 of this book), involving different degrees of ambiguity.

Arguably, in political communities characterized by consensus or by polarization, with clear and stable "we" or "we-they" feelings, there will be less ambiguity than in mixed communities with unclear identities and overlapping dividing lines. If institutional arrangements were perfect, there would be no discretion, no ambiguity, and no reason for studying accountability, except to detect occasions of misunderstanding, incompetence, and criminal acts. As held in Chapter 2, principals and agents are less likely to deviate from what they are supposed to do and there will be less ambiguity when certain institutional conditions are met, including adequate incentive structures; vertical or horizontal separation of power and expertise; effective recruitment procedures; communicative action and rational deliberation among initially conflicting parties; effective socialization, internalization, habitualization, and character formation; and relevant resources.

In such settled and well-integrated polities, where institutions work well and create modest ambiguity and uncertainty, there is likely to be little disagreement regarding who is accountable to whom, for what, under what circumstances, and according to which criteria. There is little doubt regarding who should be blamed if things go wrong. Normative concerns and causal beliefs are part of traditions, morals, socially constructed and legitimate accounts. Ambiguity and uncertainty are primarily related to the task of identifying the technically most efficient means for reaching predetermined ends within existing constraints and sanctioning violations of rules and contracts.

Unsettled and less integrated political orders characterized by weak institutions that do not work so well have a more modest ordering effect and there is likely to be considerable ambiguity and competing claims of political agency and role conceptions, representation and accountability, procedural and result-oriented assessments. Normative standards and rules are rarely exhaustive or self-interpreting. Understanding causal systems and assigning accountability is difficult. It is not always clear what has happened, why it happened, whether it could have been avoided, and whether it was good, making it difficult to establish how well different institutions or actors have performed. Under conditions of functional integration and complex and dynamic interdependencies, where the performance of one actor is dependent on the performance of others and long and uncertain causal chains with significant effects surfacing years later, the assumption that actors can be made accountable by disentangling their contribution to failures and successes is problematic (March and Olsen 1995: 157–8). The assignment of accountability may be capricious, mistaken, controversial, and politicized.

A complication is that the meaning of "accountability" becomes more complex. But accountability processes in unsettled polities and polities in transformation also provide spaces for political action and a "window of opportunity" for academic theory builders. They may help us to understand aspects of accountability largely ignored by mainstream compliance–control approaches assuming settled and integrated polities and well-working institutions. The need for such a reassessment is indicated by the current upsurge in accountability demands and claims about accountability deficits, as well as disillusion with traditional forms of representative democracy. Institutionalized practices do not work perfectly and they are less than perfectly understood.

Furthermore, the degree of ambiguity in an accountability process and the exploitation of available windows of opportunity also depend on political agency. Democracies face a dilemma. Actors may appeal to shared community and a let-us-stick-together mentality during difficult times. While a culture of compromise is likely to support the development of shared normative and causal beliefs, it also creates ambiguous lines between incumbents and opposition and makes responsibility and accountability unclear. Actors may also evoke fear and an us-versus-them mentality, thereby reducing the degree of ambiguity, but also making it more difficult to make and implement legitimate policies. Actors may respect democratic norms of argumentation and deliberation. Or the climate of debate may be dominated by hate speech, lies, and threats, creating polarization. Accountability theory has to attend to two aspects of the relationship between ambiguity and the politics of accountability: Accountability processes conceived as sense making and as a way to cope with competing conceptions of accountability and conflict.

Ambiguity and Sense Making

Democratic norms prescribe well-informed citizens able to see, understand, and respond to what power holders are doing as a precondition for sanctioning non-authorized and unacceptable behavior and accounts. Democracies are collections of interlocking communities of explanation, justification, and criticism. Making the world intelligible in normative and causal terms is central to political life and the search for identity, belonging, purpose, direction, and meaning can be as important an aspect of accountability processes as decision making, control, and compliance. Democrats are supposed to learn from their experiences and if the information available is accurate, the goals are clear and unchanging, the inferences correct, the behavior modification appropriate, and the environment stable; the process is adaptively rational and it will result in improvement over time (March and Olsen 1976: 67). Individuals, however, try to make sense of and adapt to their experiences even when events, processes, and outcomes are ambiguous; in cases where the facts are not self-evident, the causal understanding is not perfect, and the success criteria are unclear or contested. They discover or impose order, attribute meaning, and provide explanations and assessments.

The institutional approach calls attention to how accountability processes, especially in unsettled polities, provide occasions for searching for and testing collective purpose, intelligence and meaning, and political identities, including democratic citizenship based upon political equality. Accountability processes provide an occasion for exercising political visions, managing image, claiming victory, blaming, shaming, and identifying scapegoats. Possibilities arise for defining virtue and truth, during which actors discover or interpret what has happened, what different actors have done, what they are going to do, along with justifications for those actions. Accountability processes provide an occasion for distributing glory and blame for what has happened, and thus for exercising, challenging, or reaffirming friendship or trust relationships, antagonisms, power or status relationships, and for discovering self-interest and group interest (March and Olsen 1976: 11).

Under such conditions, the meaning and implications of "accountability" are defined and changed when principles meet practical situations and generate specific implications, cleavages, and relationships. As observed in Chapter 3, accounts rendered, and responses to and assessments of accounts, may be accepted as reasonable and legitimate, or they may be met with denial and create controversy. An event may be interpreted as the result of purposeful acts or a necessity, accident, or misunderstanding. Responsibility may be disclaimed and shifted to someone else, or poor results may be said to be caused by inadequate resources. Behavior may be excused, forgiven, and justified, or disapproved of and punished. The style in which an account is presented—for example, humbly submitting to criticism, expressing regret, or excusing, justifying, defending, or reframing interpretations—may be more important for responses than the act to be accounted for (Dubnick 2005).

Since learning from experience, adaptive rationality, and improvement are not guaranteed in ambiguous worlds, there is a need for introducing ideas about the processes by which beliefs and attitudes are constructed in accountability processes under such conditions. One set of theoretical ideas for understanding how actors interpret ambiguous situations and come to believe what they believe—the roots of which can be traced back to Festinger (1957) and Heider (1958)—involves different notions of consistency, balance, and harmony in cognitive and attitudinal structures. The tolerance for ambiguity varies between individuals (Furnham and Marks 2013), but imbalances are generally assumed to be unpleasant. They are drivers of sense making and change, leading actors to make efforts to move toward greater consistency and order. The more important the events observed and the relations involved, the stronger the perceived need for order (March and Olsen 1975, 1976, Weick et al. 2005).

Adaptation through interpretation is an alternative in instances where adaptation through action is impossible, and in accountability processes characterized by ambiguity, participants and onlookers are likely to try to balance (a) whether events are seen as successes or failures; (b) who or what is seen to be causing the events; and (c) whether the observer has a positive or negative relation to the assumed actor. Their cognitions as well as their assessments will be formed by the characteristics of political association and organization as well as by characteristics of individuals, including their various degrees of integration in a community and a polity.

Boundedly rational actors are unlikely to have full information and causal understanding when it comes to issues related to the terms of political order. Their interpretations and inclinations to accept information and assessments as reliable will depend on the degree to which the interpretations offered are consistent with their already existing individual belief structures, understandings, and attitudes. A participant will be active to the extent to which his judgment of events, causal interpretations, and social integration and trust relations are in balance, namely that his seeing, liking, and trusting are unambiguous. Institutions expose individuals to information in different ways, and they provide memories, making retrieval of information more or less easy. People are also likely to see different worlds as a result of variations in access to information through public documents and speeches, experts, mass media, PR agencies and spin doctors, rumors, or through friends and other trusted informants. The extent to which actors are integrated into a political community and its normative and causal beliefs affects what they see and like.

Self-evident knowledge can be expected to have strong effects upon how things are balanced and the outcome of balancing acts depends on what is ambiguous. Non-routine accountability demands are most likely to arrive when things are seen to go wrong. When social relations are characterized by clear-cut insider/outsider and friend/enemy relations and it is not self-evident whether events are successes or failures, the "establishment"—incumbents and those well integrated into the community and polity who trust the incumbents—are more likely to claim successes while the "opposition"—those outside governmental positions, less well integrated in, or alienated from, community and polity and not trusting the incumbents—are more likely to claim failures. If events are unambiguously good, the establishment will give credit to their own wisdom and deliberate decisions. Accountability processes will be dominated by image building by insiders. The opposition or dissident groups will withdraw from the interpretation process or emphasize external forces or luck. When events are unambiguously bad, causal explanations will be reversed. The opposition will attribute failure to the establishment and insiders will see failure as originating in the environment, chance, and bad luck (Olsen 1976: 346–8). There will be strong demands for accountability, explanations, and justifications. The opposition will claim that this is typical behavior of the government or governing party. The establishment will argue that "our government/party would never do such a thing."

We should, therefore, expect different patterns of activation of the establishment and the opposition in good and bad times. Non-routine accountability demands are most likely to be activated during performance crises, thus giving the opposition an opportunity to mobilize and criticize the establishment, calling attention to their mistaken decisions. Interpretations and discussions will be dominated by those who find various crises to confirm their beliefs. Outcomes are linked to deliberate decisions—someone is running the process—not to external forces or misfortunes. As a corollary, in good times we expect established leaders to do the interpreting and explaining, emphasizing the impact of their own decisions and actions. Furthermore, actors can be expected to come to trust other actors whom they see as producing events that they like and preventing events that they dislike.

Arguably, the more integrated actors are in a community and polity, the more likely that accountability processes will foster a culture of cooperation and compromise, rather than one of suspicion, confrontation, and disintegration. Accountability processes may have an integrative effect and be conducive to intellectual and moral self-development (Mill 1962: 30–35). They may ameliorate the moral qualities of individuals and society through the internalization of a democratic and civic ethos; improve communication, learning, and epistemic quality; contribute to power equalization and political equality; and help actors find meaning in life through reflection and reasoning together. The less integrated actors are in a community and polity, the more likely that accountability processes will provide a rhetorical arena for political confrontation and partisan battles, splitting rather than unifying the population. An institutional approach, therefore, goes beyond the assumption that efficient accountability is best achieved through opportunity structures, incentives, and external control motivating a self-interested agent to behave according to the desires and commands of a self-interested principal. It takes seriously the role of accountability processes as part of the set of processes of socialization, internalization, and identification through which citizens come to accept political orders, accountability regimes, codes of appropriate behavior, and substantive outcomes as democratically legitimate.

In this perspective it is not surprising that the EU—a polity more functionally economically integrated than politically, socially, and culturally integrated—experiences strong claims regarding lack of accountability, democratic deficit, discontent, and distrust in institutions and leaders in a period of economic and financial crisis. It is not surprising that identification with the EU or the member states affects whether successes and failures are attributed to "Brussels" or to national capitals. Neither is it surprising that smaller, less powerful, and oppositional political parties in the EP are exploring new ways to monitor and hold EU commissioners to account, while larger and more powerful political parties, such as the European People's Party, are reluctant to strengthen accountability regimes (Eriksson 2016). In polities, such as the EU, with fairly stable divisions between incumbents and outsiders, and where some political parties have little or no chance of coming into power in the near future, polarization and harsh criticism are also more likely than in polities with frequent changes in those who occupy governmental positions. As a result, decades of experience with European integration have not fostered rational adaptation and increasing consensus when it comes to how the Union is to be understood and assessed, what are legitimate terms of political order and orderly change, and who is responsible and should be called to account in different contexts.

The situation is further complicated because rational adaptation through accountability processes requires changes not only in beliefs but also in behavior and institutional arrangements, and because political rhetoric, which is effective when it comes to mobilizing support, gives no guarantee for programs that are working well (Barth 1993: 176–7, Klinger et al. 2001: 136–7). Reforms driven by partisan ideology rather than evidence and analysis are, for example, likely to produce perverse effects. Trust and deference are weakened through intense monitoring and complex and incoherent accountability demands and tripartite accountability relations among logics of politics, administration, and markets have turned out to be difficult to reconcile. Administrators have to decipher political decisions and legal documents, respond to a variety of pressures, and develop practical viable solutions, and it has been argued that the current wave of delegation requires a reinvention of accountability (Gilmour and Jensen 1998, Klinger et al. 2001: 134–7). Competing conceptions of accountability and competing models of the world create tensions that representative democracies have to cope with.

Coping with Competing Conceptions of Accountability

Taking as a premise that ambiguity is an inherent part of political life and not subject to enduring resolution, an institutional approach holds that there is a need for understanding how contemporary representative democracies cope with ambiguity and multiple, contested, and dynamic conceptions of accountability. An institutional approach in particular looks for institutional mechanisms that make it possible for democracies to flourish in ambiguous worlds, and when facts and causality are contested and too obscure to be established validly in terms of correctly assigning responsibility, the *politics* of accountability acquires a more important role. Accountability is seen as endogenous to democratic politics and government and as related to fundamental issues in political life.

Accountability processes provide occasions for debate and struggle, not only related to facts and causality, but also to competing prescriptions of what are acceptable authority, power, ideologies, norms, worldviews, responsibility, and accountability, namely issues crucial for the legitimacy of a political order and processes that may have unifying or dividing effects on a community. There may be disagreement regarding who shall belong to "the people," what are legitimate individual and collective identities, and to what degree citizenship shall be perceived as the primary identity and belonging. There may be conflict over different conceptions of the common good and what agenda and institutional arrangements will foster the well-being of individuals and the community at large. Contestations may, for example, involve conflicting opinions regarding how the pursuit of individual advantage and the pursuit of the common good shall be balanced.

The politics of accountability involves the pursuit of accountability within an established political order with strong institutional constraints and modest controversy (Chapter 2). But sometimes there are contestations over the terms of order and accountability processes are part of the emergence and transformation of accountability regimes and political orders, issues closely linked to competing visions of what is a legitimate political order (Chapter 3). There are efforts to change the basic rules for living together and the terms of political order, including established principal–agent relations. Accountability processes, then, provide opportunities for exploring how accountability may be enhanced, inhibited, and legitimized by alternative orders and regimes, as well as for challenging old accountability relations and processes and developing new ones. There are debates and struggles over whether and why the principles organizing and governing common affairs deserve the allegiance of citizens. Questions are raised about why specific institutions and officeholders should have the right and capacity to call to account, render, and assess accounts and to sanction unacceptable behavior and demand explanations and justifications.

What mechanisms make it possible for representative democracies to cope with ambiguity and conflicts and obtain effective accountability? For mainstream approaches assuming rational agency, decision making, control, and adaptation, understanding democratic accountability processes involves reconstructing how decisions are made, locating responsible agents, and assessing whether processes and results are acceptable and whether things could and should have been done differently. Ambiguity and conflicting causal beliefs and normative assessments are assumed to be resolved through authoritative decisions by predetermined principals and constitutional choices as well as ordinary policymaking.

The standard story of representative democracy celebrates electoral mechanisms, law making, and administrative and legal hierarchies as vehicles for imposing sanctions and securing accountability, and mainstream principal–agent approaches mainly deal with accountability in settled and well-integrated polities embracing ideas such as the sovereign people, the sovereign parliament, and the responsible minister, or some system of institutionalized checks and balances. The will of the people is expressed and control is exercised through competitive elections and a chain of dyadic principal–agent relations

(Przeworski et al. 1999, Strøm et al. 2003, Chapter 2 of this book). Mechanisms for exploring, testing, gathering support for, and authorizing accounts are assumed to be supported by institutions securing freedom of expression and organization, legitimate opposition, independent auditors, an active civil society, a free press, and free science (March and Olsen 1995: 163).

The problems of this narrative have already been addressed (Chapter 2). Democratic accountability assumes an informed citizenry that knows what powerful agents are doing, the evidence and reasons behind their behavior, and who is able to sanction unauthorized behaviors. But this ideal is difficult to realize. Problems do not necessarily originate with agents. An accountability deficit can be caused by institutions and actors who are supposed to call others to account, but lack the motivation, time and energy, knowledge, or capabilities for reliably monitoring, assessing, and sanctioning agents' behavior and performance (Considine 2002, Shapiro 2005, Busuioc 2010: 220–23). Elected and non-elected principals may provide agents with contradictory or unrealistic criteria, expectations, and aspirations, as well as with inadequate resources.

In addition, concerns regarding citizens' inability to make agents accountable need to be supplemented by citizens' responsibilities toward each other and the community at large as the foundation of democracy and ultimate source of power. The question is not solely whether representative democracies are able to live up to the expectations of citizens, but also whether citizens' expectations and demands make democracy viable and through what processes they are formed and changed. The democratic principle that power and accountability should match is not consistent with the idea of a sovereign people accountable to no one. It is, therefore, important to attend to how citizen exemption from accountability masks the contribution of ordinary citizens to democratic successes and failures (March and Olsen 1995: 153).

A core democratic belief is that democracies have a unique ability to learn from experience and to secure progress through rational adaptation and the design and reform of political–administrative institutions. Correctly assigning causal credit or blame is assumed to increase the frequency of success and reduce the frequency of failure over time as new experiences and achievements are encoded into institutions (March and Olsen 1995, Warren 2011: 523, 526). Currently, representative democracies are also reconsidering accountability relations and processes, and reformers believe in auditing and account giving as instruments for collective intelligence and improved performance (Pollitt and Summa 1997: 331). Principal–agent approaches likewise assume that "agency loss" is mitigated and citizens and legislators can cope with conflicting preferences and information asymmetry through a variety of institutional devices or institutional arrangements providing information about what agents are doing and why, as well as capacities for holding them to account (Waterman and Meier 1998, Lupia and McCubbins 2000).

Democracies *do* learn from experience on the basis of accounts. They adapt their beliefs and behaviors to new experience, but the lessons drawn do not guarantee improvement and progress. It is often difficult to give precise and valid accounts of what has happened or what could have happened, and to conclude precisely what lessons to extract. Attention is a scarce resource and some events are never accounted for. Lessons are often ambiguous and contested and they are sometimes lost. Learning may be spurious and contribute to mistakes rather than intelligence (March and Olsen 1975, March 1999, 2010). Information is gathered but not attended to or acted upon (Feldman and March 1981). The ability to implement and enforce lessons learned and decisions made varies, and new routines for information collection are not automatically followed by routines of analysis, debate, and sanctioning. Accounts may be perverted by incompetence, fraud, deception, disinformation, indoctrination, and manipulation, raising questions regarding how citizens and officeholders actually interpret the relevance, validity, and implications of accounts and how different accountability institutions support intelligence and learning (March and Olsen 1995). Deciding who to praise or blame does not necessarily depend on hard evidence, correct causal understanding, and valid normative standards. The influence of citizens usually depends on the availability of competing accounts and sources of information. Acceptance of interpretations of experience can be influenced by evidence or power (March 2010), and the ability to gain acceptance for a specific frame, type of discourse, language, interpretative community, or a particular interpretation is a source and indicator of power (March and Olsen 1995: 180).

A core democratic norm is that citizens, on the basis of their lessons from experience, should decide through what institutional arrangements they are to be politically organized and governed. However, as held in previous chapters, deliberate design and reform is only one of several institutional change processes, and it is problematic to assume that political orders and accountability regimes are designed and reformed without friction through institutional engineering. An institutional approach goes beyond the assumption that accountability regimes emerge, are maintained, and change as a result of the experiential learning and the deliberate choices of predetermined principals, or of rational adaptation to functional or normative necessities. It interprets the dynamics of accountability regimes as belonging to complex processes of institutionalization and deinstitutionalization, integration and disintegration, and an institutional agenda calls attention to how key institutions, for example, the parliament and the university, have developed through historical processes more than active agency and institutional design, and how accountability arrangements may evolve slowly in relation to repeated encounters with well-structured, recurring problems in standardized situations. What are exceptions at one point in time become more common and gradually replace historically evolved routines, normative standards, and causal understandings. In brief, political agency through experiential learning and institutional design does not guarantee rational and efficient adaptation to human purposes or environmental change, and neither do competitive selection, bargaining, deliberation, imitation, diffusion, or other adaptive processes (March 1981).

A complex, contested, and dynamic polity such as the EU illustrates the relevance of ambiguity and some of the inadequacies of the mainstream narrative. There is no unified, sovereign, and stable "people" to be served. There is no single authoritative political center formulating unambiguous mandates for agents. Principal–agent relations are in flux. Several actors hold roles as both "principals" and "agents." There are conflicting role demands and internalized identities that are mobilized differently in different settings. Resources and capabilities are not necessarily adequate for prescribed roles. Actors are required to provide accounts to a multitude of forums and satisfy multiple, contested, and ambiguous accountability claims. They are expected to do so in a variety of ways and through different channels, requiring different types of information, explanations, and justifications in terms of competing normative standards. At different points in time, different accountability relationships are activated by and in relation to elected representatives, individual citizens, specific constituencies, mass media, democratic and civil standards, laws, financial auditing institutions, epistemic communities, professional codes of good practice, and the ethos of office. There are competing and contested claims regarding what citizens want and what their interests and needs are; what normative criteria and causal understandings should have priority; and what jurisdictions and responsibilities different levels of government, institutions, and actors should have. Participants, audiences, and normative criteria are mobilized in partly uncoordinated ways and it is not clear who can legitimately call whom to account for what, or who controls relevant incentives and information. Often practice comes before theory, plans, and authoritative decisions (Olsen 2010).

In the EU, conceptions of accountability have also increasingly come to rely on non-majoritarian, guardian institutions populated by officials neither directly elected nor managed by elected officials and loosely coupled to public opinion (Thatcher and Stone Sweet 2002). Judges, central bankers, and experts are assumed to act in a principled manner, with competence, integrity, and impartiality, in accordance with laws, professional codes, the mandates of their office, and the common good. Self-control and checks and balances among guardians have been assessed as democratically inadequate and simultaneously there are perceived accountability deficits and overloads. However, a recent countervailing trend that may further complicate the situation for the EC is that the EP seems to be inclined to take its role as overseeing the executive more seriously. A reduced legislative workload may lead to higher priority being given to holding the executive to account through investigations and inquiries (Teffer 2016), even if the major parties are not enthusiastic about reforming monitoring arrangements and strengthening accountability regimes (Eriksson 2016).

The ambiguities of the constitutive treaties and different legal styles of interpretation have led to turf wars and struggles over competence and accountability, processes that can be illustrated by the birth of a new legal order in Europe. Through several partly autonomous events and decisions, and with significant elements of coincidence and chance, legal actors provided a "sufficient legal basis for the ECJ [European Court of Justice] to revolutionize European law" and create an autonomous European legal order (Rasmussen 2008: 86, 98), which has resulted in competing legal orders and ambiguous accountability relations. And, as observed in Chapter 2, similar processes have taken place related to administrative and financial accountability (Laffan 2003, Curtin 2007, Harlow and Rawlings 2007, Bovens et al. 2010, Busuioc 2010). New auditing practices and regimes have been layered on top of old ones (Mendez and Bachtler 2011).

If sense making, authoritative decisions, politicization, and polarization do not eliminate ambiguity, what mechanisms make it possible for modern representative democracies to thrive with ambiguity and competing conceptions of accountability and to create and maintain legitimacy? Modern democracies use a large repertoire of processes and it is beyond the scope of this chapter to discuss them all. It is, however, commonplace to observe that there are limits to what a democracy can digest politically at a single point in time and that democracies therefore use a variety of mechanisms to separate participants and issues in time and space and "buffer" inconsistencies and tensions (Olsen 2003, 2007: Chapter 9). Some such mechanisms, to be discussed in the following chapters, are as follows.

Attention

As held above, the search for balance and order is most significant as a driver of change when events and actors are perceived as very important and threatening. As a corollary, if issues linked to the terms of political order and the relevant decision makers are *not* seen as sufficiently important by citizens, there will be fewer efforts to create balance and consistency and fewer actors will be mobilized to make accountability demands (Chapter 6). As a result, it will be easier for a polity to reach compromises and live with ambiguity.

However, the democratic quality will arguably decrease as fewer citizens get involved in scrutinizing how power is used, holding their rulers to account, and preventing abuse of power.

Tolerance for Ambiguity

Individuals and communities have different tolerance for ambiguity. There are different propensities to think in dichotomies such as true/false, good/bad, and success/failure and for wanting clear-cut definitions and answers. Some perceive the ambiguity of situations or dynamic and heterogeneous societies in general as a threat. Others do not, or they even see ambiguity, diversity, and interaction with people holding different opinions and preferences as desirable. Coping with inconsistencies and incoherence will be easier in the latter type of communities and in polities integrated by a variety of ties and with strong socializing institutions fostering tolerance for ambiguity (Chapter 5).

Separation, Decision Making, and Organizing

When democracies face inconsistent accountability demands, normative standards, and understandings, the goal is usually seen as "striking a balance." Claims are weighed. Trade-offs are made. Conflict is resolved and equilibrium reached. However, an alternative to assuming that authoritative conflict resolution creates a stable and consistent preference order is to consider how mechanisms such as sequential attention to goals, decentralization and local rationality, and quasi-resolution of conflict, as well as slack resources, buffer inconsistencies and tend to reduce the perceived need for coordination. Rather than being collapsed into a coherent preference order through trade-offs, competing accountability claims are treated as independent constraints—"red lines" that together define a satisfying solution (Cyert and March 1963, Chapter 6 this book).

Such mechanisms are of particular importance in modern democracies, typically compound polities characterized by specialized and segmented structures, routinely limiting and curtailing tensions and perceived inconsistencies. In settled polities and routine situations accountability processes are usually "local" and institution-specific. They take place in parallel, relatively autonomous institutional spheres and existing beliefs, status, and power relationships bias interpretation toward familiar templates. Access and attention are organized separately in levels of governance and institutional spheres, allowing piecemeal decision making and adaptations and avoiding constitutional moments that are expected to generate "unnecessary conflicts" (Olsen 2003, 2007: Chapter 9, Chapter 5 of this book). In unsettled polities and uncharted waters, there are more likely to be demands for coordinated behavior and accountability relationships. Accountability processes involve the interaction of a variety of institutions and develop in a dynamic interplay between levels of governance and between institutional spheres. The pursuit of accountability and the dynamics of accountability become indistinguishable, and the challenge for democratic politics is to reach agreement about what must be coherent and unambiguous and where ambiguity and inconsistencies can be accepted.

The Pursuit of Accountability in Ambiguous Worlds

This chapter has offered an institutional approach to accountability processes in representative democracies characterized by ambiguity, uncertainty, tensions, and limited control. The approach goes beyond mainstream assumptions about political agency, decision making, and rational adaptation—namely stylized categories of predetermined, dyadic principal–agent relations, with rational decision makers making authoritative decisions through calculation of expected utility and securing rational adaptation through learning from successes and failures.

My argument is not that mainstream principal–agent approaches are not useful. Rather, I (again) hold that different approaches based upon competing foundational assumptions, including the assumed importance of ambiguity, can and should be seen as complementary rather than mutually exclusive. Theory builders need to explore competing ideas, their areas of application, their strengths and weaknesses, and the circumstances under which different processes are likely to foster or hinder effective accountability, political order, and orderly change.

The institutional approach to democratic accountability, which sees ambiguity not as the enemy of accountability, but as an intrinsic part of democratic politics and accountability in contemporary Europe, addresses both settled and unsettled polities. It emphasizes the importance of institutional routines, standard procedures, cognitive templates, and resources. However, it also holds that political and organizational decision making is sometimes messy. The fluidity, inconsistencies, and conflicts of political life—incompletely reconciled desires and understandings that evolve in the context of pursuing them, variable participation, and shifting legitimacy of resources—make it difficult to correctly assign causal responsibility, credit, and blame. In a context of democratic norms emphasizing human will, understanding, and control, as well as responsive and accountable government, these norms foster demands for calling actors to account for things that happen even under ambiguous and uncertain conditions where there is limited control. They also make possible sense making and accountability politics related to the terms of political order.

One reason for rethinking ambiguity and the politics of accountability in the context of European transformation is that many citizens perceive the world as confusing and threatening. Those hit by unemployment, poverty, and social deprivation feel that they have good reasons for being disappointed and angry. Others fear terrorism, war, loss of identity, or climatic breakdowns. There is disenchantment and discontent and a collapse of expectation of peace, prosperity, and enlightenment inspired by a belief in progress. Accounts have been demanded as well as volunteered and, consistent with an institutional approach, well-established ideological templates and stereotypes have been used to create meaning and "balance" in cognitive and attitudinal structures. It is not surprising who attributes responsibility to the "establishment," European or national politicians, neo-liberalism, capitalism and "big business," populists, nationalists, "the South," "the North," "the East," or "the West," immigrants, or Islam.

A possible next step for students of ambiguity and accountability politics is to explore in some detail the actual *interaction* of coexisting accountability institutions and networks organized upon competing conceptions of what accountability is all about and contested ideas about what institutional arrangements will foster effective accountability. In settled and differentiated polities and routine situations it can be fruitful to study the internal operation and the dynamics of single, relatively autonomous accountability institutions structured according to different principles and rules, for example, legislative–executive relationships, administrative hierarchies, independent courts and legal accountability, ombudsmen, auditing institutions, market–consumer arrangements, and mass media. However, there is also a need to examine democratic accountability in less settled and differentiated polities that have to cope with competing analyses and prescriptions. Accountability regimes are never fully integrated or accepted by everyone. Tensions and disputes are endemic in and between institutions. There are collections of more or less tightly coupled action programs determining possible actions over a range of circumstances that satisfy complex sets of standards, goals, rules, requirements, and constraints. In periods of discontent there will most likely be demands for coordination of the various accountability institutions.

Another possible next step is to examine exactly how change in accountability regimes happens and the conditions for orderly change. A key aspect is the stabilizing and destabilizing factors and frictions in change processes, including deliberate design, rule following, bargaining, deliberation, experiential learning, rational adaptation, diffusion, competitive selection, and evolving historical processes. One part of such an agenda is to explore how incentives and internalized behavioral codes interact in influencing adaptation of ideas, behavior, and institutional arrangements. Another part is to examine how accountability processes and different institutions for training and socialization contribute to fostering individuals and political cultures characterized by tolerance for ambiguity, for example, democratic and civic identities and humanist and law-abiding citizens.

Chapter 5 deals with *one* mechanism that possibly may help democracies thrive with ambiguity and inconsistency, namely the separation of political talk and political action. Democratic agents are supposed to speak the truth so that there is consistency between what they do and what they say. Still, the tension between cultural demands for responsible and accountable actors and the difficulties of establishing responsibility and accountability may contribute to a separation of talk and action. A puzzle to be explored is whether democratic norms and democratic practices under some conditions may be separated and inconsistent without any mass mobilization of disillusioned citizens trying to close the gap between what power holders do and how they explain and justify their behavior, outcomes, and the terms of political order.

5

Accountability and the Separation of Talk and Action

Democratic Rhetoric and Democratic Practice

A democracy is a community of action and authoritative decision making, but also a community of sense making, explanation, education, and justification. Governance involves shaping history, as well as trying to understand it and being willing to learn from it (March and Olsen 1995: 44, 146). A democratic ethos of responsibility and accountability, together with a norm of honesty, prescribes that agents acting on behalf of the community tell the truth about what they have done and why. Accountability and popular control benefits from consistency between what agents actually do and what they say: How they describe, explain, and justify their actions.

Still, it is commonplace to observe inconsistencies between talk and action (Meyer and Rowan 1977, March 1984, Brunsson 1989). An actor may try to satisfy some with talk, some with formal decisions, and others with action and achievements. When what actors say is consistent with what an audience wants to hear, talk may contribute to acceptance; the same is true for formal decisions, even when they are not implemented and have no practical effects. Separation of talk and action is likely in conflictual situations in particular, when accountability demands are perceived to be inconsistent, problems have no solution, or there is disagreement about what the problem is (Brunsson 1989, 2007). There is, for example, often a loose coupling between how major public-sector reform programs are presented and talked about, and actual reform action and outcomes (Brunsson and Olsen 1993, March and Olsen 1995: 196).

As already mentioned, in contemporary Europe, democratic institutions and actors face multiple, inconsistent accountability demands and contradictory normative success criteria. They need to explain and justify their performance, structures, processes, and symbols to a variety of forums (Bovens et al.

2010, Busuioc and Lodge 2016). A single accountability arrangement can also be based upon contradictory elements. An arrangement can, for example, be founded on trust and shared norms as well as on distrust and detailed control regimes (Lægreid and Neby 2016). Inconsistent and conflicting demands are, however, likely to create problems (Koppell 2005).

This chapter, therefore, explores factors that make it possible for a polity to thrive when there is separation between official rhetoric and practice and still avoid accountability demands regarding the terms of political order and, as a corollary, under what conditions accountability processes are likely to generate demands for more consistency between what is said and done. I devote special attention to how the likelihood of different accountability patterns is affected by how a polity is integrated—how it is tied together by political association, organization, and agency.

To shed light on these issues, I take Norway and the EU as examples of two different types of polities. The former has a fairly settled and well-integrated political order while the latter is an order still in the making. Norway and the EU are different in many ways, but this chapter focuses on a few of the mechanisms that can buffer inconsistency between talk and action. A polity's ability to thrive with gaps between rhetoric and practice is likely to depend on its political association, history, and conflict patterns. Trust in institutions is likely to give decision makers a relatively wide margin of discretion and allow gaps between official self-presentation and practice. Accountability demands, then, may come from unusual, non-standard events that are either meaningless or difficult to make sense of and integrate into routinized beliefs and practices that are taken for granted. Demands are also more likely when a society is confronted with another society with a significantly different history, making people realize that their universe does not represent an inevitable and unalterable "objective reality" (Berger and Luckmann 1967: 103, 107). Crises of trust and confidence are likely to have an effect in terms of creating more accountability demands and mobilizing more issues, participants, and audiences. Frustration and dissatisfaction, or pride in the established order, can, however, increase or decrease the chances of eliciting public attention and accountability demands.

The more capable political institutions are of learning from experience and solving problems sequentially through stepwise reforms rather than allowing historical cleavages to accumulate (Lipset 1963: 71, 79), the less likely that accountability demands will involve questions of inconsistencies between talk and action and issues related to the terms of political order. Polities provide few or many institutionalized opportunities for debate, contestation, and citizen involvement, making accountability demands regarding the political order more or less likely. Different forms of political organization also have different capacities for buffering talk–action inconsistencies through mechanisms such as local rationality, sequential attention to goals, and slack resources (Cyert and March 1963, Chapter 4 of this book). In addition, power holders are more or less restrained when it comes to promising performance, thereby affecting citizens' aspirations, expectations, and responses differently. Decision makers may, through their different promises/performance balances, generate disappointment and discontent or legitimacy and allegiance. The wider the gap between what is said and done, the more likely that accountability processes will involve demands for more consistency between practices, explanations, and justifications of the existing order and its cognitive, normative, and power foundations. Crises of confidence created by unkept promises are likely to have a mobilizing effect leading to more accountability demands, participants, and audiences. Moreover, political actors may believe, or not, in the possibility of bridging talk–action gaps through the deliberate design and redesign of institutional arrangements, making accountability demands more or less likely.

Accountability in an Era of Discontent and Reform

Over the last three or four decades, the two most important forms of political organization and governance in Europe—the nation-state and the EU—have been heavily criticized. Reformers inspired by New Public Management have claimed that states, and welfare states in particular, do not achieve their objectives. They are inefficient, not sustainable financially, and they lack popular support. Reformers have given priority to accountability based on market-like mechanisms and managerial accountability for results, efficiency, and budgets. There has been structural fragmentation and specialization and a variety of agencies have been granted contract-based autonomy (Verhoest et al. 2012, Lægreid 2014, Christensen and Lægreid 2016). Less attention has been given to the traditional formal legal forms of control and accountability through the parliamentary chain of governance and the traditional form of a unitary, hierarchical public administration. Public administration has been perceived as a technical vehicle for implementing and enforcing authoritative decisions and as an enterprise producing goods and services in competition with other producers. Reformers have assumed that enhanced accountability would improve performance and efficiency (Lægreid 2014) rather than create accountability overload and reduced performance (Halachmi 2014).

The link between administrative reform, accountability, and performance has, however, often been weak (Christensen and Lægreid 2016). Performance audits and accountability mechanisms have not always improved performance (Reichborn-Kjennerud 2013), and there is a perceived need to go beyond a narrow concept of managerial accountability (Van Thiel et al. 2012: 435). Questions about how agency autonomy and accountability can be combined as domestic administrations have become part of a European administrative order and international networks have attracted little public attention (Egeberg 2006, Curtin and Egeberg 2008, Trondal 2010, Busuioc et al. 2012).

European integration has been advocated as a remedy for the weaknesses of the nation-state. The founders of the European Community saw integration as an antidote to nationalism and it is still commonplace for European leaders to warn against a return to nationalism. Nevertheless, political cleavages have cut across member states' boundaries only to a limited degree; mostly member states have lined up against each other in cumulative and polarized ways (Lefkofridi and Schmitter 2015, Schmitter and Lefkofridi 2016).

The EU is still an unsettled polity. It is a large-scale experiment in integration and an attempt to deliberately change the political organization of a continent through institution building in an already densely institutionalized context (Olsen 2010). A new European polity is emerging, built on several competing normative and organizational principles. But there is little agreement regarding what a desirable future political order looks like in terms of territorial borders, a shared agenda, and institutional arrangements. There is also disagreement regarding how the existing order and its foundational principles and dynamics can be described, understood, and justified. Actually, the EU has become increasingly controversial and contested. It cannot take popular support and legitimacy for granted. Rather, leaders and electorates have drifted apart (Mattila and Raunio 2012). The discontent with the Union has been growing with opposition to integration in general or to specific forms of integration and terms of political order. Possibly, the "leave" majority in the "Brexit" referendum has increased the possibility of EU disintegration.

A result of these developments has been that accountability processes increasingly have become related to different ideas regarding what are the legitimate terms of political order. There have been demands for explanation and justification of how shared rule and self-rule (Elazar 1991: 12), interdependence and independence, unity and diversity can be balanced; where authority, power, responsibility, and accountability should be located and how they should be legitimately transferred between levels of government; and what role democratic politics should have in relation to other institutional spheres, such as competitive markets, an independent judiciary, free science, and religion. In brief, the EU's ability to flourish with a separation of talk and action seems to have become more difficult, and the rest of this chapter tries to shed some light on variations and shifts in a polity's ability to thrive with talk–action inconsistencies by comparing Norway and the EU.

Norway: "Successful" Separation of Talk and Action

The official Norwegian self-understanding is embedded in a grand narrative of national independence, self-governance, and democratization. The narrative celebrates the sovereign people, governing itself through a sovereign nation-state and with a sovereign parliament (Stortinget) as the institutional frame for representative government, securing legitimacy (Olsen 2014a, 2015b). The popular will is expressed through competitive elections, law making, and hierarchy (Olsen 1978). There is a chain of authorization from the people to the legislature, the government, the public administration, and back to the people; and there is a chain of accountability going in the opposite direction. There are competing stories about Norwegian democracy, but the main ones are organized around the events in 1814, when Norway split from the Danish–Norwegian state, entered a union with Sweden, and got its own constitution; and in 1905, when the Swedish–Norwegian union was dissolved and Norway gained its national independence. The national holiday, May 17, features displays of patriotism and national community in the form of parades of schoolchildren rather than military parades.

The Norwegian political self-understanding and the idea of a parliamentarian chain of authorization and accountability is close to the assumptions usually made by rational choice principal–agent approaches to accountability. Indeed, Norwegian political practices are influenced by these ideas. However, practices have changed more than their official explanations and justifications. There have been incremental pragmatic reforms with attempts to build broad support and legitimacy, but without much principled debate. Of special importance was the "great compromise" in the 1930s between capital, labor, and the state, organized around social peace, economic productivity, and redistribution through the public sector. The compromise created a new power balance by combining an open-market economy with a norm of reduced social inequality and increased social protection and security. Government became accountable for a redistributive agenda and the welfare of society. Accountability relations and the border between the public and the private realms were blurred, with citizens as members of interest organizations and carriers of socio-economic rights. There was a gradual introduction of corporative representative structures with the integration of organized interests in public policymaking. Focus was on agreeing on decisions, but not necessarily on explaining or justifying them. Since then, Norway has become part of a variety of European and international regimes. The country is not a member of the EU, but it is heavily integrated into, and dependent upon, the Union's activities and legal system. National borders have become less important and it is more difficult to identify unambiguously what the national government can legitimately be made accountable for.

In Norway, as in the other Scandinavian countries, "democracy" has become a meta-norm that includes not only representative political democracy but also social and economic democracy, with an emphasis upon social equality and security, a relatively large public sector, and willingness to redistribute resources (Allardt et al. 1981). Reforms have been based on a sense of common purpose and understanding of the rules for living together. Historically, alongside disagreements about policies and criticism of politicians, political parties, and governments, a fairly widespread agreement has developed regarding the terms of political order and how disagreements should be handled.

As in other democracies, Norway's political order is characterized by some enduring, unresolved tensions and conflicts rather than by rational consensus, consent, and stable harmony. There is a combination of partly conflicting normative and organizational principles embedded in a variety of compromises, and it is not obvious how democratic ideals will be interpreted in different institutional settings. The order is based on a balance of representative and direct democracy, majority power and minority rights, and an intervening welfare state and a liberal Rechtsstaat. It involves tensions with regard to the appropriate role of laypeople, elites, and experts, how public opinion is to be legitimately formed and changed, what is to count as "the will of the people," and the right relation between the nation-state and competing communities and belongings (Olsen 2014a). There is a need to find a legitimate balance between the collective ideal of a sovereign people and the individualistic ideal of the sovereign individual (Olsen 1990), and between building broad compromises through appeals to community and unity and giving the population clear political alternatives by demarcating what divides the population.

As a result of historical experiences, political and social institutions have become infused by shared tacit understandings of appropriateness, reason, and justice, including what is important to agree upon and what is acceptable to disagree about. The collective life of citizens has been defined by a widening sphere of taken-for-granted routines and procedures. There has been institutionalization of "normal" and legitimate ways of interpreting and handling tasks and situations, embedded in a relatively integrated set of differentiated but interconnected offices, roles, functions, powers, rights, duties, responsibilities, and accountabilities. In difficult situations, a major concern has been to maintain and further develop community, cooperation, trust, and peaceful coexistence. Efforts have been focused more on coping with specific problems than on confrontations over ideals and principles; these have included attempts "to find a reasonable balance," to arrive at "a better allocation of tasks," and to "remove unnecessary rules and interventions," combined with an aversion to "theories," "abstract principles," and "hypothetical questions" about what constitutes good democratic order. The result has been a political order characterized by a fairly low level of conflict and confrontation, somewhat ambiguous compromises, informal arrangements, and shared tacit understandings (Olsen 2014a).

Although Norway, through practice, has developed a political culture, tacit norms, and understandings that make appeals to widely accepted standards of appropriate conduct, reason, and justice possible, the grand narrative and the written constitution (Grunnloven) are of limited help for understanding how Norway is organized and governed politically. There is a weak connection between the written constitution, actual legal practice, and the "living" political order. The 1814 Constitution is one of the oldest functioning constitutions in the world, and a leading Norwegian lawyer has characterized the document as outdated and out of touch with current reality (Sejersted 2013, 2014). For example, the constitution still has the king selecting his advisers, and more is said about the royal family than about the executive power. The corporative system of representation, local self-government, and Norway's relation to the EU have little or no place (Olsen 2015b).

There has not been any major revision of the written constitution since 1814, nor has anyone in Parliament suggested such a revision. Major reforms have been seen to create unnecessary conflict. In contrast, there have been a large number of limited reforms through stepwise, non-coordinated processes, often without clear substantive implications (Sejersted 2013: 65–6, 70). The formal inclusion of parliamentarism in the constitution in 2007 took place more than 100 years after it became political practice, and then with few practical consequences (Sejersted 2014). A value paragraph was written into the constitution in 2014, but it contains many tensions and does not prioritize between competing values. The paragraph can be interpreted in several ways, and it is difficult to say exactly how it will be used. Furthermore, both these changes came about as byproducts of other processes. They were not based on any popular demand nor on planned reforms to solve a specific problem (Michalsen 2014). Generally, there have been few attempts to formulate new normative and organizational principles or to identify the shifting conditions for democratic accountability and popular legitimacy and support.

Unused Occasions for Calling Rulers to Account

Accountability demands regarding the terms of political order have largely been a non-issue, and the reason is not that the public and their elected representatives have not had occasion for making such demands. There have been several unused occasions. One of these was the celebration of the 200th anniversary of the written constitution in 2014, when citizens were officially invited to discuss the future of Norwegian democracy. Another was the publication of three critical official Norwegian government reports—one based on a five-year study of power and democracy in Norway (1998–2003), the second looking at Norway's relationship with the EU, and the third analyzing the July 22, 2011, terrorist massacre of 77 people.

The Norwegian government had high aspirations for its official celebration of the 1814 Constitution. The major theme was the importance of democratic government and its current challenges and the public was invited to reflect on and debate the terms of political order. This framing generated expectations about new ideas and actions regarding how Norway should be organized and governed politically in the future. However, these expectations were not met. The event ended up being mostly a nice birthday party, with some updates to existing legal arrangements and rhetoric linked to existing narratives and doctrines. The jubilee did not contribute to an improved understanding of how the political order actually works and develops. The political milieu did not use the anniversary to discuss which political order is desirable and possible in an increasingly heterogeneous society with growing international dependencies. Minor changes were made to the written constitution—language changes and the addition of some human rights. But it was, throughout the process, emphasized that these reforms were not meant to change legal or political realities in Norway (Olsen 2015b).

It may be argued that an anniversary is not the right context for discussing accountability and the terms of political order. However, the Norwegian public and its elected representatives also refrained from using other occasions presented by official committee reports and academic literature. The study of power and democracy in Norway from 1998 to 2003 was concerned with the withering of popular government (NOU 2003: 19). It was asked whether the ongoing development implied a "goodbye to popular government" (Tranvik and Selle 2003, Selle and Østerud 2006). Studies were concerned with the juridification of politics and it was argued that transfer of sovereignty to the EU made it less clear whether Norway was still a sovereign state (Østerud et al. 2003: 55).

Europautredningen, a commission established to analyze Norway's agreements with the EU, asked how Norwegian authorities weighted democratic concerns compared to other concerns such as market access and economic competitiveness in practice. The commission concluded that it was problematic to assume national sovereignty because Norway, as a non-member without formal influence in the EU, had become part of a European legal order, so that Norwegian politics and society were influenced by an increasing number of European rules and decisions (NOU 2012: 2, Sejersted 2013: 103). Other studies have shown that the Norwegian public administration has become part of both a Norwegian and a European administrative order (Egeberg 2006). It has also been argued that Norway's special relation to the

EU undermines the constitution as a basis for democracy (Eriksen and Fossum 2014).

The mandate of the 22 July Commission was established to analyze and draw lessons from the attacks on the government quarter in Oslo and the youth camp of the governing Labor Party at the island of Utøya, in which 77 people were killed and many were wounded. The commission documented that routines that work well under normal conditions do not necessarily do so under exceptional circumstances with unknown tasks and great uncertainty. Important institutions—first and foremost the police—were strongly criticized for their handling of the situation. Most analysis focused on the system's capability to implement and enforce decisions and on future preparedness for situations most Norwegians did not believe could take place in their country (NOU 2012: 14, Fimreite et al. 2014).

None of the reports evoked accountability demands or principled debate about the terms of political order. Public authorities were not worried about the country's democratic quality. Rather, there was a democracy-is-us response from the government. Norway's relation to the EU was portrayed as unproblematic in democratic terms. Democratic challenges were seen to be related to how Norway could help other countries develop democratic institutions. Norway, furthermore, had great economic advantages from European market access and was seen to share the basic values of the EU. The July 22 tragedy was met with emotional appeals to community, democracy, openness, and the rule of law. The government was criticized, but much of the criticism was related to specific events such as why a street was not closed for traffic. The opposition in Parliament did not call for a vote of no confidence. The judicial proceedings against the terrorist were carried out according to *Rechtsstaat* principles. There were rose parades and crowds singing the popular song "*Sammen skal vi leve*" [Together we shall live]. But there was no principled discussion regarding the best kind of political community and rules for peaceful coexistence. There were no questions about what normative and organizational principles are most likely to make a "living democracy" possible or about how the government, or others, could and should be made accountable for the terms of political order.

Why No Accountability Demands?

It is an apparent paradox that Norway, which ranks as a well-organized and well-functioning democracy in international comparisons, has been heavily criticized in three different public reports, which provided alarming diagnoses of the current and future functioning of Norwegian democracy. However, this kind of public criticism may also work as a safety valve, contributing to incremental reforms and making discontent and accountability demands regarding the political order less likely. In spite of a gap between official self-presentations and political practice, citizens seem to differentiate between the legitimacy of the democratic order and the legitimacy of specific policies, political parties, governments, and institutions. Norwegian data are consistent with the observation that democracy in the sense of free, competitive elections and popular participation does not alone guarantee legitimacy. Nor does it create a good society and prevent poverty and economic inequality, high infant mortality, low life expectancy, illiteracy and unequal access to education, unequal gender relations, or absence of subjective feelings of well-being. A well-functioning polity with institutions able to solve important problems also requires that public authority be exercised in a non-corrupt, reliable, neutral, and competent way (Rothstein 2011, Holmberg and Rothstein 2012).

Four percent of the population says that they are very satisfied with how democracy works in Norway. 67 percent are somewhat satisfied, 22 percent are not very satisfied, and four percent are not satisfied at all (Strømsnes 2003: 180). The population sees its own participation as less important than achieving good public services and efficient use of tax money. Being politically active is not a moral duty and the role of the citizen is to a large extent decoupled from participation in political parties. Citizens want to be taken into account more than to participate. They are interested in politics, but they rank family, friends, free time, and work higher. Good citizenship is related to making up one's mind in an independent way, taking part in elections, following laws and rules, showing solidarity, paying taxes, and being concerned with the welfare of others. A good society is one where all people can use their faculties, people take responsibility for one another, there is economic safety and prosperity, and people follow the rules and are self-confident, critical, and hardworking (Strømsnes 2003: 162–3, 179, 192). Parliament wants power—but within limits. Elected representatives have the formal power to ultimately decide, but they realize that other institutions and actors need a certain amount of autonomy in order to do a good job. Public administration—"the bureaucracy"—and organized interests may be both criticized and praised.

The attitudes and opinions of citizens and elected representatives probably reflect that the Norwegian polity is a settled, compound, and historically developed political order based on many ties and forms of integration, and not on utility calculation alone. The "living" political order is a result of historical processes more than of deliberate choices by constitutional assemblies at constitutional moments. Gradual state-building and nation-building processes have provided action capabilities, national homogenization, and a community feeling. The result is a territorial state with elements of a functional state, nation-state, Rechtsstaat, democratic state, and a welfare state with socio-economic citizenship. Due to the polity's small size, it is fairly easy to anticipate what other leaders and citizens will accept, and political and organizational leaders have prioritized maintaining community by searching for compromises and avoiding decisions that are unacceptable and unlikely to be obeyed. Political promises have rarely been completely out of touch with what it was possible to deliver in practice. As a result, Norway usually ranks near the very top in international comparisons when it comes to citizens' trust in authorities and each other.

It is, therefore, unsurprising that political practice in Norway is not dominated by a hierarchical chain of authorization and accountability between predetermined principals and agents. The political order reflects compromises between institutions founded on competing normative and organizational principles—institutions likely to be held accountable in relation to democratic representative majority decisions, Rechtsstaat norms and principles, the norms and beliefs of a national culture, expertise and scientific and professional standards, economic realities, organized interests, mass media and public opinion, and a variety of European and international standards and rights regimes.

Why then is the separation of the official narrative and political practice so unproblematic in Norway? It may be due to elements of deceit and manipulation and strategic use of information by agents. There are, however, other possibilities. An institutional approach suggests that talk and practice are partly institutionally separated. Practice might be related to functional prerequisites. The great narrative and related rituals might be rooted in the normative environment (Meyer and Rowan 1977, March 1984, Brunsson 1989, 2007), having a unifying effect on the population.

In a compound, historically developed polity such as Norway, characterized by deliberation, bargaining, and compromise, it is difficult to objectively say how accountability ought to be attributed. Ambiguity and uncertainty can lead to image management, blame games and the politics of accountability. When this has happened in Norway to a very limited extent, several factors have probably contributed. Well-developed trust relations provide a relatively wide margin of discretion for decision makers. The quality of democratic governance has been interpreted as satisficing, allowing other interests and values to be part of the definition of good government.

Arguably, Norwegians do not relate accountability to an abstract ideal of democratic political order. When citizens do not mobilize and call rulers to account for discrepancies between the way the political order is officially presented and the way it works in practice, it may be because citizens use pragmatic tests—both historical, to evaluate whether things are better than before, and comparative, to compare Norway to other countries. A strong community feeling and national identification, stepwise pragmatic reforms, and sequential problem solving and conflict resolution have prevented the accumulation of tension. There have been no major crises of performance or confidence. Of 14 European countries studied, Norway was the one least affected by the 2008 fiscal crisis (Randma-Liiv and Kickert 2016). Oil money and slack resources have reduced the demand for consistency between talk and action and prevented widespread discontent and accountability demands related to the political order. Grand principled debates about the terms of political order have been seen as a possible source of unnecessary conflict and thus avoided.

In brief, the Norwegian case indicates that talk–action gaps are unlikely to attract much public attention as long as citizens are relatively satisfied with their everyday lives, and as long as decision makers routinely anticipate what citizens accept as reasonable and just, exercise some degree of self-restraint, and largely stay within citizens' zones of acceptance. A question, then, is under what conditions the (near) consensus is likely to be challenged and shaken so that rulers are called to account for the terms of political order and for ongoing political developments.

Without a Road Map

While striving for order, democracies also need to preserve flexibility and prevent excessive rigidity that might generate decay in the long run. Democratic politics can be seen as an ongoing search for political order, with free public debate and an organized opposition legitimately challenging existing arrangements. Democracy is ideally a continuous, experience-based self-regulating process of learning and adaptation. Through freedom of expression and organization, political debate, and competition in free elections, democracies are assumed to have the ability to test established truths and normative principles and create progress based upon reason and experience. Democracies do not always make good decisions, but they learn from experience and they can call rulers to account and even remove them.

Within this framework, the three democracy alarms—involving contestation, public criticism, and legitimate opposition in a fairly well-functioning democracy—are not necessarily a sign of a democratic crisis; they may provide occasions for learning and improvement. Even if learning processes are not perfect, to the extent that political institutions respond to and learn from alarms, they can be a source of reform and adaptation that reduce the likelihood of accountability crises and rapid and radical breaks with the existing order. Norway's challenge is related to a further development of the ability of everyday politics to learn and adapt, more than to making possible grand reforms at constitutional moments.

The Norwegian political style has contributed to a system of governance that has been adaptive under post-World War II conditions, in practice if not in official self-understanding. Political–administrative institutions have been fairly successful in handling "normal times" and well-known tasks using institutionalized routines and standard operating procedures. The absence of accountability demands regarding the political order may, however, partly be due to the fact that the order has not been seriously challenged during this period. The recent criticism regarding democratic failure and alarming developments, therefore, raises questions about how well Norwegian democracy is prepared for a more turbulent period with new national and international conditions (Olsen 2014a). Will the system be able to learn and adapt to a highly dynamic and interdependent world involving geopolitical, economic, cultural, demographic, information technological, and climatic changes? Will it be able to cope with a higher level of conflict and develop *new* historical compromises in a situation where the standard identities and cleavages of industrial society, emphasizing economic production and distribution, meet increasing competition from a growing number of other cleavages? Will the system be able to counteract the assumed reduced ability nation-states have when it comes to solving important societal problems and simultaneously securing high democratic quality with a more heterogeneous population, more open national borders, rapidly changing international environments, unknown and complex problems, and a more difficult economic situation?

A not completely unrealistic scenario is that calls for accountability related to the terms of political order will be more frequent and stronger as a result of growing domestic heterogeneity, increasing international dependencies, and reduced economic slack. It is not obvious that Norway will be able to combine its welfare-state tradition with the neo-liberal economic and neo-constitutional legal ideas that have provided premises for many public-sector reforms over the last few decades, a period with reduced popular trust in representative democratic institutions and reduced interest in traditional forms of political participation and party membership. Accountability demands may become more frequent because citizens see national identity and self-governance as threatened, generating conflicts over immigration and the composition of the population. Incremental reforms and appeals to common responsibilities and shared standards about what is reasonable and just may not secure compromises if the national common culture and the traditional integrating opinion and norm-forming processes are weakened. Appeals to equality and redistribution may be less successful in a more multi-cultural society, especially if public finances are weakened by declining revenue from oil and gas and if the allocation of private resources becomes more skewed.

A basic question is whether effective public problem solving and production of welfare services are enough to keep citizens satisfied, or whether democracy and the absence of order-challenging accountability demands are possible only if citizens share certain fundamental values, attitudes, and understandings with intersubjective validity. More specifically, the question is whether democracies need democrats who are carriers of integrating democratic values and virtues, that is, people who are willing to defend the political community and long-term concerns, and not only participate in short-term actions in the pursuit of narrow self-interest.

Today it is less clear what the Norwegian (and Scandinavian) dreams and visions for the future are and how Norway's well-established pragmatic problem-solving routines may be combined with more principled thinking about the terms of order and the rules for living together. There is no agreed-upon road map suggesting what is needed to successfully cope with future challenges. There is no new narrative or great compromise that is likely to mobilize public support and become institutionalized. Possibly, Norway will provide another example of the danger of success, that is, a successful welfare state where commitment to old purposes, structures, and solutions makes learning and adaptation to new circumstances difficult.

To avoid such a negative outcome there is a need to develop more principled thinking *without* losing the ability to pragmatically solve problems and reduce conflict. One such challenge is related to the problem of reconciling conflicting attitudes toward European integration and the EU, itself a dynamic and unsettled polity. It has been argued that the EU is not likely to break down as long as it successfully fulfills key functions for the Union's economy and society as a whole (Schmitter and Lefkofridi 2016: 3). Over the last decade, an increasing number of people have wondered to what degree the EU is capable of filling such functions any longer.

The EU: "Unsuccessful" Separation and the Terms of Order in Dispute

The idea of Europe as a unified political system has a long history (Heater 1992). Efforts to increase integration into a larger organized polity have, however, historically had to compete with efforts to defend the autonomy of the basic components (Rokkan and Urwin 1983: 14). Like other polities, the EU faces the questions of how to achieve the gains of integration without destroying the autonomy and the identity of the units integrated (Deutsch 1966: 253), how much and what forms of unity the components can tolerate, and how much and what forms of diversity a political order can tolerate (Olsen 2007: 24, 107, 2009b).

Most of the time, integration into a larger organized order competes with the desire for autonomy among the order's component units. It is difficult to find and maintain a proper balance between system integration and unit autonomy. System coordination and coherence tends to foster efforts to protect the distinctive character of the components. Likewise, differentiation of subsystems and integration of each component is likely to generate demands for system coordination, control, coherence, and consistency (March 1999). How integration processes unfold depends on whether the basic entities, or some of their parts, will have to give up constitutive characteristics when entering a larger unit and thus on how well the identities and key characteristics of the larger and smaller units match (Brunsson and Olsen 1998: 32–3). At issue is what ties a group of individuals with different interests, values, worldviews, life plans, and resources together in a political entity organized for collective action and how to balance the desire to develop a common identity and a capacity for joint action and the desire to protect the specific identity and autonomy of the component units.

A polity constituted solely on calculated utility is generally less stable than one based on habit and even more so than an order upheld by legitimacy regarded by citizens as exemplary or obligatory (Weber 1978: 31, 33). The challenge of integration for the larger system and the component units is least daunting when they are constituted on functional expediency and utility alone. The more a polity is founded solely on expected advantage, the more entrances into the system, accountability demands, and exits will depend on the comparative effectiveness and efficiency of available organizational alternatives. Cycles of integration and disintegration will follow shifts in the comparative efficiency of different units. No constitutive identity, commitments, or emotions are involved. To join or not, and to allow in component units or not, is decided based on the calculation of the comparative benefits of existing alternatives. The dilemma of keeping an original identity and becoming part of a larger entity will be more problematic in organizations and polities held together by a strong shared identity, loyalty, and legitimacy. The dilemma of safeguarding autonomy and identity will be conspicuous in particular when both the larger system and the component units are held together by strong constitutive cultural or political identities (Brunsson and Olsen 1998: 31–4).

The Treaty of Rome (1957) left undefined the precise meaning of integration and the mechanisms through which "an ever closer Union" and the elimination of internal frontiers could be achieved. A key characteristic of the European way of coping with unity and diversity has been not to formulate a *finalité politique*—an agreed-upon political philosophy, a coherent blueprint for a desired future, and a strategy for achieving it. There have been specified procedures and timetables and gradual shifts in meaning rather than operational goals and desired end states (Kohler-Koch 2005).

However, a (stylized) functional vision of European integration has been that functional integration in terms of interdependence and social integration in terms of trade and travel contact would create a need for political integration in terms of European-level governmental institutions, which in turn would generate cultural integration and a common identity. The process of European integration and the construction of a supranational European political system was expected to cause a significant decline in the normative role of the nation-state, its governing capacity, trust, and legitimacy (Caramani 2004: 8). A scenario of historical discontinuity in the political organization of Europe was foreseen—that is, an integration process whereby most of the state's tasks, support, and resources would be transferred to institutions at the European, regional, or local levels, and political actors would shift their loyalties, expectations, and political activities toward a new center, whose institutions possessed or demanded jurisdictions over the pre-existing national states (Haas 1968, Schmitter 1996).

Functional efficiency and substantive advantage were the most significant founding rationales of the European Community. It was the presumed superiority of the community's problem-solving capacity over that of the traditional nation-states which largely motivated its foundation in the 1950s (Preuss 1996: 219). A belief in integration was embedded in the view that aggressive nationalism and nation-states were a danger to peace. The state, furthermore, had lost its superior technical performance. It was functionally obsolete and unable to cope with new challenges and opportunities. The new political organization of the continent was meant to ensure peace and prosperity. For some, "the law of progress" had made states and nations unviable and doomed to disappear (Hobsbawn 1992).

Since then, the EU has come to define itself in terms of expected utility, geography, socio-cultural values, and constitutive political–democratic principles. Still, explanations and justifications of integration have primarily been functional and apolitical, with reference to practical results, voluntary cooperation, consensus seeking, expertise, and indirect democracy derived from the member states. Unification has been portrayed as an efficient way to create a win–win situation with advantages for all and no losers. In addition, it has been argued that the ties that held nation-states together do not work anymore and that the state can no longer provide the appropriate framework for the maintenance of democratic citizenship. The claim has been made that modern democracies have to loosen the connection between ethnicity and cultural homogeneity and political citizenship (Habermas 1996b: 137).

The EU has, in practice—through institution building, including the development of administrative capabilities at the European level—become a competitor to the inherited state order and the intergovernmental paradigm and logic (Egeberg 2004, 2009, Curtin and Egeberg 2008, Trondal 2010). But the chain reactions of integration based on interdependence, social contact, political–administrative institution building and identity building foreseen by functionalists have been far from perfect. Claims that the state has lost its predominant role in political life have been founded on hopes and fears, as well as analysis. Explanations and justifications of European integration have been embedded in strong but contested beliefs in depoliticization, self-regulating competitive markets, and powerful non-majority institutions as the embodiment and disinterested carrier of reason, objective knowledge, justice, or necessity—institutions that therefore should be insulated from politics and public opinion.

Partly inconsistent foundational normative and causal beliefs are reflected in cumbersome and contested institutional arrangements, characterized by a combination of organizational principles and forms rather than the purification of a single principle or form (Olsen 2010: 54). Practice has been formed through several constitutional compromises and opt-outs, reflecting different conceptions of a desirable Europe. Incremental changes have produced a complex patchwork of rules and regulations (Preuss 1996). There are shifting institutional power balances, considerable variation in integration, and centralization of authority and power across policy sectors (Leuffen et al. 2013), and a variety of horizontal forms of accountability (Schillemans 2008). Allocation of authority and accountability has often been implicit and indirect. When, for example, the EP and the Court of Justice of the European Union hold the EC accountable for what agencies are doing, they (tacitly) assume that the EC has and should have power over agencies. In turn, this may reduce the complexity of an accountability regime in the interface between national and European forums, make the system more transparent, and create more uniformity in the application of law (Busuioc 2013, Egeberg and Trondal 2016, Egeberg et al. 2015).

Generally, institutional developments have been less a matter of choice and an overall vision than a byproduct of events and attempts to cope with the most dramatic problems of the day (Mény 2012: 159). New institutional relations have been shaped in polycentric, open processes with a broad range of possible developments. There has been interaction between actors whose roles and functions have not been predefined by an overarching concept of legitimate political order and unity. Competing principles of legitimation and opposing forces of integration and disintegration have been driven by agents that are partly formed through the process itself (Preuss 1996: 218). Outcomes have been artifacts of specific policy decisions and events outside political control (Hooghe and Marks 2001: 36, 117). No single decision-making authority has been in control and nobody can now claim to govern the EU (Majone 2014).

For example, during the financial and economic crises since 2008 supranational actors such as the EC and the Central Bank took on more discretionary powers. They themselves were instrumental in generating this change, in spite of a decline in support for European integration among governments and the public. Sudden and radical changes, with potentially huge implications for the balance of power in the EU, were caused by an unprecedented crisis situation, a need to restore confidence among financial market actors, and mistrust among member states. The future of the Union was seen to be at stake. Yet, changes did not happen overnight and through a "big bang" but rather through a series of compromises (Dehousse 2015: 10, 17, 21–2).

A conclusion is that the EU is still an unsettled polity struggling to find a balance between the whole and the parts, between unity and diversity, coordination and autonomy, order and flexibility. There are debates and conflicts over how Europe should be organized and governed politically and competing conceptions of integration and what kind of unity and diversity the EU can live with. Part of the struggle involves what role democratic politics and government should and can have in the future European order—that is, to what degree and in which ways ordinary citizens should and are able to determine how polity and society are to be organized and governed and how power holders are to be held to account. Recent developments in the EU have raised questions about the conditions under which deliberate institutional reform is a process primarily involving executives and experts, and the conditions under which it involves wider popular mobilization with accountability demands regarding the limits of technocratic and executive legitimacy (Olsen 2007: 46–7). Ambiguous and uncertain situations make the objective attribution of accountability more difficult and open the way for accountability politics, image management, and struggles over whom to blame and hold to account.

Occasions Used for Calling Rulers to Account

The EU has, over the last few decades, provided several occasions for public debate and accountability demands related to the terms of legitimate political order. A long sequence of treaty reforms creating perceived "constitutional moments" has led to struggles over the cognitive, normative, and power foundations of political union. The citizens of various member states have used these occasions for calling rulers to account, for example by rejecting draft treaties through referendums. However, post-referendum processes have, in many instances, modified the public will expressed through the referendum.

For example, the 2001 Laeken Declaration, committing the EU to more democracy, transparency, and efficiency, started a constitution-making process and the Convention on the Future of Europe, established in the same year, aimed at widening and deepening the Union. The European Constitutional Treaty was signed in 2004 but rejected in Dutch and French referendums in 2005, only to reappear later in a somewhat revised form. Irish voters said "no" to the Nice treaty in 2001 and to the Treaty of Lisbon in 2008. Yet both came into force after some modifications. The Treaty of Lisbon was implemented in 2009, followed by the consolidated versions of the Treaty on European Union and the Treaty on the Functioning of the European Union (2012). Furthermore, the Greeks voted against accepting the EU bailout conditions (2015), but the conditions were later accepted by the Greek parliament.

Whereas few noticed that Greenland in 1979 voted to leave the EEC, and a possible Greek exit was seen by many as a greater problem for Greece than for the EU, the British vote of 52 percent to 48 percent to leave the EU has created a new situation and a feeling of crisis in Europe. But once again, there are good reasons to believe that post-referendum processes will affect what the leave vote really comes to mean. The result will depend on the political processes triggered by the vote in both the UK and the EU. There is a broad range of possible future developments, and available theory and facts do not allow any precise predictions of what will actually follow.

For the UK, the movement to leave the EU was nested in deep internal conflicts in the two major political parties, and concerns about future relations between England, Scotland, and possibly Northern Ireland. For the EU, there is a need to accommodate Britain as a major European power and trading partner and simultaneously avoid a result that creates a domino effect of other member states calling referendums over EU membership, with possible exits as a result. The uncertainty is also influenced by less than precise rules for exiting the EU. The situation illustrates that the need for flexibility in politics (see Chapter 3) sometimes makes rules incomplete, unclear, and even chaotic. The uncertainty about the implications of a member state exiting, and the necessity of leaving room to cope with particular needs and unseen circumstances, have led to the EU having formulated only some basic elements of the withdrawal process (Hillion 2015: 135, 142).

More generally, there has been political mobilization from the mid-1980s accompanied by a shift from a "permissive consensus" to a "constraining dissensus" (Hooghe and Marks 2001, 2009). In the view of the EU's founding fathers, ordinary people were not ready for European integration and leaders had to do what was necessary in a critical situation. Since then it has become more difficult for elites to restrict public debates and conceal popular discontent (Stratham and Trenz 2013). The political organization of Europe has become an increasingly more important cleavage, with tensions between eurozone and non-eurozone, creditors and debtors, East and West, and South and North. Some want to go forward toward "an ever closer union," and in some member states the satisfaction with democracy in the EU is slightly higher than the satisfaction with democracy in their home country (Hobolt 2012: 100, 101). Others have claimed that the EU is non-democratic, non-accountable, and secretive and they want power to be transferred back to the member states. Cross-border protest movements have challenged the political order and a theme has been the gap between what political leaders say and what they do. Protests have often come from the losers: The unemployed, low-skill, immobile people who have not had their living conditions improved, but rather have seen a growing inequality in welfare and life chances. Euroskeptic parties and social movements are, however, far from in agreement regarding what the problems are and what kind of political order is desired (Szczerbiak and Taggart 2008, Usherwood 2013).

Observing that many citizens feel that representative democracy in the Union does not work well, the EU has made several attempts to counteract the perceived democratic deficit and regain trust and legitimacy by engaging citizens. Discourse regarding European citizenship formally entered the European Community's agenda in the early 1970s, driven by a perceived need to generate a sense of belonging (Jenson 2007: 59). The Committee of Independent Experts, initiated by the EP with a mandate to study allegations regarding fraud, mismanagement, and nepotism in the EC, concluded its harsh criticism by claiming that there was "a growing reluctance among the members of the hierarchy to acknowledge their responsibility. It is becoming difficult to find anyone who has even the slightest sense of responsibility" (Committee of Independent Experts 1999: 144). In its more recent attempts to bring the EU closer to its citizens, the EC has observed that Europeans want representative institutions and political leaders to find solutions to major societal problems at the same time as they increasingly distrust institutions and policymakers or are not interested in politics. Improved accountability was among the five principles of good governance assumed to counteract the loss of confidence and meet the expectations of the citizens, together with openness, participation, effectiveness, and coherence (European Commission 2001). Still, reforms from above have not prevented declining public support and more skeptical or hostile public opinion. Rather, they have triggered blame games and accountability demands.

Despite the EU winning the Nobel Peace Prize in 2012, the belief that the experiment of European integration is "condemned to succeed" has been shaken (Spinelli Group 2013: 11). Reforms involving further integration have been met by defense of national sovereignty, identity, and established welfare arrangements. There is reduced public support for both the enlargement of the EU and the widening and deepening of integration. The principle of open borders and free movement of people has been challenged, partly as a result of refugee and migration crises. In contrast to the idea that "the way forward" involves further integration, there is greater awareness of the lasting limitations of European political integration, and it has been argued that it is necessary to recognize the end of the unitary project. "The need for deeper integration in the EMU [European Monetary Union] policies will make the continuance of a common legal and institutional order unlikely" (Fabbrini 2014: 12). People have come to realize that the EU will not, in the foreseeable future, become a democratic polity (Scharpf 1999: 200). The EU has accepted several opt-outs in order to reach treaty compromises. Conflict patterns have become increasingly complex. There is an "uneasy marriage of supranational and intergovernmental methods" and a need to regain confidence in Europe (Dawson 2015: 55, 118).

It has become commonplace to claim that the EU is in a state of emergency and facing an existential crisis (Menéndez 2013, 2014). There is no time for business as usual (European Commission 2015) when the EU has to deal simultaneously with (a) economic and financial crises; (b) employment, distributional issues, and socio-economic rights; (c) managing its common borders at a time of mass migration and refugees; (d) responding to terrorism; (e) coping with climate and environmental sustainability; and (f) facing democratic deficit claims and accountability demands related to explaining and justifying the terms of political order. The EU risks falling apart. Concern and criticism are not limited to critics of the integration project. The founding members have (even before Brexit) become concerned about the state of the European project and they want to strengthen cohesion in the EU (Joint Communiqué 2016).

In brief, there is a crisis of integration, a growing gap between words and deeds, and a divorce between elites and peoples. Ordinary people are on average more skeptical or anti-EU than elites. The present state of affairs might not be acceptable for long and there is a need for major reforms of the governing institutions (Mény 2012). Why, then, has the EU not been able to maintain the kind of "successful" separation of talk and action that Norway has?

Why is Separation No Longer Possible?

The EU aims at integrating established polities with different constitutive rules, traditions, and capabilities (Bogdanor 1996: 135, Eriksen, Fossum and Menéndez 2004, Fossum and Menéndez 2011). The population of the EU is, however, a hundred times that of Norway. The level of trust in authorities and fellow citizens is considerably lower, probably making the margin of discretion narrower for policymakers. Heterogeneity also makes it difficult to reach legitimate collective decisions. Successive enlargements have created more heterogeneity and mass migration across cultures has contributed to conflict. Whereas treaty reforms have been perceived as necessary in order to cope with ongoing crises, they have been difficult to achieve.

EU leaders have not been afraid of using big words and making great, and sometimes unrealistic and unachievable, promises. The aim of the Lisbon Strategy, devised in 2000, was to make the EU the most competitive and dynamic knowledge-based economy in the world, capable of sustainable economic growth with more and better jobs and greater social cohesion. In 2010 it was (again) time to be bold and ambitious and get Europe back on track and offer a sense of direction (Barroso 2010). Europe 2020 promised "a strategy for smart, sustainable and inclusive growth," a high-employment economy delivering economic, social, and territorial cohesion, combating poverty and social exclusion and reducing health inequalities (European Commission 2010: 17). The Treaty on Stability, Coordination and Governance in the Economic and Monetary Union envisioned a stronger, deeper, and extended single market as a strategy for fighting economic nationalism and developing ever closer coordination of economic policies within the eurozone (European Council 2012).

The EU has not always delivered as promised and crises have shaken a fragile political order based upon multiple compromises and "an intersection of several treaties" (Fabbrini 2016: 94). Some critics have claimed that the EU intervenes too much in national politics, business, and the in the lives of individuals. Others have held that the belief in a free-market economy and self-regulating markets securing economic growth, efficient allocation of resources, economic rights, and free movement has been more important than the belief in democratic participation. According to these critics, economic (ordo)liberalism, the 2008 financial crises, and austerity policies have spelled disaster for countries such as Greece. They have also undermined the functionality of the institutions and policies of Continental and Scandinavian welfare states (Everson and Joerges 2012, Scharpf 2015). The space of politics has been reduced (Mény 2012: 157) and a suspicion has been that restoring trust in the EU among actors in financial markets has been more important than restoring trust among ordinary citizens. Criticism of the proposed dispute settlement mechanism, as part of the EU–US Transatlantic Trade and Investment Partnership, has involved similar complaints. Investors' rights will be protected by arbitration panels staffed by trade lawyers handling disputes in secret and bypassing ordinary courts. The arrangement will constrain governments from making legislation regarding health, social, and environmental protection. Depoliticization has been presented as a functional economic necessity. But critics have argued that settling public matters involving competing values, interests, and understandings in private or expert settings does not make them "apolitical" (Mény 2012: 162).

Among euroskeptics such suspicions were amplified when the former president of the EC, Jose Manuel Barroso, was hired by the US investment bank Goldman Sachs as an advisor and non-executive chairman of its international businesses in 2016. The bank played a central role in the 2008 financial crisis and it helped Greece to hide parts of its deficit in the early 2000s. Yet, confronted with the criticism of Barroso's decision a spokesman for the EC referred to existing rules. Eighteen months after leaving office Barroso had no obligation to notify the EC and the spokesman saw no problem. Others saw Barroso's decision to work for Goldman Sachs as "morally and politically deplorable" and "outrageous and shameful." It was also observed that nine of Barroso's former commissioners have gone to work for big business after their terms ended in 2014 (Zalan 2016).

Accountability demands have been related to both performance and process, reflecting that the EU is not solely based upon substantive performance. The EU is to a large extent a community based upon legal acts and "integration by law." Integration through law was not supposed to overrule "the political" (Joerges 2010: 70), but the court has fashioned a new legal order—a juridification of the political sphere (Azoulai and Dehousse 2012: 354). Judge-made law has played a crucial role in European integration processes, taking part in a contest among prescriptive conceptions of society (Shaw 1996: 241). The court's role has been expanded and integration through law has prioritized liberalization and deregulation. The Court of Justice of the European Union has committed itself to furthering the progress of integration, ensuring the uniform application of EU law, irrespective of the particularities of national law. Court decisions have ignored the foundations of the social and political constructions of solidarity. More protection has been given to economic liberties than to worker safety, consumer and environmental protection, and institutional asymmetries, and high consensus requirements have made it difficult to correct these effects (Everson and Joerges 2012, Scharpf 2015). The courts have, through controversial law making and expansive interpretations, extended the rights of non-national beneficiaries of public and collectively financed health care at the expense of domestic taxpayers and insurance funds (Scharpf 2010: 237).

The financial and economic crises have, however, also shifted patterns of authorization and accountability toward executive federalism (Fossum 2016a), and legal scholars have claimed that legitimating decisive action by the requirement of necessity and a state of exception has trumped the traditional legality of the *Rechtsstaat* (Somek 2013: 575). The principle of the rule of law and *Rechtsstaat* principles has been broken in the handling of the financial and economic crises. Euro summits, improvisation, unconventional processes, and institutional practices have taken place outside the institutional frameworks of EU treaties and national constitutions. The division between eurozone members and non-members has challenged the equality of member states. The institutional balance of the EU has changed and the community method has been weakened. The space for democratic politics has furthermore been constrained by the increased power of non-majoritarian institutions at arm's length from political processes and democratic accountability, such as the EC, the Court of Justice of the European Union, and the European Central Bank, all of them engines of further integration. Powerful agencies have also been placed outside the traditional administrative hierarchy and their democratic legitimacy is problematic. It is unclear who controls them and ensures that legislation is faithfully executed and the legitimacy of decision makers and decisions can be traced back to citizens (Chamon 2016). The constitutional basis for assessing the establishment and empowerment of EU agencies has eroded (Orator 2016). There is no unified legal order or legal hierarchy. There is conflict between legal orders and principles and no single institution can claim to have ultimate authority (Goldoni 2012: 386).

Competing claims regarding accountability and talk–action gaps are often based on different normative principles and standards. On the one hand, critics can refer to the treaties, which state that the EU shall be founded upon representative democracy. The (Maastricht) Treaty on European Union (1992) for the first time explicitly said that the Union was to be founded on the principles of democracy and fundamental human rights. It was observed that there was a need to counteract the image of an elite project with limited popular information, debate, and involvement (European Commission 1992). The Copenhagen criteria (1993) made "liberal democracy" a requirement for membership, assuming institutions that guarantee democracy, together with the rule of law, fundamental human rights, respect for individuals and minorities, a well-functioning economic market and the capacity to cope with competition in the EU, and staff and resources to make it possible to implement the *acquis communautaire*.

Whereas the EU claims to have established democracy at the European level, the democratic ideal has been realized only to a limited degree. Democracy and democratic accountability have not had the same status as the single market, economic freedom, and integration by law. There are numerous claims of a democratic deficit and lack of democratic legitimacy. A "façade of democracy" hides the real power holders (Streeck 2014: 177), and parliamentary accountability is "remarkably weak" (Weiler 2012: 251). There are disagreements over the desirability of a fully-fledged European parliament on a par with the parliaments of the member states and the role of democratic government in managing the economy (Jachtenfuchs et al. 1998). Likewise, the emerging role of national parliaments in the EU is deeply contested. The EP, for example, views the role of national parliaments as marginal and there are competing models of parliamentary scrutiny (Cooper 2016). In contrast to the parliamentarian turn, it is also argued that rights are better protected by courts than by democratic legislatures and electoral accountability. Courts help to uncover and address the pathologies of democracies by holding legislatures accountable. Judicial independence ensures that the court is immunized from the pressures of the ordinary political process and is a necessary complement to democratically accountable decision making (Kumm 2007: 2–4, 15–16).

In the EU, there is no institutionalized opposition and only weak institutional arrangements for channeling discontent and protest (Mény 2012: 162–3). A study of four categories of initiatives to mobilize ordinary citizens, including the European Citizens' Initiative, also concluded that there have been few results in terms of activating rank-and-file citizens. There have been more rhetoric and symbolic gestures towards "doing something" than improved participatory mechanisms and increased democratization (Boussaguet 2016). It has been held that

> at heart, member governments do not consider that European integration is about democracy, even if they claim to be concerned about the democratic deficit. In the final analysis, member governments continue with the integration process because they are economically dependent upon it and because they perceive it to be a potential means of reasserting themselves, albeit as a collectivity, in a way impossible for them alone. (Warleigh 2002: 114)

On the other hand, there is limited agreement on the specific nature and causes of the deficit (Fossum 2016a). It can be argued that the EU was never intended to be a polity resembling existing liberal democracies (Hooghe and Marks 2001: 41). Its governance structure was not designed for democratic accountability, and European citizenship is still a vague concept (Weiler 2012: 251). There is a modest will to further integrate Europe politically and there are voices raising doubts about democracy's normative status, and the possibility and desirability of democracy in the EU (Majone 1998, Moravcsik 2004). In any case, European democracy has to be different from national democracies. It is neither possible nor desirable to try to democratize the European polity completely or immediately. People are not prepared to exercise democratic rights and the only option is to improve the EU's democratic quality stepwise (Schmitter 2000: 42, 115).

Discontent, accountability demands, and the breakdown of a "successful" separation of talk and action depend on how disputes are settled. Leaders may have unifying or dividing effects (Olsen 2007: 6), and a democratic challenge for the EU is that there is a lack of appropriate institutions for political leadership (Mény 2012: 162–3). The EU has a constitution but lacks an ethos and telos to justify it, and it is not clear who is the constituent power (Weiler

1996: 106, 107). If EC (EU) law has an ethic, it is economic liberalism (Shaw 1996). Because the ordinary political channels for airing support and discontent from citizens do not work well, opposition in the EU is often directed towards the order itself. Revolt becomes necessary because the polity has failed to integrate opposition within government and to provide criticism with an outlet (Mair 2007: 6). In addition, the EU and European integration are often not attractive issues for domestic political parties, which fail to debate EU affairs and offer clear alternatives because they often deviate from their voters by being more supportive to European integration, and they are internally divided. Mainstream parties have reached agreements and made grand coalitions, leading the way for Euroskeptic parties (Kröger and Bellamy 2016). Contestation in national elections and EU elections is not about issues that each of the channels can influence. Votes in both channels have become increasingly irrelevant to the output of their respective systems. Because democratic decision making is marginal to the workings of the European polity at the supranational level, it also tends to lose its value in the working of various component polities at the national level (Mair 2007: 11, 14). There is a divorce between "politics" and "policymaking" (Papadopoulos 2013: 19, 20), with "policy without politics" at the EU level and "politics without policy" at the national level (Schmidt 2006, 2007). Politicization and democratization are seen as threats to the Union's ability to govern effectively for the people.

Discontent, accountability demands, and the breakdown of a "successful" separation of talk and action can also be related to limited resources and the fact that the EU's resources do not match its aspirations. National governments are not willing to transfer the powers and resources the EU "needs" (Spinelli Group 2013: 5), and they frequently use "the bureaucracy in Brussels" as a scapegoat for their own mistakes and unpopular policies. The EU lacks the power to do what is asked of it because institutions are not endowed with the resources and power required to fulfill their mission and achieve their goals (Barroso 2013: 11). There is limited capacity to act, limited means of coercion, and modest taxation and fiscal abilities. Compared to well-developed welfare states, EU budgets give little room for redistribution. The EU, furthermore, has limited institutional capacities for creating a political community with a strong collective identity, cultural unity, and integration based on common values and purposes.

An institutional approach assumes that a well-functioning democracy needs democrats. Democracy does not only rest on getting incentives right, it also needs active and well-informed citizens, representatives, and officials who act as carriers of a democratic faith. At issue is whether the EU needs a firmer foundation than expediency and expected utility in order to function as a democratic polity, and whether some shared European identity and a sense of collective purpose is necessary for a well-functioning EU. Arguably, there is a need for a form of legal framework for integration which preserves cultural diversity within Europe without creating a divisive European identity (Shaw 1996: 250, 252). Compared to economic and political issues, the spiritual and cultural dimensions of the European project have, however, had a modest place in debates (Biedenkopf et al. 2004, Battista et al. 2014). European identity was assumed to be an outcome of, and not a precondition for, European integration. European institutions were to be built in the absence of Europeans (Hooghe and Marks 2001: 51).

It was, nevertheless, claimed early on that "unless a new loyalty to the European idea can be fostered more rapidly than has thus far proved possible, the difficulties and conflicts arising from the attempt to integrate Western Europe may grow rather than diminish" (Frey-Wouters 1965: 477). A more recent claim is that the old forces of cohesion, the desire for peace and prosperity, and external threats, are losing their effectiveness. The forces of unity and cohesion are to be found in the common culture, in the values, morals, customs, and expectations of Europeans (Biedenkopf et al. 2004: 5–8). However, there is no unified and homogeneous people, a *Staatsvolk* upon which European-level political institutions can be built (Eriksen 2005: 260). Most citizens see the national community as the predominant frame of reference for solidarity (Whelan and Maître 2009). There are few signs that Europeans are eager to sever the link between citizenship and the native state in any major way (Jones 2012: 699). There is no evidence of a shift in mass loyalties or that European identity is replacing national identities (Fliegstein et al. 2012). Rather, there is a re-emergence of nationalism and thinking in terms of national sovereignty.

In sum, the "unsuccessful" separation of political talk and political action in the EU has in this chapter been discussed in relation to political association, organization and agency, and what ties a population together or drives it apart. I have argued that the growing accountability demands related to the terms of political order are a result of the EU being an unsettled order still searching for a way to achieve unity in diversity, or, in Elazar's (1991: 64) terms, unity without homogeneity and diversity without disunity. Accountability demands and the breakdown of a "successful" separation of talk and action are related to the fact that the EU, to a large extent, has based its legitimacy on performance, expected utility, and mutual advantage. Much has been promised, yet the EU has faced significant performance crises. It lacks institutional channels for airing discontent and opposition and also for political leadership. Resources have not always matched policy aspirations and there have not been slack resources buffering external shocks and inconsistent accountability demands. There is considerable socio-cultural heterogeneity and limited trust in authorities and fellow citizens. The EU also lacks a strong collective identity, solidarity, and trust, as well as strong socializing institutions able to generate a shared identity and collective purpose.

Now the EU faces accountability demands related to the terms of political order. The Union is a polity exploring the possibilities and limits of integration, but it also illustrates the limits of deliberate design and reform of political institutions for achieving desired results (Olsen 2010). Efforts to improve the EU's democratic quality and the accountability of power holders have not prevented increasing accountability demands related to the terms of political order. Can the gap between talk and action be bridged by changing talk or action, by generating a new narrative or a new deal?

A New Deal or a New Narrative?

Democratic accountability processes can trigger changes in formal legal institutions, practices, and substantive outcomes. Or, they can trigger a search for meaning and new narratives and changes in interpretation of concepts such as democracy, citizenship, legitimacy, and accountability. The EU is a meeting place for competing narratives of political order, but the second option is impaired by a tendency in the EU establishment to use a technical, apolitical language of necessities, together with a tendency to assume that well-informed citizens will approve further European integration. Lack of support is seen as a question of lack of information or giving priority to narrow self-interest rather than the European interest.

Renationalization is portrayed as a danger. As conflict has escalated, popular opposition has (by some) been labeled populist, reactionary, racist, and xenophobic. Misunderstanding has been used as an explanation, and not only in relation to ordinary citizens. For instance, when the German Association of Magistrates, a judicial umbrella organization, argued that setting up an investment tribunal court as part of the Transatlantic Trade and Investment Partnership is illegal, that there is neither a legal basis nor a need for such a court, the response from the EC was that the arrangement had been misunderstood (Nielsen 2016a, b).

Neither are dialogue, the will to compromise, mutual understanding, and legitimacy facilitated by the language used by (some) critics of the Union. Rather, deepened division, confrontations, and polarization are likely results of statements such as "Brussels disdains democracy and luxuriates in unaccountability" (Varoufakis 2016). Likewise, "A Manifesto for Democratizing Europe," formulated by the Democracy in Europe Movement 2025, holds that while unelected technocrats in Brussels are appealing to democracy, liberalism, freedom, and equality as slogans, they betray and mystify those terms when in government. They present a highly political, top-down, opaque decision-making process as "apolitical," "technical," "procedural," and "neutral" (DiEM25 2016).

Scholarly accounts also offer competing understandings of how the EU is organized, functions, and develops, including the well-known divisions between the (new) intergovernmentalism (Bickerton et al. 2015, Fabbrini 2015) and scholars who see supranational institutions as gaining power (Schimmelfennig 2015, Dehousse 2015). Yet it is difficult to make sense of ongoing developments within existing understandings of EU integration (Dawson 2015: 55, 118) and there is also a search for a new European self-understanding (Biedenkopf et al. 2004, European Commission 2004).

The "New Narrative for Europe" initiative invited citizens, and in particular artists, intellectuals, and scientists, to debate the future of Europe. Europe was seen to require a collective normative commitment and positive emotions that could reconnect citizens with European ideals, give a sense of direction, inspire hope for the future, and mobilize energy and participation. Europe was presented as a moral and political responsibility which had to be carried out not only by institutions and politicians, but by all Europeans. There was a need to go beyond the story of securing peace through economic performance and growth founded on a belief in self-regulating markets. Well-functioning political institutions require an understanding of what Europe as a state of mind stands for—the European heritage of philosophy, art, and science. The declaration on the New Narrative for Europe invited a story about what it means to be a European in the twenty-first century and Europe as an identity, idea, and ideal. Europe needed a societal paradigm shift in terms of a revolution of thought. It needed "to be positioned as the world champion of sustainable living and to be a driving and inspirational force in setting and implementing a global agenda for sustainable development" (Battista et al. 2014: 128).

It has, however, been asked whether a grand narrative educating the people is needed, or whether the challenge is to listen to what people have to say and live up to European ideals (Battista et al. 2014: 126, 129). A follow-up study of the "New Narrative for Europe" showed a deep cultural schism, both among and between politicians and officials in Brussels and people from the cultural milieu. The process had severe problems because of different logics and operational modes. What for some was an effort to provide a unifying narrative and cultural integration was, for others, a superficial propaganda exercise. There was a near failure to deliver a narrative and only a modest ability to disseminate the new narrative across Europe (Kaiser 2015). The process stands in sharp contrast to the role cultural elites played in nation-building processes in many European states, including Norway (Eisenstadt and Rokkan 1973/1974).

A belief in a new narrative also faces competing accounts of the nature and effects of group identification—that is, people's self-conception and to what degree they see themselves as part of a collectivity; how important a part the group is of an individual's own identity; how motivated they are by the norms and duties imposed by the group; how willing they are to give priority to the goals of the collective over their personal goals; and how much they are willing to honor, revere, and submit to the group's norms, symbols, and leaders. Because individuals hold multiple identities linked to various groups to which they simultaneously belong, it matters how integrated and consistent such belongings are (Roccas et al. 2008). But, as already mentioned, the EU has limited control over educational and socializing institutions, including civic education for citizenship.

It is, however, not obvious that the other option—namely, reforming institutions and practices in order to create redistribution and "a new deal"—is easier to achieve than changing talk and dominant narratives (Olsen 2010). Nevertheless, authorities often emphasize the importance of such reforms. In a world of tectonic geopolitical, economic, and technological change there is a need to adapt the institutional architecture. It is out of the question to go back to the old normal. A new normal has to be shaped. Reforms should aim to make the EU more effective, efficient, and democratic. Yet it is also observed that controversies about the division of labor between the national and European levels will never be conclusively ended (Barroso 2013).

Reform proposals have multiplied and a frequently suggested solution is to strengthen parliamentary scrutiny and control of the executive in order to enhance the democratic legitimacy of the EU. Yet there are different conceptions of representative democracy and of how horizontal patterns of authorization, learning, and accountability can supplement traditional vertical lines (Fossum 2016a). Republican intergovernmentalism proposes a "democratic reconnection" to counteract the disconnection between domestic democratic institutions and EU policymaking, as well as making citizens' authorization and accountability to the people more important by giving EU matters a more prominent place in domestic democratic processes, national parliaments, and political parties (Kröger and Bellamy 2016). Germany's finance minister, Wolfgang Schäuble, has suggested a separate eurozone parliament for countries using the euro, to allow them to integrate more closely—a suggestion interpreted by some as an attempt to dismantle one of Europe's biggest symbols of unity (EurActive 2014). Former president of the European Central Bank Jean-Claude Trichet has proposed "an economic and fiscal federation by exception of the euro area" with strong powers of intervention by European-level institutions under specific circumstances, legitimized by a key role for the EP, yet taking into account the subsidiarity principle and the role of domestic parliaments. The scope of intervention by federal institutions should rely on the principle of "as little as possible in normal times, but as much as necessary in exceptional times" (Trichet 2013: 10). The Democracy in Europe Movement 2025, which is against both the current EU order and a return to a nation-state order, has proposed a Constitutional Assembly with representatives elected on transnational tickets and a sovereign European parliament respecting national self-determination and sharing power with national parliaments, regional assemblies, and municipal councils (DiEM25 2016). However, little is said about the precise division of power, and the proposal, like most others, does not present a road map that explains in detail how the desired developments can be achieved in practice.

In the absence of crises of even greater proportions than those the EU has faced so far it is uncertain whether changes in talk or action will bridge the talk—action gap in the foreseeable future; yet Brexit is seen by some as an impetus for triggering such crises and creating a new historical discontinuity. It is also uncertain whether the EU's ability to live with the existing gap will improve. Existing institutional arrangements and political leaders are likely to affect future developments. But developments in cultural heterogeneity, collective identity, feelings of community and trust, political institutions and policy styles, and slack resources are also likely to be influenced by external and internal shocks and an ecology of loosely connected processes, rather than being governed by a single dominant process or identifiable group of actors.

* * * * *

Norway and the EU are, in many respects, different when it comes to political association, organization, and agency, and thus also when it comes to the social, institutional, and behavioral bases of political order. Both claim to combine economic freedom and social equality and protection. The balances and the realism of promises have, however, been rather different, generating different degrees of trust in government, different degrees of accountability demands related to the terms of political order, and different success when it comes to living with separation of political talk and political action. Nevertheless, both Norway and the EU are now without a road map in a complicated, dynamic, and threatening situation where few dare to predict where the continent is headed.

Regarding accountability demands and "successful" separation of talk and action, much will depend on how many and what participants and issues are mobilized in the time to come. For students of democratic accountability, a challenge is to shed light on factors affecting varying degrees of public attention and citizen involvement in generating accountability demands related to the terms of political order, assessing accounts rendered, and possibly sanctioning unacceptable behavior and accounts. Chapter 6, therefore, explores the varying and shifting public attention to, and significance of, accountability processes. The chapter looks at how accountability processes may attract few or a variety of participants and issues, and the explanatory power of political association, organization, and agency.

6

Political Order and Citizens' Involvement in Accountability Processes

An Upsurge in Accountability Demands

The democratic vision that citizens should decide how they are to be organized and governed politically makes accountability arrangements, as relations between rulers and ruled, crucial for citizens' influence and the democratic quality of a polity. However, in contemporary democracies, most citizens, most of the time, do not spend much time and energy discussing the terms of the political order under which they live. They are usually even less involved in calling power holders to account for the order and how it is developing. Nevertheless, from time to time there is an upsurge in accountability demands. There is discontent. The level of conflict is high. A variety of participants and issues are mobilized, and an increasing number of accountability demands with an order-transforming potential become part of larger debates and struggles over the terms of political order. The relevance of such processes beyond institutionalized accountability routines is illustrated by the fact that over the last few decades accountability has become a buzzword and even an obsession (Lerner and Tetlock 1999, Borowiak 2011, Dubnick 2011, Pollitt and Hupe 2011, Bovens et al. 2014, Wright 2015, Chapter 1 of this book).

This chapter explores how the upsurge of accountability demands may contribute to improved insight into how political order affects the likelihood of mass participation and a growing number of accountability demands. The chapter deals primarily with accountability processes related to the foundations of the political order and the role of rank-and-file citizens. At issue are when and why we can expect popular mobilization and increased calls for accountability, and what drives demands for explanations, justifications, and possibly even sanctions of the performance of power holders and the accounts they offer. I analyze the varying attention to, and the perceived significance of, accountability processes and why accountability processes sometimes attract considerable public attention and citizen involvement, whereas at other times they escape public notice and are dealt with through institutional routines.

An increase in non-routine demands for accountability is likely to reflect discontent with the established order and/or its development, and I interpret the recent obsession with accountability as part of a struggle over the rules for living together in a political community. The aim of the chapter is to explore how the varying attention to and involvement in accountability processes on the part of citizens may be related to the foundations of the political order and its social, institutional, and behavioral bases. Thus, I examine how the likelihood of citizens being mobilized to make or support accountability demands may be affected by three aspects of political order (Chapter 1): *Political association* and the possible effects of different mixes of unity/diversity, trust/mistrust, and the historical experiences of a political community; *political organization* and the possible effects of the ordering rules, routines, ideas, and resources of different institutions, including their organized channels of access for rank-and-file citizens; and *political agency* and how the actual use of institutionalized opportunities for citizen participation may depend on individual motivations and action capabilities.

I assume that these kinds of issues are particularly relevant in areas where and eras when established orders are undergoing transformations, and a premise of this chapter is that these issues can be fruitfully studied in the context of the political organization of contemporary Europe. Currently, the European state-centered order is challenged by Europeanization, internationalization, and devolution, as well as competing ideas about the legitimate role of democratic politics and the public sector in society. There are claims about a democratic deficit, the withering of the nation-state, the hollowing out of representative institutions, a legitimacy crisis, and an accountability gap. Simultaneous, popular support for the EU and further political integration in Europe is declining.

In order to address these claims, I use a dynamic conception of democratic accountability and invite the discipline of political science to rethink what democratic accountability is all about—that is, what democratic accountability is assumed to accomplish and how political orders affect accountability processes, as well as how order-maintaining and order-transforming accountability processes affect political orders, their democratic quality, and the possibility of civilized coexistence. I argue that theorizing the relationship between political order and democratic accountability brings political science back to some enduring issues related to how and why humans constitute themselves in political communities and how different institutional arrangements contribute to democratic politics as a way to rule divided societies without undue violence or elimination of diversity. Accountability processes related to the terms of political order call attention to competing ways of thinking about political life and popular self-government, including the kinds of activities that constitute democratic politics and governing; the kind of agenda a political community sees as legitimate; the institutional arrangements within which politics and governance typically take place and their organization of authority, power, responsibility, and accountability; acceptable ways of handling conflicts; and the conditions for legitimate and orderly change.

However, while accountability is vital for democratic government, it is also costly in terms of time, energy, and resources. As a result, democracies are constantly searching for and contesting mutually acceptable balances between authorizing and restraining their elected and non-elected agents and holding them to account.

The Effects of Political Order

An accountability relation involves actors obliged to render an account to other actors in a domain under specific circumstances, with the latter having the right and resources to require, assess, and sanction the account rendered. Accountability processes involve facts, causality and moral–ethical standards, as well as authority, power, and action capabilities. They can be order maintaining or order transforming. They can be conceived of as apolitical and technical processes or as political processes.

When accountability processes are seen as apolitical and technical, designed to police, sustain, or strengthen an existing order, the challenge is to make sense of what happens and why, that is, to detect errors, malpractice, or criminal acts, to attribute responsibility, and to control and sanction incompetent and unruly agents. As argued in Chapter 2, accountability is then a question of correct reporting, truth finding, and securing compliance with the established regime. Accountability assumes (near) consensus about political order and normative standards and implies enacting a polity's repertoire of routines and fulfilling role expectations, duties, and commitments. Accounting and auditing specialists and lawyers interpret and respond to experience using the templates and standard operating procedures of institutions and professions. They attribute responsibility, call the responsible parties to account, and recommend sanctions. The challenge is to secure effective accountability and improve the democratic quality and efficiency of government by incorporating experience into new routines. Accountability, conceived as politics *within an existing political order*, also assumes that most people accept the order as legitimate. There may be causal uncertainty or disagreement about what is true and justifiable. Accountability processes, nevertheless, take place within institutional frames and the orderly transfer of powers. Rank-and-file citizens play a modest role and so do accountability demands with an order-transforming potential.

Citizens' mobilization and increasing demands for accountability are likely to reflect extensive discontent with the causal, normative, or power foundations of an order or its development. Politics exists because individuals do not agree, and there is a perceived need to find compromises a community can live with (Crick 1982, Mouffe 2005, Hay and Stoker 2009). In situations where a few individuals make binding decisions on behalf of a community, democratic norms prescribe that they should be accountable to its citizens. The greater the power of the decision makers, the more important it is to establish effective accountability mechanisms (March and Olsen 1995: 152). As a consequence, more aspects of accountability have to be treated as endogenous to democratic politics, and accountability as a neutral technique has to be supplemented by accountability as politics, including public reasoning and contestation over what is a possible, reasonable, and just political order.

Accountability politics related to the terms of political order usually take place in contexts and situations where established institutional arrangements have limited legitimacy and public support and there is no dominant interpretation of what counts as a legitimate order. Determining who is accountable to whom and for what is part of the processes through which political order is formed, maintained, and changed. In such processes, authority, power, and trust may be gained or lost (Olsen 2015a). The politics of accountability involves (a) struggle over political association—the borders of political entities and who shall belong to "the people," collective identity, dividing lines, and how to live together; (b) political organization—what are legitimate roles, rules, and resources of good governmental institutions; and (c) political agency—what are legitimate individual actions, motivations, and resources in different institutional contexts.

A democratic hope is that discontent with specific governments, institutions, political parties, politicians, and policies can be combined with trust in, and support of, the political order. Citizens may oppose the incumbents in office and still respect the office, and there may be reservoirs of favorable attitudes that make them tolerate policies they are against (Easton 1975). Arguably, the ability to criticize policies and personnel, the ability to impose sanctions on decision makers who do not act in accordance with their mandates, and the ability to replace governments provide a safety valve for loss of trust in and revolt against the political order (Olsen 2010).

Accountability theory, nevertheless, cannot assume agreement on political order. A political order is an institutional arrangement for allocating tasks, mandates, authority, power, information, responsibility, and accountability.

At times, and in some areas, political life is highly institutionalized. There are well-defined boundaries, institutionalized rules and practices, shared normative and causal understandings, and adequate collective resources. At other times, and in other places, political life is less orderly. Boundaries are less well defined. There are fewer and weaker institutions and enduring divisions and antagonisms, such as competing allegiances and loyalties, opposing normative and causal understandings, and insufficient common resources. Over time, political life achieves or loses structure, and the nature of order changes (March and Olsen 1998: 303–4).

An institutional approach holds that in normal times in settled and highly institutionalized polities, accountability processes are likely to be dominated by apolitical and technical processes aimed at control and maintaining order, and with a limited role for ordinary citizens. When political orders are weakly developed, contested, or in transformation, public attention and citizen involvement are more likely to increase. Accountability processes are politicized and they can become order transforming (Chapters 2 and 3). The following sections, then, explore in more detail how citizens' participation in and the political significance of accountability processes are likely to be affected by the political association and historical experiences of a society, its political organization and institutional arrangements, and political agency and actors' motivations, resources, and capabilities.

Political Association: Unity, Diversity, and Experience

Individuals associate and dissociate in a variety of ways and demands for accountability are likely to be affected by what unites and divides a population. There may, or may not, be functional, social, political–institutional, and cultural integration (Chapter 1). Cultural integration implies some degree of common values, norms, sentiments, trust, and understanding. There are shared ideas regarding what individuals think they owe each other; what freedoms, rights, and duties they associate with citizenship; and their expectations about the degree of solidarity and the legitimate forms and intensity of conflict. Individuals may be selfish and associated by the calculation of individual or group advantage embedded in contracts. Or they may be tied together by a shared civic identity, we-feelings, and an ethos embedded in a pact prescribing what is appropriate, reasonable, and just. To belong to a community means to conduct one's life in ways that are accepted by the community. Behavior is governed by prescriptions and routines based on a logic of appropriateness derived from an identity or role (March and Olsen 1989, 1995).

Accountability is a virtue as well as a mechanism (Bovens 2010) and democratic ideals assume that freely associating individuals accept each other as autonomous and equal citizens. "The people" are supposed to decide collectively what kind of society is worth living in and give mutually acceptable reasons for how they should be associated and live together. However, the democratic form of association is at best an achievement and cannot be taken for granted. The belief that democratic citizenship dominates all other identities has to be held up against the possibility of relations characterized by deep-seated distrust and hate and an existential battle between groups that see each other as threatening their respective forms of life. A friend/enemy relation may be dominant, especially in exceptional situations of crisis and emergency (Schmitt 1976).

Much depends on which identities are evoked through accountability processes and to what degree citizens redefine their sense of identity (Roccas et al. 2008) and their conception of what is appropriate during accountability processes. An increasing number of groups seem to see themselves as discriminated against and oppressed and they present demands for change in the terms of political order. Processes of accountability and orderly change are likely to be affected by whether ideas about what is reasonable and just are related to national sovereignty, European community, social class, race, ethnicity, gender, religion, language, and so on. They are also affected by the conditions under which different group identities prescribe involvement—whether through ordinary, institutionalized channels or through illegitimate actions and taking up arms.

Democracy, as a legitimation principle, does not prescribe the terms of association precisely. It is unclear who is to be included in "the people"—whether demos should be constituted on the basis of territoriality, history, nationality, ethnicity, commitment to specific political principles, or being subjected to or affected by government rule and laws (Goodin 2007, Näsström 2011, Chapter 1 of this book). The latter criteria are also complicated by the fact that an increasing number of problems, crises, and disasters—characterized by threat, urgency, and uncertainty—are of a transboundary and dynamic nature (Boin and Lodge 2016). In addition, democracy gives few clear and stable answers when it comes to what accountability is supposed to accomplish and what role citizens are supposed to have when it comes to calling rulers to account. Neither does the term give a recipe for how democracy and other legitimate values are to be balanced (Dahl 1989, 1998, Rothstein 2011).

The term "democracy" provides only vague guidance because it refers to developmental processes of reflection, reason giving, and contestation, rather than to static normative and organizational principles. Accountability processes involve more than implementing and enforcing the preferences of predetermined principals. They provide an occasion for contestations of how normative and organizational principles are to be legitimately interpreted and applied. Democracy is an arrangement for developing and transmitting identities and beliefs (Dahl 1989) and encompasses demands for explanation and justification regarding what democratic association is for and what it means to act democratically. It entails searching for purpose, direction, and meaning, and attempting to make the world intelligible in normative and causal terms. Intelligence, virtue, and community are products of political action and interaction (March and Olsen 1995, Olsen 2014b, March 2015).

An implication of the imprecise nature of democracy is that accountability theory needs to take into account that citizens may disagree over forms of political association and that they may change their minds, rather than sticking to specific and stable normative and organizational principles. There are likely to be different and shifting visions of how autonomous democratic politics should be in relation to society and disagreement over whether popular participation and representation should have priority in relation to other values and interests, including security and economic rationality. Competing visions of political association are likely to generate different accountability demands, suggesting that it may not be fruitful to assume a static type of association and cleavage structure that is predetermined and exogenous to democratic politics. Rather, accountability can be related to dynamic conceptions of association. For example, both internal differentiation and large-scale migration across cultures create heterogeneity and dynamics that complicate the balancing acts involved in governing a territory and population—namely, reconciling unity and diversity, coping with unresolved conflict, making binding decisions while remaining a political community, and reconciling order and flexibility and collective action capabilities and individual freedom.

It is useful to assume that history matters and that forms of association and accountability demands are influenced by experience with the trustworthiness of representatives, officials, and fellow citizens gathered over generations. People can come to believe that decision makers have to be continuously monitored, kept under scrutiny, and held to account in order to prevent misuse of power, or that they are trustworthy and behave reasonably and justly most of the time (the Scandinavian countries in the post-World War II period being an example). The more mistrust a people has in its decision makers and each other, the more likely that agents are tightly monitored and called to account and the higher the chance that there will be public mobilization and increased accountability demands with an order-transforming potential.

Different forms of association based on different mixes of unity, diversity, and experience affect *the potential* for accountability demands. The extent to which demands materialize depends on the capabilities of political institutions to deal with diversity and disputes in legitimate ways. Any theory of accountability, therefore, will benefit from an exploration of how citizens' participation and accountability demands are affected by the institutions that frame the roles of citizen, representative, and non-elected official and organize actors, issues, cleavages, arguments, and resources in or out of politics. Participatory, representative, and guardian democracies create different access for, and require different motivation and capabilities of, citizens, thus generating different accountability relations.

Political Organization: The Ordering Ideas, Routines, and Resources of Institutions

Democratic theory usually portrays the individual citizen as the key political unit. Modern political life, however, unfolds within and between large-scale, resourceful organizations and formally organized institutions. Institutions are markers of a polity's identity, vision, and history, and they do not adapt easily to deliberate reforms or shifting circumstances (March and Olsen 1989, 1995). An institutional approach, therefore, gives priority to the organizational basis of accountability—the institutions that tie citizens together or keep them apart and the implications of vesting intelligence, norms, interests, authority, and resources in institutional practices. It explores what institutions matter and how their characteristics and legitimacy affect citizens' participation and the significance of accountability processes: Namely, how institutions empower and constrain actors; influence what discretion actors have and how it is used; authorize some actors to act on behalf of a community and regulate access to decisions; accommodate or suppress issues; affect the likelihood of violent conflict; and help or hinder citizens to hold rulers to account.

The approach attends to how reliable and competent behavior can be achieved through coercion, rules, incentives, deliberation, bargaining, recruitment, education, socialization, and habituation (Olsen 2013, 2014b, 2015a). Acceptable behavior can be secured through the external control of opportunity and incentive structures, which make the expected utility of complying greater than that of not complying. Self-control can be achieved through character formation, which ensures that codes of appropriate conduct are understood and respected, even when behavior is not monitored (Olsen 2013: 460–1, 2014b: 110). The more routines of external and internal controls are seen as legitimate and trusted, the less likely it is that there will be mass mobilization, detailed monitoring, and intense accountability demands. Corollary, the more suspicion there is of ineffective mechanisms, and the more conflict, the more mobilization, monitoring, and accountability demands there will be.

Political organization theory has for some time considered the territorial state to be the prevailing form of organization. The state has been conceived of as a sovereign unitary actor with constituent power, expressing the public will. Norms prescribe a clear allocation of authority, power, responsibility, and accountability. Focus is often on formal legal rules. Language is shaped by industrial society. Governmental institutions are interpreted as instruments, apparatus, and machinery, and the result of organizational engineering and structural choice.

In practice, contemporary democracies are compound, complex, and dynamic orders that try to reconcile competing normative and organizational principles across levels of governance and across institutional spheres. Powers and responsibilities are dispersed between territorial levels of government, institutions of government, and private groups with their own power base. State sovereignty is challenged by Europeanization, internationalization, secession, devolution, dehierarchization, and visions of a networked polity and society and of competitive markets. There are competing visions of the role of democratic politics in society and of what are considered legitimate issues for political contestation and for binding, collective decisions. Institutions are infused with different ordering ideas about what is to be achieved, how, and why. They have routines and standard operating procedures, resources, and some autonomy, and they distribute benefits, burdens, and access opportunities differently. Citizens participate in a variety of ways and authorize several institutions to act on their behalf. There is varying trust in majority rule, hierarchical command, legal rules, corporatist bargaining, markets and price systems, expertise, civil society, and fellow citizens.

Under such conditions it is probably not fruitful to assume a sovereign center or principal with normative and coercive authority, command, and control. There are multiple channels of accountability, including a variety of mechanisms for rendering, assessing, and sanctioning accounts, competing and contested accountability demands, and appeals to different audiences and normative standards (Bovens et al. 2010). The importance of elections and hierarchical authorization and accountability depends on the varying and shifting power of votes and elected assemblies (Rokkan 1966). Appointed and self-appointed guardians of order, reason, truth, justice, freedom, and equity have to be held accountable to (some version of) the foundational principles of a democratic political order. The same is true of organized interests, financial actors, private enterprises, lobbyists, religious leaders, and mass media (Moncrieffe 1998).

An implication is that accountability theory has to consider non-electoral and non-hierarchical mechanisms of accountability. It has to explore how different accountability regimes and oversight systems facilitate and distort information flows differently (Boin and Lodge 2016) and how different institutions require different motivations and capabilities of citizens (Elkin and Soltan 1999). For example, compound polities have different mixes of three (stylized) forms of access structures (Cohen et al. 1972, Olsen 2015a, Chapter 3 of this book) suggesting different roles for citizens in accountability processes.

Participatory democracy and open structures allow all citizens and issues access to all decision opportunities. Everyone and everything are permitted, yet no one or nothing is required. A democracy is a community of explanation and justification and informed consent is the basis of governmental authority (March and Olsen 1995: 146, 150). Citizens have the right to call rulers and each other to account in terms of democratic standards. They ideally have influence through referenda, direct administrative contact, courts, opinion polls, citizens' juries and rights of inquiry, protest demonstrations, civil disobedience, and media activity. Still, confidence in rank-and-file citizens has varied over time (Friedrich 1942) and modern democracy requires citizens to let representatives act on their behalf. A challenge is to organize governmental institutions in ways that make elected representatives and non-elected officials, as well as other power holders, responsive without the continuous participation of citizens while simultaneously holding them accountable to the public for their (in)actions.

Representative democracy and hierarchical structures are the most legitimate form of order in contemporary democracies. Popular votes and legislative decisions are decisive. There is a chain of authorization and accountability with free public debate, competitive elections, majority law making, and parliamentary and administrative scrutiny as key accountability mechanisms. The elected is agent and the electorate is principal. Public administration is agent and legislative, executive, and judicial institutions and citizens are principals.

However, there is more to democracy than majority decisions and guardian democracy, and specialized structures imply institutional differentiation with institutions at arm's length of citizens and elected representatives. Institutions, legitimized by their missions, mandates, foundational rules, expertise, and integrity are supposed to be the guardians of reason, rule of law, inalienable rights, and freedoms and to constrain majority politics. There is institutional autonomy and separation of powers or institutional power sharing with checks and balances where institutions founded upon different causal and normative beliefs and resources monitor and control each other.

The complications of theorizing democratic accountability and citizens' influence in compound polities when the relative importance of open, hierarchical, and specialized structures are ambiguous or contested can be illustrated by the EU. The Union is a meeting place for competing ideals and narratives of political order. There is no unitary and stable "people" with a shared identity or notion of accountability. Accountability demands are based on different conceptions of the nature, purpose, and desired future of the EU. They vary among those who see the Union as an intergovernmental, supranational, or regulatory entity (Bovens et al. 2008, Bovens et al. 2010). There are appeals to cohesion and solidarity, yet disagreement about facts and causality. The EU's foundational treaties involve long lists of normative criteria justifying the Union, but they say little about the relative importance of each (Rose 2013: 32). There is disagreement about the proper balance between market, judicial, and expert power and political–democratic institutions. In brief, Europe faces a struggle over enduring issues related to the terms of political order, including the balance between territorial levels of government and between institutional spheres; the relation between the sovereign people and the sovereign individual and between collective and individual responsibilities; the appropriate realms of majority decisions and inalienable rights and freedoms; and the importance of citizen involvement compared to peace and security, economic competitiveness, and prosperity, religion, and equal life chances.

The EU claims to draw its legitimacy from its citizens, and their trust in the Union depends on perceived benefits of membership, a lack of corruption, and trust in institutions (Arnold et al. 2012). Considerable resources have been used to prevent and detect fraud and corruption. There is well-developed horizontal accountability through institutional checks and balances. Still, critics hold that there is a democratic deficit. EU institutions, they argue, are unrepresentative, non-transparent, and not accountable to citizens. Financial crises have fueled new demands for accountability and one strand of criticism is that EU leadership has prioritized the Single Market. Economic freedoms are largely insulated from political–democratic processes and political accountability is marginalized. The confidence of financial actors is more important than citizens' trust. Important reforms have been made without treaty changes and the community method has been sidelined during the financial crisis. The role of the Troika and selected executive leaders in austerity policies has been criticized. Lobbyists are too influential. The investor–state dispute settlement mechanism of the Transatlantic Trade and Investment Partnership is problematic. Institutional asymmetries redistribute power, dismantle social protection, increase poverty and social inequality, and reduce the EU's and the member states' capacity to deal with global capitalism. Within the current institutionalized veto system, feasible democratic reform will not solve these problems. Persistent minorities make majoritarian government problematic. There is a need to deconstitutionalize some economic rights and increase the room for political maneuver, but there is little enthusiasm for reforms requiring treaty revisions (Scharpf 2015).

The EU has elements of a guardian democracy (Dahl 1989: 320). Legitimacy claims have been based on problem solving and service-delivery efficiency more than popular participation and democratic process. The EC, the Court of Justice of the European Union and the European Central Bank are not directly accountable to citizens. The EC presents itself as an independent and objective guardian of the foundational treaties. The Court and the Bank legitimate themselves as expert institutions. Critics, however, hold that guardians extend their mandates, empower themselves, and eschew democratic accountability and control. Many citizens are ambivalent or have lost faith in the European project. There are protest parties and skepticism about the vision of "an ever closer union." Enlargement projects are replaced by possible departures from the Union. An EU collapse is a thinkable scenario. There is a perceived need to (re)gain the trust of citizens and bridge the gap between those who govern and the governed.

History has mattered. The EU's governance structure was not designed for democratic accountability, and parliamentary accountability is still "remarkably weak" (Weiler 2012: 251). There is a lack of genuinely European parties, a limited space of public communication, and the connections between the results of elections and political developments are loose. The referendum is an instrument to sanction rulers and enforce accountability, but citizens cannot vote government out of office (Rose 2013). Consensus style policy-making makes it difficult to attribute accountability, thereby expanding the space for accountability politics and blame games as well as providing opportunities for actors to cultivate their reputation and legitimacy (Busuioc and Lodge 2016).

A possible lesson is that mass mobilization and intense accountability demands are likely in polities in transition where competing conceptions of accountability regimes and political orders collide. When developments are seen as disappointing or threatening, and institutionalized access opportunities are limited, citizens are likely to use open structures and possibly take to the streets. The terms of order are influenced by historic and existing power relations. The ability to call others to account and remain unaccountable is an indicator of power (Day and Klein 1987: 9) and accountability demands are likely when power relations, and the causal and normative beliefs and interests on which they are based, are challenged or changed. Political conflict can be a source of incremental change or of the breakdown of an old order and the emergence of a new one based on different principles. Conflict can be an engine of learning, emancipation, and progress or of suffering and destruction, or tensions can escalate due to a tendency to find mitigating circumstances for friends and blame adversaries.

Arguably, mechanisms of institutional specialization, separation, and autonomy help the EU to cope with inconsistent accountability demands that create conflicts and stalemates at constitutive moments (Olsen 2007: Chapter 9, 2010). Still, the more complex, conflict-prone, and dynamic a political order is, and the more interdependence, power sharing, and compromises it accommodates, the more room an order has for accountability politics and competing interpretations of what has happened, why it happened, whether what happened is good, and whether things could have been done differently. Under such conditions, it can be an insurmountable task to objectively disentangle the contribution of specific actors and institutions, attribute responsibility, blame, and praise, and hold actors to account democratically (Easton 1975, March and Olsen 1995: 157–8). Sometimes there are fact-free claims of accountability deficits (Bovens et al. 2010) and "emotional storytelling" (Galston 2010).

Political institutions, however, provide a framework that affects but does not determine how things are understood, justified, and acted upon. Institutions exist because a sufficiently high number of citizens believe they exist (Searle 1995) and democratic institutions need the support or acquiescence of the governed. They require continuously renewed collective confirmation and validation of their constitutive rules, meanings, and resources, and it is difficult for public officials *not* to give accounts without losing legitimacy. Accountability and orderly change are supported by legitimation of critical reflection, debate, and organized opposition. But what is the role of political agency and how motivated and capable are citizens when it comes to participation in accountability processes related to the terms of political order? When are accountability processes likely to take place within specialized apolitical or hierarchical political structures? When are open structures more important, attracting many participants and issues? The next section considers the role of shifting citizens' motivation attention, resources, and action capabilities.

Political Agency: Individual Motivations and Capabilities

Accountable government implies purposeful agency—discretion, will, reasoning, and deliberate choice—rather than determinism (a divinely ordained or natural order) or pure chance, and it is consistent with democratic faith to argue that "choice in politics is both possible and necessary." Things do not need to be the way they are. In a democracy, "the last word goes to the politicians and in the end, via the process of accountability, to the voters." Political leaders have significant control and can be assigned responsibility. Their decisions can be understood and assessed by citizens (Lewin 2007: 180, 182).

Nevertheless, conceptions of well-informed citizens calling power holders to account on issues that are important to them (Hutchings 2005) have to be held together with an old observation. Whereas there have been fierce struggles over the right to participate in politics, some political systems have found reasons to define political participation as a duty and they have made voting in public elections obligatory. Being a citizen does not appear to be an important role, nor political participation an intrinsic good. Participation in public affairs is regarded with indifference by vast numbers of citizens. Popular interest in political matters remains sporadic. The average citizen seems to find the exercise of political rights burdensome, boring, and often lacking in significance. Politics possesses little prestige. The individual increasingly seeks political satisfaction outside the traditional area of politics (Wolin 1960: 353).

In brief, the idea of well-informed, rational, and active citizens calling their rulers to account is a democratic norm that is not always realized, and accountability theory cannot assume that access opportunities are used continuously. The entire population is rarely activated. People may lack motivation and/or action capabilities. Thus, if it is assumed that accountability processes normally are dominated by professionals and the standard operating procedures of specialized and hierarchical institutions, and that most citizens are unlikely to participate most of the time, when are open structures likely to attract large numbers of citizens and issues and accountability demands with an order-transforming potential?

High degrees of citizens' satisfaction and trust are likely to foster passivity. High degrees of discontent and distrust are likely to foster activity. Relevant resources and action capabilities facilitate action, but pure despair over deteriorating living conditions and life chances can also have a mobilizing effect. Increased mobilization and accountability demands are likely to follow from changes in knowledge, norms, and power relations that generate discontent and disillusion with an order's cognitive, normative, and power foundations. These are situations where the basic assumptions on which a political order is instituted are discredited as being illegitimate, inefficient, immoral, or exploitive. Existing explanations and justifications are no longer seen to make sense. Trust is eroded and prescriptions not obeyed. Citizens can gradually lose faith in institutions and actors, or specific events can lead to radical change. Increased demands for accountability are especially likely when expectations, aspirations, and dreams are generally disappointed, when there are unsatisfactory explanations and justifications, or when conflicts are seen as urgent and threatening.

Whereas citizens' participation, their accountability demands, and how they attribute blame and accountability depend on what different power holders have done, such processes are also affected by how decision makers respond to criticism and demands. Peoples' attempts to make sense of what has happened, why it happened, who is to be blamed for what has gone wrong, who is to be called to account, and who is to be sanctioned can be part of a framing contest where actors present situations as more or less disastrous and unavoidable, defending themselves and blaming others (Resodihardjo et al. 2016). Such struggles over the terms of political order are likely to attract attention and activate accountability demands.

However, calling rulers to account and sanctioning them normally requires adequate resources and alternative sources of information. For democracies, it is difficult to reconcile the ideal of political equality with increasing socio-economic inequality. Power based on number of votes competes with power based upon economic, organizational, informational, and military resources and accountability demands are likely to be affected by citizens' action capabilities. While citizens may not call rulers to account because they are satisfied with their performance, they may also be inactive because they believe they have no chance to make a difference; for example, if they are disillusioned and feel apathetic, fatalistic, or powerless, or if they think that politics is none of their business, and that politicians are corrupt and do not listen to people like them (Amnå and Ekman 2014).

Calls for accountability may follow from shifting attention. During normal times, most political–administrative decisions are made without public attention. Accountability processes are driven by routine scrutiny involving accountants and auditors, political and organizational leaders, and ready-to-use narratives that provide explanations and justifications and assign praise and blame. The public is activated by extraordinary events, disasters, performance crises, scandals, or conflicts. Unexpected major threats may evoke appeals to unity, activating citizens within institutionalized channels of participation or to issues that divide a population, mobilizing citizens in disruptive forms.

The public is also likely to be activated by more enduring political contestation over the terms of political order. Changes in the international discourse over the last few decades have generated more and different accountability demands related to the terms of political order. Claims have been raised because institutionalized expectations have not been met and also because causal beliefs, success criteria, and power relations have changed. The contestation of (most) forms of authority and the demands for direct democracy and democratization of all major social institutions made during the 1970s have, since the 1980s, been replaced by economic neo-liberalism, individualism, and ideals of commercial life, together with neo-constitutionalism and ideals of protecting individuals against political authorities through legal guarantees. Anti- and apolitical impulses have been nurtured, discrediting politics and the public sector and calling renewed attention to threats of state coercion, majority tyranny, and "bureaucracy." Preventing government from abusing political power and doing harm and protecting the freedoms of individuals by reducing the public agenda, demanding rule-bound exercise of political authority, and giving priority to social, economic, and cultural institutions have been prioritized over enabling government to solve common problems.

The New Public Management ideology has, for example, been a driving force for public-sector reforms and new accountability demands (Lægreid 2014) and the "reinventing government" movement has used a less anti-political and more apolitical language, advocating better rather than less government and public services (Saint-Martin 2001). The public sector has been assumed to work better and cost less when using standardized measures, quantifiable performance indicators, administrative control systems, and when customers and clients are empowered. Belief in network governance and making public officials accountable via market-like mechanisms has replaced belief in hierarchical government. Priority has been given to economy and efficiency—to *how* issues rather than *what* and *why* issues.

New problem definitions and accountability demands have followed from democratic elections and shifts in governmental power. Politicians have contributed to anti-political attitudes and accountability demands by creating unrealistic expectations, promising more than they can deliver in order to win elections, and describing opponents in negative terms, tendencies strengthened by a "culture of cynicism" in the mass media (Hay and Stoker 2009). The realm of democratic politics has been challenged by end-of-history narratives portraying global markets and the liberal constitutional state as the institutional foundations of society. Traditional political democratic rights have been dismantled through transnational processes—free-trade agreements and international dispute-settlement bodies protecting investors and private economic rights, with a norm-making and polity-building character across policy areas (Isiksel 2013: 194). The room for political maneuvering has also been affected by a rights revolution and the transfer of "an unprecedented amount of power from representative institutions to judiciaries"—the empowerment of a juristocracy (Hirschl 2004: 71). Some wonder whether the "rule of law" has become a "rule of lawyers" (Kratochwil 2009).

The reforms illustrate that accountability processes are part of a struggle over people's minds, their expectations, and their aspiration levels, and accountability demands are likely to depend upon citizens' *zone of acceptance*, what they see as acceptable alternatives (Simon 1957: 12, March and Simon 1958: 140–41). Citizens' zones of acceptance define legitimate purposes, powers, methods, and outcomes, and the ruled are unlikely to call decision makers to account if rulers routinely anticipate what citizens see as legitimate, exercise self-restraint, stay within the zones of acceptance, and report about their practices and results to the satisfaction of citizens. Amnå and Ekman (2014), for instance, observe the importance of standby citizens. These are citizens who are informed, competent, resourceful, and interested in politics, yet remain inactive. They trust political institutions and actors. Accountability is assumed to be taken care of by those whose duty it is to do so, and specialized actors and routines are seen to work reasonably well. Standby citizens are willing and able to participate, but not continuously, and not as long as they think their concerns are attended to even when they do not participate in active supervision, monitoring, and sanctioning of rulers.

These are patterns that offer many points of resemblance with the attitudes of Norwegian citizens described in Chapter 5. Likewise, the EU illustrates that discontent and distrust may have a mobilizing effect. However, the EU also illustrates that disengagement is an alternative to increased accountability demands and that efforts to strengthen citizens' involvement are not always successful. As part of the Union's attempts to change its image, the year 2013 was declared the "European Year of Citizens," dedicated to citizens' rights in shaping the future of Europe. The Citizens' Initiative, which gives European citizens the right to petition the EC, however, requires organizational muscle. To be taken up by the EC, an initiative has to be backed by at least one million citizens from at least seven member states, with a minimum number from each state. The EC promises to examine initiatives, but is not obliged to propose legislation.

The results of this and several other participatory mechanisms have been modest (Boussaguet 2016). An example is the "New Narrative for Europe" initiative. This initiative invites citizens, and in particular artists, intellectuals, and scientists, to debate the future of Europe. Europe is seen to need a new narrative, a collective normative commitment, and positive emotions that can reconnect citizens with European ideals. Europe is presented as a moral and political responsibility that has to be carried out not only by institutions and politicians, but by all Europeans. Nevertheless, it has been questioned whether a top-down grand narrative educating the people is needed, or whether the challenge for political leaders is to listen to what people have to say and live up to European ideals (Battista et al. 2014: 126, 129, also Chapter 5 of this book).

The European case also raises questions about the degree to which "rulers" actually rule and control the terms of political order and therefore can legitimately be called to account when these terms shift. A new multi-level and multi-centered order is evolving through complex interactions between supranational, intergovernmental, and transnational processes rather than following a single master plan of institutional design (Olsen 2007, 2010). A democratic vision is that democracies are able to change incrementally and adapt to a variety of opportunities and challenges. Yet the importance of intention and consistent structural choice in the development of political orders varies. The degree to which political institutions are, or even can be, deliberately structured and restructured is contested, and sometimes they are evolving incrementally over time as an unplanned artifact of historical processes (Mill 1962, March and Olsen 1983, Olsen 2010). Institutions formed under specific historical circumstances are used to solve problems in quite different historical–political contexts. Complex and dynamic orders composed of multiple interacting components are unpredictable and uncontrollable. Feedback is more or less fast, reliable, and easy to interpret. There are complicated loops and imperfect learning (March and Olsen 1975, March 2010). Institutional change characterized by coevolution, rather than a single dominant process and driving force, makes it difficult to objectively attribute responsibility and facilitates political contestation over who is accountable for what, as well as what constitutes appropriate accountability regimes and a legitimate political and societal order.

It may therefore be useful for accountability theory to examine under what conditions institutional choice is a tool for pre-established principals, so that they can legitimately be called to account, rather than to take for granted that political–administrative institutions and traditions are easily malleable. It may also be useful to examine the belief that experiential learning secures improvement, or, in other words, that progress is guaranteed through a self-organizing and self-correcting polity driven by free debate in civil society, electoral competition among political parties, pluralistic bargaining among interest groups, competitive markets, or scientific and technological progress.

Actually, theories of accountability have to address both limitations in rulers' control and citizens' democratic obligations. First, given the particular roles, relations, and powers that structure democratic politics, acting well is political virtue. However, action is demanded, or believed to be demanded even when governments are impotent with respect to the issues they face (Philp 2010). Governing implies making efforts to improve things under conditions of ambiguous or conflicting values, unobtainable objectives, causal uncertainty, inadequate resources, and uncertain control. Second, the observation, that accountability problems can be located in principals rather than agents (Schillemans and Busuioc 2014) has relevance for citizens as the ultimate source of democratic power. Making unattainable accountability demands may cause trust in the political order to decline—a possibility more likely if it is correct that the ancient idea that citizens, as responsible members of a political community, are accountable to each other for their performance, is alien to modern democracies (Borowiak 2011: 93, 97).

To conclude, the upsurge in accountability with increasing demands for explanations, justifications, and sanctions can be interpreted as a positive democratic phenomenon. Under ideal democratic conditions, when representative institutions are working well, most citizens do not spend much time thinking about, or trying to influence, the terms of political order and calling their agents to account. However, many of today's European citizens have good reasons for their discontent and distrust. Many of them are more capable and demanding, and they increasingly have confidence in their own political opinion. There is less deference to hierarchies and less fear of authorities

(Hay and Stoker 2009). Authority has become reflexive rather than based upon subordinates' willingness to follow commands of authorities and superiors while holding their own assessment of alternatives in abeyance (Simon 1957: 126).

Increasing accountability demands can, however, also be interpreted as overburdening democracies with unsolvable problems and unreasonable expectations (Crozier et al. 1975: 9). Elected representatives and governments are called to account for things they do not control or control only to a limited extent. There are many resourceful and well-organized special interests making demands. At the same time the status and powers of those who are supposed to be the guardians of the common interests have been weakened. They are not able to cope and the result is reduced trust in democratic politics and government.

Theorizing Citizens' Involvement in Accountability Processes

Theorizing the role of citizens' attention in democratic accountability processes involves issues ranging from whether a single rule is broken or a budget misused to contestations over the foundational terms of political order. It involves approaches ranging from bookkeeping and the discipline of accounting to institutional approaches viewing the development of accounts as a core task of governance, on a par with developing political identities, normative standards, codes of appropriate behavior, organizational capacities, and political adaptiveness (March and Olsen 1995: 44–5, Chapter 1 of this book). Some prefer a restricted use of accountability linked to specific institutional spheres and actors, in particular elections, voters, and formal legal hierarchical authorities. This chapter has presented a dynamic conception of what accountability means and implies under different institutional circumstances and the possible roles of ordinary citizens. The recent obsession with accountability has been interpreted as part of a struggle over the terms of political order in a period when the legitimate position of different territorial levels of government and the role of democratic politics in society are contested in Europe. In a period such as this, more is at stake in accountability processes than an apolitical and technical clarification of facts and causality and disciplining incompetent or unruly agents.

To theorize citizens' involvement in accountability processes implies exploring multiple and dynamic accountabilities in different contexts as well as attending to some timeless aspects of political organization—that is, to combine an interest in a changing study object with a return to some enduring issues in the study of government and politics including the causal, normative–ethical, and power bases of different orders and the role of citizens in constituting and changing the terms of political order and accountability regimes. Rather than assuming highly institutionalized and static democracies, we can, as suggested in Chapter 1, see accountability processes as part of an historical struggle between order and reform (Mill 1956: 57–8) and a possible transition to a new and yet unrealized or unrecognized political order (Bendix 1968: 9).

Historically, Europe has experienced many forms of political organization: The city-state, the feudal state, the empire, the nation-state, and the territory of Christendom. As earlier political orders have evolved and become outdated, they have come to embody ignorance, superstition, prejudice, oppression, and obstacles to progress. There have been institutional breakdowns due to war, civil war, revolution, counterrevolution, and coup d'état. The nation-state has been alternately hailed as an agent of civilization and condemned as a source of human disaster. Since World War II, Europe has tried to adapt to the loss of world hegemony, a global redistribution of power and new interdependencies, the fall of the Berlin Wall in 1989, the economic and financial crises since 2008, climate and environmental challenges, terrorism, large-scale migration, and a refugee crisis. Now, a new type of polity is emerging, activating enduring issues about political organization, the terms of order, and the role of rank-and-file citizens. Who shall be part of the political community? How much unity and diversity is viable? What do citizens expect from government and from each other? What are acceptable agendas, purposes, and normative standards? How is government to be organized? What are legitimate instruments for interfering in the lives of citizens? How can rulers be held accountable?

Mainstream political science has, however, shown only modest interest in developing behavioral theories of political organization after World War II, in spite of the fact that students of political life historically have viewed establishing and maintaining political order as a core governmental task (Wolin 1960). They have seen well-organized institutions as a precondition for civilized coexistence and have explored how political organization affects the well-being of citizens. Many factors may have contributed to the modest interest in political organization and "living" political institutions. There has been considerable formal legal institutional stability in Western democracies during the period and strong democratic legal norms regarding how political institutions ought to be understood. Academic specialization has focused on single institutions more than the political order at large. "Idealist" political theory, assuming normative standards and rights exogenous to politics, has generated a "displacement of politics in political theory" (Galston 2010: 386–7). Political science and organization theory have not regarded each other as particularly relevant (Olsen 1991), a tendency that has been strengthened as organization theory has migrated to business schools.

This chapter has invited students of politics to rethink what democratic accountability is supposed to accomplish, the role of ordinary citizens, and the possible relevance of political association, organization, and agency. It is likely to be fruitful to contextualize assumptions of normative democratic thought and principal–agent approaches, which treat key aspects of accountability processes as exogenous to democratic politics and assume that accountability is secured by an arrangement of institutions linked in a neat sequence of separate action. The world is divided into sovereign states, within which opinions and preferences are freely formed in civil society and a public sphere. Rulers are selected, authorized, made accountable, and removed through competitive elections. Elected representatives make laws binding for all. Accountability requires consistency with the law and representatives scrutinize how laws are executed. The rule of law assumes a clear distinction between making the law and enforcing it, and between the realm of politics, public administration, and the judiciary. Effective accountability mechanisms safeguard the ability to learn from experience and guarantee orderly transfer of power, survival, and progress.

These assumptions are not reliably met in contemporary democracies. State borders are increasingly porous and influence goes in many directions. Action is interconnected with extensive feedback loops and outcomes are difficult to predict and control. The formation of opinion and preferences is affected by resourceful, organized actors, a professional communications industry, new communication technologies, and social media. Citizens participate in a variety of channels beyond elections. Colliding democratic visions generate different accountability demands. The role of democratic politics is uncertain and the Westminster ideal of a sovereign parliament, authorized to do anything except bind the next parliament, has limited support. The politics–administration dichotomy is problematic, as are assumptions about administrative hierarchies. Courts make, as well as interpret laws. Learning is imperfect and experience does not guarantee rational adaptation, equilibrium solutions, and improvement.

* * * * *

It should be obvious that this chapter has not aimed to provide final answers about how political order affects how accountability processes work in modern democracies, what role rank-and-file citizens have in practice, and under what conditions there is likely to be mass mobilization and accountability demands with an order-transforming potential. Rather, it has raised some issues and invited debate, and called for empirical studies of the social, organizational, and behavioral basis of political order and democratic accountability.

The chapter has addressed how citizens' participation and the political significance of accountability processes are likely to be affected by varying and shifting terms of political order. A dynamic conception of democratic accountability suggests that (a) political association involving different mixes of unity/diversity, trust/mistrust, and historical experiences generates different *potentials* for mass mobilization and order-transforming accountability demands; (b) political organization and institutionalized behavioral routines, ordering ideas, and resources make a polity more or less able to cope with divisions and generate acceptable solutions, thereby affecting the *felt needs* and the *options* for the ruled to hold rulers accountable; (c) political agency and individual motivations and capabilities influence which available options are *actually used* by citizens.

Chapter 7, the final chapter, returns to how democratic accountability, political order, and orderly change are interrelated and affect each other. It also asks what studies of accountability processes in an era of transformation can tell us about the possible reconciliation of order and flexibility, continuity and change, unity and diversity, and about what insight they offer about the shifting meanings of key terms such as democracy, politics, the sovereign state, and constitutional choice.

7

What Accountability Processes in an Era of Transformation Tell Us

Reconciling Order and Change

This book has explored the organizational–institutional basis of democratic accountability. It has asked how political order affects accountability processes and how accountability processes affect political order and orderly change. The starting point was the claim that students of democratic accountability need to attend to accountability processes in both unsettled and settled polities (Chapter 2), and to address order-transforming as well as order-maintaining accountability processes (Chapter 3). Dichotomies between settled and unsettled political orders and order-maintaining and order-transforming processes should not, however, be allowed to overshadow the fact that democracies—more or less settled and integrated in different ways—strive to reconcile order and change. Neither should the dichotomies be allowed to hide that accountability processes—namely, demanding, rendering, assessing, and responding to accounts—are part of such balancing acts.

Citizens want and search for order. They also resent order. Living together in politically organized communities requires participants to be subject to some degree of ordered rule and authority. There is a need for shared interpretations of acceptable terms of political organization and government and ideas about the legitimate role of citizens, elected representatives, non-elected officials, and other power holders. In other words, political orders must have an ethos with codes and rules of appropriate behavior, cognitive understandings, normative standards, and resources and collective action capabilities embedded in institutions. Yet political orders are not neutral. They mobilize a certain bias (Schattschneider 1960). Political order assigns different roles to individuals, groups, and institutions and there is likely to be resentment against the discipline imposed by the order at large and against specific roles assigned by an order (Connolly 1987: 142). Only rarely is there an alternative that is the first choice of all groups. Authorities inevitably satisfy some groups more than others (Gamson 1968: 111), and discontent is a likely source of accountability demands.

Democratic accountability is an idea that involves facts and causal understandings, moral standards and commitments, and authority power relations embedded in a variety of institutions. Accountability implies agency, power, and discretion, as well as a distinction between authorized and non-authorized behaviors. Democratic norms dictate that those who exercise power should be accountable to those over whom they rule. Rulers have a duty to describe, explain, and justify what they have done and not done and why. They should speak the truth and not deceive the ruled. Stories and arguments are supposed to be rational, logical, and true, as well as reflecting what is viewed as right and morally acceptable in a community. A surge in accountability demands invites questions about what factors trigger such demands, the normative standards used to assess both behavior and the accounts rendered, and what resources and capabilities are mobilized. Accountability processes have to be analyzed from cognitive, normative, and authority–power perspectives.

A *cognitive* perspective focuses on facts and causality—what has happened, how and why, and to whom causal credit or blame should be assigned. In a polity, it may be taken for granted how truth is to be established, for example by the help of specialized institutions and experts. But understanding causal mechanisms can also be problematic. It can be difficult to objectively and unambiguously assign facts and causality for political events. There can be disagreement regarding what has happened and why it happened.

A *normative* perspective attends to the norms and ethical standards used to decide what praiseworthy and blameworthy behaviors are and what counts as acceptable explanations and justifications. There may be agreement, or enduring contestation over normative criteria, how they are to be understood and weighted. There is often a need to take into consideration criteria and claims that are difficult to reconcile.

An *authority–power* perspective looks at how resources and action capabilities are distributed, how they match responsibilities, and when they are activated. At issue is whether resources and capabilities are allocated, exercised, and controlled in ways that hold rulers effectively to account and whether institutions at the same time protect citizens, elected representatives, and unelected officials from being held accountable for things that are impossible for them to do or control.

The dynamics of cognitive, normative, and authority–power aspects of democratic accountability are different. They are not necessarily synchronized and they may alternately be sources of political continuity and change. In modern democracies there are competing attempts to mobilize the necessary motivations and capabilities for demanding, rendering, and responding to accounts. The resulting complexity and ambiguity make it difficult to create consensus about what has happened, who has done what, whether what has happened is good or not, what was politically feasible, and who had the resources and capabilities necessary to secure legitimate outcomes. A space is opened for accountability politics, which like democratic politics generally, involves the handling of tension and conflict (Chapter 4). The quality of democratic institutions depends on their success in balancing not only continuity and change, but also unity and diversity and system coordination and unit autonomy—that is, the ability to act in a coherent and purposeful way and at the same time respect and accommodate legitimate diversity and disagreement (Olsen 2007: 22).

Accountability processes, then, can be a source of both political continuity and political change. On the one hand, modern democracies try to develop rules for living together, embedded in fairly stable institutions. Well-functioning institutions foster conflict resolution, legal certainty, and predictability. Accountability processes help police deviance from the established order and re-establish order. On the other hand, democracies require flexibility and change. They legitimize public criticism and organized opposition as part of efforts to learn from experience and adapt to complex and shifting circumstances. Accountability processes can be part of debate and contestation over the terms of order, and possibly contribute to the development of a new order.

I have argued that mainstream principal–agent approaches take too many aspects of accountability processes for granted and treat them as exogenous to democratic politics and governance (Chapter 1). By relaxing several mainstream assumptions, I have gone beyond the view that accountability processes are solely concerned with making predetermined agents do what predetermined principals want them to do and that principals decide success criteria and control incentives, whereas agents control information and expertise. Accountability regimes and processes have not been understood exclusively, or primarily, as technical, neutral processes that uncover accidents, incompetence, or illegal acts. They have been seen as a crucial aspect of popular self-governance and political order—a political mechanism related to how authority and power are distributed, exercised, controlled, and transformed. Accountability has been interpreted as governance by feedback, with citizens serving as a sounding board, as part-time participants, and as a democratic safety valve.

One aim of this book has been to shed light over the politics of accountability and the interaction between democratic accountability, political order, and orderly change in an era of European transformation. Another has been to explore what studies of accountability processes in an era of transformation can tell us more generally about political life, order and change, unity and diversity, and how the upsurge in accountability demands invites reconsideration of assumptions and understandings of democratic government, including key terms such as democracy, politics, the state, and constitutional choice.

Accountability: A Source of Political Order and Change

Accountability is sometimes embedded in institutionalized agreements and routines regarding what qualify as accountability mechanisms (Bovens 2010: 960). Accountability is perceived as an institutionalized authority relationship between a predetermined principal and a predetermined agent acting on the principal's behalf. Accountability processes can be routinized or triggered by the perception that something has gone wrong. They are mechanisms for the principal's control and learning and for order maintenance. The task is to ensure effective accountability: To observe whether agents fulfill their responsibilities, whether they act in accordance with the principles and rules on which the order is based, and to sanction inappropriate behavior.

There are good reasons for studying order-maintaining accountability routines in contemporary democracies, for instance, how electoral systems, legislatures, administrative hierarchies, courts, ombudsmen, auditing institutions, organized interests, mass media, and professions contribute to effective democratic accountability and order maintenance. Accountability processes are part of a struggle against accidents, incompetence, corruption, and the misuse of power and a means for maintaining political order. The problem is often seen to be located in the single actor, the operator. Yet there are good reasons to study the effects of system properties and who is called to account for how operators are recruited, educated, and trained and for the design of the opportunity and incentive structures within which they work.

The claim that all societies need order and continuity has long historical roots. Without order, the argument goes, there will be a loss of confidence and trust, making community life problematic. Order has been motivated by religious, legal, political, and economic reasons. A religious order must be faithfully followed because it is divine. It is eternal, based on God's Commandments, and behavior has to be accounted for at the Day of Judgment. In legal thinking, a core principle is *pacta sunt servanda*—agreements must be kept. The principle has been based upon conceptions of natural law; benefits in terms of public security; and the economic benefits for investments and trade following from honoring voluntary, self-imposed obligations embedded in private contracts (Wehberg 1959).

Modern democracies, however, also need flexibility—learning and adaptive capabilities that make it possible to cope with shifting circumstances and new experience. Democratic ideals (and to some degree democratic practices) invite continuous discourse and contestation. There are evolving interpretations of institutions and their scope of application. There may be new cognitive understandings, changing normative standards, and shifting power relations, making the existing terms of order problematic and contested. The order may be seen to breach rules of rationality and logic, or it may be viewed as unreasonable and unfair. Dividing lines and coalitions may change.

Accountability demands may be triggered because substantive outcomes or structures and processes are outside what citizens are willing to accept, or because citizens do not find the explanations and justification given acceptable. Citizens disapprove of what is happening and they are not willing to comply. Discontent may be related to a single actor, decision, or institution, or to the order at large. Accountability demands may be a result of a general lack of trust or disagreement over what is a desirable political order. An example is conflicting models of a legitimate European political order (Jachtenfuchs et al. 1998). Accountability demands are also affected by available resources and capabilities and what different actors are strong enough to do, that is, the resources that can be mobilized behind accountability demands and the organized capability to initiate, redirect, or derail, for example, a reform process.

A cognitive perspective on democratic accountability calls attention to how knowledge and beliefs are developed, communicated, certified, and acted upon. Reducing accountability deficits requires improvement in terms of developing institutional mechanisms capable of organizing experience in the service of improved learning (March and Olsen 1995: 199). There is a need to clarify which institutional arrangements are likely to foster accounts that support a democratic order and the ability to learn from history, as well as which information systems are likely to improve understanding of facts and causality and develop enlightened public understanding.

These are important issues. They are, however, often related solely to "how" questions and not to "what" and "why" questions. They deal with how political–administrative actors can do what they are doing more effectively and efficiently, avoiding political contestation over what they ought to do and why they ought to do it. A cult of efficiency, in theory and practice, might be a modern way of overstressing means and neglecting ends (Selznick 1957: 135).

Democratic learning is not only linked to understanding facts and causality, but also to the shifting normative criteria used to define a legitimate accountability regime and its mechanisms for calling decision makers to account, rewarding, or punishing them. One challenge, then, is to understand how accountability processes contribute to the dynamics of political identities and roles, that is, how a society of free individuals can create and maintain a political culture characterized by an ethos of civic virtue, duty, and obligation. The self-interested, autonomous, and calculating individual assumed by rational principal–agent approaches, as well as national identities, civic identity, and rule-following bureaucrats, are all products of long and complex historical developments. There is a need to explore in which time periods and also in what institutional contexts accountability processes function as schools of democracy by contributing to democratic identities and roles through education and socialization.

The observation that political accounts are often constructed in encounters among contending accounts (March and Olsen 1995: 175) calls attention to the authority–power dimension of perceived accountability deficits. There are competing claims not only to superior knowledge and expertise, relevant norms, and interests, but also to what are legitimate authority and power relations. Creating, allocating, regulating, sustaining, and mobilizing organized resources and capabilities are tasks of democratic governance. Governments are supposed to empower and constrain actors, and democratic norms of political equality require public authorities to regulate the use of private resources in different institutional spheres and to modify the effects of unequal private power. Democratic theory usually assumes that responsibilities and powers are well matched. Actors have the resources required to accomplish tasks, follow the rules, and reach the goals they are responsible for. They can be called to account for things they actually do control.

This book, however, has linked accountability demands and deficits to the more or less perfect matching of responsibilities and capabilities. Demands on officials are frequently beyond the capabilities of their offices. Democracies often seem to mandate public services without providing the resources necessary to implement them (March and Olsen 1995: 125, 134–5). Furthermore, what are interpreted as legitimate authority and power relations are not governed solely through deliberation and rational arguing, but also through negotiations and power games. Struggles over accountability are influenced by both institutionalized and individual capabilities and whether they are activated or not. An institutional approach to democratic accountability, therefore, is concerned with how different institutional arrangements distribute resources in ways that make it more or less possible for different actors to behave in accordance with democratic codes of behavior, and with how arrangements affect their capability to demand, render, assess, and respond to accounts. A challenge for accountability theory is to analyze how polities in practice allocate, explain, and justify political capacities, how they regulate the use of authority and resources, and how well capabilities and responsibilities are matched. There is a need to study where the necessary capabilities for demanding accounts and for rendering and responding to accounts are located, when and how they are mobilized, and whether there is a need, assessed by democratic norms, for reallocation of authority and power in order to reduce accountability deficits.

In the next sections I look at how an institutional approach that challenges several key assumptions of mainstream principal–agent approaches invites questions about what accountability processes in an era of transformation can tell us more generally about political life and why it may be fruitful to reassess terms such as democracy, politics, the sovereign state, and constitutional choice in order to make sense of contemporary politics and government. These are terms frequently used in both political practice and academic studies. They are also terms that are slippery and contested, and often interpretations of what they mean and imply are part of accountability politics, challenging old understandings and generating new ones. I approach these terms as follows:

a) "Democracy" as a belief system and a normative standard for assessing, criticizing, and justifying what is to be accepted as a legitimate order; what is appropriate political association, organization, and agency; and what explanations and justifications are considered acceptable.
b) Politics as a special type of purposeful activity and process. Political agency involves both decision making and sense making, including the development of common or competing normative ethical standards, understandings, and authority–power relations.
c) The sovereign territorial nation-state as a form of political organization and identity, providing the framework within which key ideas about democratic politics, government, and accountability have developed historically, and which for some time has been seen as the "natural" framework of accountability discourses.
d) Constitutional choice as having a key role in orderly change. The ideal of constitutional-structural choice is often portrayed as a basic democratic political process. It is the hallmark of democratic self-governance, national sovereignty, and the rule of law, celebrating demos as the ruling body. The people alone can authorize and legitimate the basic rules of political organization and governance.

Democracy: The Struggle Continues

Legitimacy is a precondition for effective government and democracy is the dominant principle of rightful rule in contemporary Europe. A democratic political order is an institutionalized arrangement for allocating, exercising, and controlling power and for making power responsible and accountable. A democratic vision is that citizens decide how they are to be organized and governed politically. The will of the people is the basis of the authority of government and for the rules of coexistence. Citizens are assumed to control their own fate and history and democratic politics is a specific way humans try to manage their lives and cope with the tensions and conflicts of living together. Where the government is concerned, being accountable to the people and securing the consent of the population are important parts of such efforts.

These visions and mainstream principal–agent approaches make strong assumptions not only regarding what accountability is all about but also regarding democratic politics and government in general, including who are principals and agents and what the relationships are between them. This book, however, argues that it cannot be assumed that democratic theory and practice always provide clear criteria for how authority and power, responsibility, and accountability are to be organized or how different types of conflict are to be legitimately solved in different institutional contexts. Adherence to the majority principle implies that there are tensions without any objective scientific answers to the question of which moral and organizational principles should have priority. Neither can it be assumed that effective aggregation of individual preferences, exogenous to politics and government, generates a consistent and stable collective preference function. At issue is under which conditions accountability processes actually work as a mechanism for securing *democratic* order and orderly change—that is, when and whether they contribute to transparency, informed citizens and officials, and popular control and when and whether they foster learning from experience and progress by increasing the frequency of successes and reducing the frequency of failures and disasters.

I have proposed that rather than assuming an established democratic order based upon static normative and organizational principles, it may be useful to acknowledge the indeterminacy of the term "democracy" and see its content as a shifting product of an ongoing and open-ended debate and struggle over normative ideals and institutional arrangements. Democratic accountability discourses *are* constrained by historical practices and academic theories. Democracies, nevertheless, invite debates over explanations and justifications and different interpretations and prescriptions of accountability are embedded in different conceptions of democracy. There is contestation over what democracy and democratic accountability mean and imply in different contexts and time periods.

Due to the (near) hegemonic normative status of democracy as a legitimating principle in polities currently called democracies, public debate is rarely formulated as an issue for and against democracy as a form of political organization and governance. Historically, however, the meaning of the terms "democracy" and "the people," and their respectability, have varied over time (Friedrich 1942, Hanson 1989). There has been as much attention to the problems of democracy as to the benefits. Democracy has been viewed as an unstable and dangerous form of government. It has been argued that the masses, in contrast to the elites, are driven by passions rather than reason. Compared to their wise and virtuous rulers, ordinary people have been seen to lack both understanding and virtue. It has been commonplace to argue that there is a need to constrain majority power and prevent the population from being seduced by demagogues. It has also been argued that "the will of the people" is a fiction. It is necessary that a few rule and exact obedience by force or other means from the many (Richter 1995: 70). The demos, in the sense of a shapeless mass, never "govern" large associations (Weber 1978: 985). Throughout history a variety of forms of government have been labeled democratic based on numerous and contested criteria and it is impossible to judge any democratic order as superior to all others in all respects (Dahl 1996: 179, 182, 1998).

In spite of the normative status of democracy and frequent references to Lincoln's "rule of, by and for the people," there is still considerable uncertainty, cynicism, and hostility toward democratic politics. Moreover, democratic government is seen to cause waste, harm, and injustice. The possible tension between, on the one hand, what is good for the people and in their interest and, on the other hand, what they want has been given renewed attention as treaty reforms in the EU have been rejected in referendums. "Populism" has again become a negative word. In the academic literature it has for some time been claimed that the term "democracy" has lost its meaning (Hanson 1989: 86). We live in an age of "confused democracy" where democracy can mean just anything (Sartori 1987: 6) and it is necessary to address the ambiguous character of the foundational standards and principles of democracies (Connolly 1987).

For these reasons, I have interpreted democracy as an historical, spatial, contextual concept rather than as a universal one. Contemporary European contestations over who is accountable to whom, for what, under what circumstances, and with what consequences have been interpreted as part of a struggle over what "democracy" will mean and imply in the future. I have suggested that it is not unusual that democracy is supported in words more than in action and shown that democracy is not the only or even the dominant source of legitimacy in contemporary democracies. Most citizens are conditional democrats and it is uncertain how strong the commitment to democracy is and what it implies. Democratic concerns compete with several other concerns, in particular economic ones, both in the EU, with its assumed democratic deficit, and in presumably well-functioning democracies such as Norway (Chapter 5).

Norway has given priority to market access over democratic participation and influence in the EU and at home. In the EU, a well-functioning common market has often been seen as more important than a political union and democracy. Primacy has been given to economic competitiveness and freedoms and to the struggle over the organization of the world economy and capital markets more than to social security, reduced inequality and welfare state-like arrangements. Government has been supposed to support market competition rather than to tame markets. Financial and economic crises have been seen as creating exceptional situations where economic rationality and "necessities" have required exceptional political processes rather than the use of institutionalized democratic processes and routines. Opponents of this development have, however, wondered what restrains and prevents a political majority from using their power to radically redistribute wealth and life chances in a world of increasing social and economic inequality. They have claimed that rather than leading to prosperity and geopolitical influence, economic interdependence and integration have created social inequality, cultural disintegration, and political confrontations.

In sum, the term "democracy" offers limited guidance when it comes to how the boundaries of European polities are to be drawn and who is to be included and excluded. It is of limited help to appeal to the principle that the people shall decide when there is conflict over who shall belong to the people. There are disagreements over what a desirable collective identity looks like, ethical–moral standards, and what the shared political agenda should be, as well as over what weight democratic concerns should have compared to other values and interests, such as security, prosperity, and maintaining community, loyalty, and trust. Political organization and the allocation, exercise, control, and accountability of authority and power—that is, how powers and responsibilities between different territorial levels of governance and between different institutional spheres shall be balanced—are contested. This includes what influence and autonomy democratic government and politics shall have in relation to economic markets, legal systems, religion, experts, and so forth, and what the proper role of citizens, elected representatives, appointed officials, and other power holders should be. "Democracy" does not specify in detail the relative importance of direct participation, representation, and trust in the competence and integrity of non-majoritarian institutions. Likewise, there are different opinions about the legitimacy of government instruments, such as regulation, redistribution, organization, education, and socialization. Public-sector reforms, for example, continuously focus on vague and apolitical terms such as "better regulation" and "reducing the bureaucracy" and there is a declining willingness to accept redistribution and transfer of money both within and across national borders. Finally, there is disagreement over what processes can be used to secure orderly and legitimate change.

It is unlikely to be fruitful, therefore, to always assume that democratic politics have primacy and that the number of votes in public elections and public authority dwarfs other resources. It cannot be taken for granted that elected representatives and public officials manage power relations, regulate the use of private resources, and decide people's living conditions and life chances. Instead we must look at how public authorities depend on the cooperation and support of others, how majority politics is continuously competing with other power centers claiming autonomy and influence based on economic, religious, military, organizational, technological, and professional resources (Weber 1978: 1164, Ferguson and Mansbach 1996: 10, 60). There is a struggle over how numerical democracy, founded on formal equality among citizens and the power of numbers, should be balanced with power based upon organization, capital, expertise, and other unequally distributed resources. As Stein Rokkan argued, votes count, but resources decide. Public authorities always need the consent and participation of corporate groups that control key resources, and political systems vary extraordinarily with regard to how the votes of mass electorates count in national decision making (Rokkan 1966, 1999: 254, 261). An implication is that accountability theories have to address the accountability of *all* powerful actors, not only elected representatives and non-elected public officials acting on behalf of the public.

When theorizing democratic accountability, it is necessary to take into account not only political optimism based upon ideals of freedom, equality, authority, and voluntary compliance but also historical and contemporary observations of inequality, injustice, lack of freedom, failure, decay, and breakdowns. To borrow from Schattschneider's analysis of American politics more than half a century ago:

> The struggle for democracy is still going on. The struggle is no longer about the *right to vote* but about the *organization of politics*. Nowadays the fight for democracy takes the form of a struggle over theories of organization, over the right to organize and the rights of political organizations, i.e. about the kinds of things that make the vote valuable. (Schattschneider 1960: 102)

Accountability processes have, in this book, been seen as part of the struggle over the organization of government and politics, over order and change, unity and diversity. Effective democratic politics is likely to foster accountability demands. Demands for explanations and justifications are likely to modify the terms of political order. A key issue, then, is the actual vitality and democratic quality of accountability politics and the role of ordinary citizens in such processes.

Politics: A Side Show for Most Citizens, Most of the Time

Politics and government are usually portrayed as purposeful activities, with political agency aiming at some degree of citizens' control over their own fate and society. Rulers are assumed to make choices that bind the ruled while the ruled are assumed to hold rulers to account. Accountability is a mechanism by which the people try to influence authorities by demanding that they explain and justify their purposes, behaviors, and results. Citizens may call power holders to account in attempts to change a specific decision, remove the people who made the decision, reform the institution within which it was made, or modify or replace the order at large. According to democratic theories, citizens may take the role of *overseers*, asking what has happened and why, and clarifying facts and causality. They may act as *judges*, asking whether what has happened is appropriate, whether explanations and justifications are acceptable, and what reasonable sanctions might be. Citizens may also act as *normative political theorists and institutional designers*. They may ask what the terms of order ought to be in the future and what it takes to realize desired outcomes. Or, citizens may simply support or reject accountability demands initiated by others, whether they claim to represent the people, the majority, reason, justice, God, or the oppressed.

Accountability processes provide mechanisms through which democracies cope with tensions that often do not have any universally accepted and enduring solutions. Coping with conflict is likely to foster demand for explanations and justifications. But how important are accountability processes for political agency and active citizenship, and do accountability processes foster effective participation of citizens in shaping and reshaping the political order under which they live? An observation in this book is that accountability demands, and in particular demands related to the political order, most of the time are not central to the everyday life of ordinary citizens in modern democracies. Inaction is more likely than active political agency (Chapters 5 and 6). So if accountability processes are likely to involve mass engagement only under certain conditions, how can the rare moments when "We the people" speak be recognized (Ackerman 1993: 171–2)? What facilitates and impedes effective citizenship, and why the recent outburst of mobilization and upsurge in accountability demands?

Trust in an existing order and in authorities often results in inactivity while discontent leads to action. But democratic deficits do not always generate discontent and discontent is not always translated into action. For example, gaps between official narratives and political action do not necessarily produce discontent, nor do they result in accountability demands if citizens think their living conditions are by and large satisfactory (Chapter 5). Accountability processes may or may not capture public attention. They may mobilize many or few participants and issues. Participation is not necessarily constant over the processes studied and both motivation and capabilities vary across institutional contexts, issues, and time periods (Chapter 6). There is no reason to assume that citizens have much motivation, virtue, activity, or influence. But neither are there reasons to assume that they lack these things. Fast shifts in both participation levels and problem definitions are sometimes possible.

For example, in the early 1960s being a citizen was not necessarily considered an important role, and political participation was not seen as an intrinsic good by citizens (Wolin 1960: 353). Politics in liberal societies was portrayed as a "sideshow in the great circus of life." According to this view, citizens are not continuously searching for political participation and influence and they do not fully mobilize all their resources (Dahl 1961: 305). The political mobilization during the 1960s, in particular among students, is reflected in Wolin's co-edited book on the Berkeley student revolt (Lipset and Wolin 1965) and Dahl's "After the Revolution" (Dahl 1970). It took little time before the dream of an "Arab Spring" was transformed into an Arab nightmare. Likewise, a fast shift in problem definition is illustrated by the migration issue. A few years ago it was concluded that "modern European societies have been modified more by the departure of its residents than the entry of newcomers" (Freeman 2006: 636). Now, a decade later, mass migration and refugees are seen to create economic problems for Europe, challenging European values and identities, and changing power relations between political parties. Generally, the degree of political mobilization and changes in problem definitions related to the terms of political order have increased in Europe. Power holders have been called to account for what they have done as well as for what they have not done. The European integration project and its legitimacy are not as secure as they appeared only a decade ago.

Democratic visions combine a belief in direct participation of citizens in political life with a belief in developing institutions that work with competence and integrity without continuous citizen participation. In well-functioning democracies, accountability processes take place most of the time within acceptable institutionalized frameworks and without many citizens participating. Under normal conditions, accountability demands are likely to activate a limited number of institution-specific actors and normative criteria (Chapters 2 and 6). Arguably, non-elected officials have also become more important for securing accountability, as they have for political–administrative life in general (Vibert 2007).

Accountability demands and mass mobilization depend on how authorities use their powers. Demands and mobilization also depend on how behaviors are explained and justified, and sometimes post-event processes are as important as the original actions or non-actions of power holders (Chapter 3). Misuse of power and accountability demands are rather unlikely in settled orders where institutions work well (Chapter 2). In such contexts, compliance is secured through external controls of opportunity and incentive structures; thus the expected utility of complying is always greater than that of not complying. Reciprocal control is established through vertical or horizontal separation of power and expertise, checks, and balances. Congruence in norms, understandings, and role expectations is achieved through recruitment. Reliable and competent behavior is guaranteed by selecting and removing actors with certain characteristics to/from office. Agreement is reached through communicative action and reciprocal discovery of normative validity and the best argument through deliberation among initially conflicting parties. Self-control is achieved through socialization, internalization, habitualization, and character formation, making the appropriate norms and codes of conduct understood and respected. Available resources make it possible to follow behavioral prescriptions and proscriptions (Chapters 2 and 4). When such institutionalized routines work perfectly, there is no discretion and no reason to study accountability relations. Authorities anticipate what citizens find acceptable and citizens are frequently consulted. Authorities are responsive, or they are able to convince citizens and make them change their minds. Accountability demands are limited to detecting misunderstandings, incompetence, and criminal acts.

The recent upsurge in accountability claims, complaints about democratic deficit, discontent with outcomes and the ways in which conflicts have been handled, and disillusionment with traditional forms of representative democracy suggest that European practices are less than perfect (Chapter 1). Weakly settled institutional arrangements, turbulent times, and external shocks make it more likely that there will be conflict over the terms of political order and the legitimacy of government. Accountability processes are likely to be order transforming more than order maintaining (Chapter 3). Increased accountability demands follow from performance crises and degradation of living conditions, collisions between cultures, and changes in available resources and capabilities or in their distribution. Accountability demands may be generated by reduced life chances, relative deprivation, insecurity, and fear. Citizens may become alienated because they do not have adequate resources to make themselves heard and, as a final option, they may exit from the system. However, rising expectations and new capabilities may also generate accountability demands.

Accountability processes involve ambiguity and sense making as well as decision making (Chapter 4) and comprehending the role of citizens' aspirations, expectations, resources, involvement, and influence requires understanding the dynamics of citizens' zones of acceptance—the zones within which decisions are seen as authoritative, legitimate, and binding (Chapter 6). The likelihood of accountability demands depends on how authority is exercised, explained, and justified. If there are attempts to carry authority beyond a certain point, disobedience is likely to follow, depending, however, on the sanctions that authority has available to enforce its commands (Simon 1957: 12, 116). Citizens are searching for satisficing alternatives, solutions they "can live with." While a political order may have a fairly coherent, consistent, and stable set of criteria defining what is "satisfactory," there is not necessarily agreement about how a satisfactory solution should be defined. The standards themselves, including how they are set and modified, are part of how a situation is defined (March and Simon 1958: 141, 175). They are inherent parts of the politics of accountability.

We may be able to better understand accountability deficits in contemporary democracies, therefore, if we do *not* assume that accountability is secured only, or primarily by active citizens, elections, and elected representatives. As this book suggests, mass popular participation can be seen as a *safety valve* rather than the dominant mechanism of democratic accountability. Accountability is most of the time taken care of by specific institutions through mechanisms of political–administrative and judicial hierarchies, through institutional arrangements of checks and balances, and by the representatives of organized interests and popular movements. In modern, compound polities, the division of powers and the systems of checks and balances go beyond Montesquieu's categories of legislative, executive, and judicial powers. Specialized and differentiated governmental institutions relate to each other and to society and citizens in multiple ways. A variety of institutions are seen as crucial for securing democratic accountability. Elections, parliaments, and political oppositions are important elements of the accountability system. But in addition, there is a complex arrangement of watchdog entities and institutions guarding their own identities and territories and routinely holding each other to account. Arguably, anticipation of what citizens will accept is, under normal conditions, as important for democratic accountability as citizens' responses after the fact.

The mix of legitimate participants, normative criteria, causal beliefs, arguments, and resources varies across institutional contexts and over time. Appropriate behavior and acceptable accounts are likely to be defined by what is politically feasible, consistent with a plausible interpretation of law, economically viable, culturally appropriate, and administratively, scientifically, and technically possible. Aspiration levels and expectations are determined through historical battles and they may be structured around fragile compromises. There are several competing dividing lines and only rarely are conflicts between elected principals and a unitary front of non-elected agents. For example, public administration, and in particular higher civil servants are key actors, yet they play on different and competing teams (Lægreid and Olsen 1984).

The recent upsurge in accountability demands indicates that not even these institutional arrangements work to the satisfaction of the citizens of contemporary Europe. There is a growing gap between citizens' zones of acceptance and rulers' performance, and an important aspect of the gap is related to how European integration and processes of internationalization challenge the territorial nation-state as the main framework of political governance, identification, and accountability. Historically, citizens' civic identity related to the nation-state has had to compete with identities related to (among others) political ideology, territory, social class, ethnicity, race, religion, language, and gender. Now, nation-state identities and powers increasingly have to compete with European and humanitarian–cosmopolitan identities and powers. Therefore, making sense of the wave of accountability demands and determining what lessons can be drawn from ongoing accountability processes can be facilitated by an understanding of the challenges the territorial nation-state is facing.

The State: Declared Dead, but Won't Lie Down

For some time, the territorial community organized as a nation-state has been the most important institutional setting for democratic self-governance and politics. Democratic practices and ideologies, as well as academic theories of democracy, are closely connected with the historical development of the territorial state as the main form of political decision making and identification in Europe (Eisenstadt and Rokkan 1973/1974, Tilly 1975). In Europe a single (Roman) empire was transformed into a bewildering complexity and extraordinary diversity of political entities (Rokkan 1999: 153, 315), but the French Revolution and the Napoleonic wars left behind them the idea of the nation-state and the ideal of popular sovereignty. The emergence of the sovereign state implied that a territory was brought under a unified administration with an organized capacity for collective action. All citizens were declared equal before the law, and nation-building processes created cultural standardization by penetrating bastions of primordial local culture (Rokkan 1999: 162, 218, 284). There was also a gradual ascendance of state law over other types of law, and a value system beyond economic concerns and calculated benefits (Weber 1978: 56, 901–3).

It has been assumed that the state is a successful form of political organization due to its technical superiority and because there is a belief in its legitimate order and the integrating capacity of historically developed cultural ties, identities, and belongings. Nationalism is a doctrine that assumes that the world is divided into nations with unique identities and characteristics, each with a right to govern itself. The nation-state has created national integration and diversity between nation-states. "The ideal of homogeneous territorial nation-states has haunted Europe for centuries up to the present day" (Caramani 2004: 289).

A Europe organized into discrete territorial units, nation-state sovereignty, and exclusive territorial borders is, nevertheless, a relatively new idea. The state is only one of many collectivities with which people can identify and to which they may be loyal (Ferguson and Mansbach 1996: 13, 56). Whereas the state is still the main subject of the loyalties of citizens and the primary institutional arrangement for democratic governance and accountability, the primacy of the state has been challenged by other levels of governance and by resourceful non-governmental organizations. The EU, an increasing number of human rights-giving and rights-policing international regimes and courts, and transnational organizations and networks have constrained the right and capacity of states to unilaterally control their territories and populations. Focus has been on the inability of nation-states and national democracies to solve important societal problems. It has been argued that the state is withering, and that it is doomed to disappear (Hobsbawn 1992).

The EU has been seen as part of a development reversing the trend of national unification and European diversification (Caramani 2004). There is a dedifferentiation of the continent following a five-century-long process of differentiation and the formation of a political order based upon territorial, sovereign states (Bartolini 2005: xii). Modern Europe is a complex compromise between aspiration to universality and manifestations of difference (Jones 2012: 700). There are different traditions and ideologies regarding state sovereignty, national identity, the role of democratic politics in society, and European integration. Contemporary Europe is characterized by complex and dynamic multi-level and multi-center institutional arrangements (Hooghe and Marks 2001). The continent is testing its functional capabilities and trying to determine which collective identity is likely to be perceived as reasonable, just, and acceptable by citizens. There is a search for a legitimate political order (Olsen 2007, 2010).

An implication is that students of democratic accountability can easily be led astray if they base their analysis on traditional formal legal prescriptions of "the state" as a polity and form of human association and government characterized by the formation of a single center with the capability of controlling territory and population, and clear-cut and dyadic principal–agent relations. It is unlikely to be fruitful to portray the state as a unified, centralized, and hierarchical organization with a sovereign parliament when accountability processes in contemporary Europe in reality are taking place in diverse, interdependent, and interacting compound polities with complex overlapping centers of governing and accountability.

Modern liberal democracies are states characterized by separation of authority, power, responsibility, and accountability across levels of governance and institutional spheres. There is a variety of interdependent and interacting institutions based on different purposes, values, interests, understandings, and resources. Democracies have complex configurations of accountability institutions, each with their own normative criteria, resources, and red lines.

Rather than fostering a sovereign center claiming to represent the public will and the common good as the ultimate source of authority and with the right to demand accounts, liberalism is "the art of separation." Liberalism erects walls between institutional spheres as a method for reducing the probability of open conflict, creating liberties and constraining majority power (Walzer 1984: 35). There is a need to accommodate a variety of accountability demands referring to competing cognitive understandings, normative standards, and preferred authority–power relationships.

Whereas the weaknesses of the nation-state have been pointed out—specifically that it is too small for the big tasks and too big for the small tasks—there has been less attention to how increasing the size of a political entity may generate heterogeneity. Identification is an important mechanism of integration (March and Simon 1958) and a lack of shared identity, unity, solidarity, and cohesion are likely to reduce citizens' willingness to comply, making it more difficult to operate in a consistent and coherent manner and generate acceptable solutions. For example, the EU's increasing size has provided it with more resources and capabilities. However, the upsurge of accountability demands reflects that its increasing size has also created more heterogeneity and made it more difficult to achieve agreement about how the EU, including its accountability arrangements, should be organized and governed.

There are, for example, tensions between supporters of supranational and intergovernmental arrangements and between post-national and national visions and ideals. Some argue for an ever closer and even more connected union. Others prescribe exit from the EU, or a transfer of powers back to the member states. There are struggles over the institutional balance between and within each level of governance and over what is a preferable balance between the public and the private realms. The role of ordinary citizens, their elected representatives, bureaucrats, judges, experts, and organized interests are contested. Some argue that the democratic political organization of Europe needs a new integrating narrative, a collective identity, democrats, and Europeans. Others argue that political organization is a question of getting the incentives right. Whereas elites talk about a new *narrative* as a means to encouraging citizens' involvement and loyalty (Chapter 5), protesters want a new *deal* that will improve their well-being and life chances (DiEM25 2016).

Accountability processes are an important part of these dynamics. European integration and the claimed erosion of state sovereignty have opened the door for accountability politics related to the terms of political order. Tensions between levels of governance and between institutional spheres have created a need to accommodate a variety of accountability demands based upon competing cognitive understandings, normative standards, and preferred power relationships (Bovens et al. 2010). Collisions between state traditions also contribute to tensions and accountability demands and there are increasing tensions between member states and between member states and "the bureaucracy in Brussels." There is growing distrust of leaders and a gap between elites and ordinary citizens when it comes to how national sovereignty and European governance should be balanced. The European integration project has become more contested and more uncertain (Chapter 5).

Although the territorial nation-state has been declared dead by some, national identity is alive and well, and the nation-state does not seem to be willing to lie down. Nation-states are still entities with collective action capabilities and integrative capabilities, providing a framework for accountability politics and contributing to some degree of institutional continuity. There are, however, countervailing change processes. Functional interdependencies and integration are likely to generate demands for cooperation and common problem solving across national borders, as are social integration, travel, and trade. However, "anti-Brussels" attitudes and demands for national sovereignty are fostering developments in the opposite direction, making further political–institutional integration problematic. Weak institutions for debate, education, and socialization at the European level, together with mass migration across cultures, make cultural integration difficult to achieve.

The result is that future developments are difficult to predict. For students of democratic accountability it becomes important to comprehend possible processes of orderly and legitimate change. To what degree are Europeans capable of deliberately choosing how they are to be organized and governed politically and what role are accountability processes playing in the ongoing changes in the terms of political order?

Orderly Change: Constitutional Choices and Evolving Historical Practices

In this book, accountability processes have been interpreted as a possible part of larger processes of establishing, maintaining, reforming, and eliminating political orders. The normative and organizational principles on which the European political order is founded, as well as its legitimacy, have been seen as in flux rather than as fixed. There are ongoing processes of defining and redefining what is politically necessary, possible, desirable, and acceptable. It has been suggested that political orders and accountability regimes are likely to emerge and disappear in different ways, depending on historical experiences and what ties a political community together and what keeps it apart. Orders and regimes founded on expediency and mutual advantage or on internalized belonging to a political community with a specific identity are likely to follow different development patterns. Accountability processes involve both decision making and sense making that may contribute to the processes through which causal and normative beliefs about an appropriate order are developed, modified, or abandoned, and authority, power, and responsibility are distributed and redistributed.

Now, once again, the political organization of the European continent is being contested and leaders are being called to account. The terms of political order and visions for the Europe of tomorrow are in transformation. There is institutional reassessment and conflict with regard to how the borders of political communities should be drawn and what agenda they will have in common. There is disagreement regarding how authority and power are to be legitimately allocated, exercised, controlled, and made accountable between territorial levels of government and across institutional spheres. It is unclear what kind of political agenda and interinstitutional balance will be perceived as reasonable, just, and desirable by European citizens in the future. It is not even obvious that Europe will avoid disorder, violence, capricious rule, and armed conflict.

Theorizing democratic accountability, then, implies exploring the role of accountability processes in transforming individual and collective actors with divergent ideals, interests, understandings, and resources into a politically organized cooperative with common purposes and rules, relatively enduring collective commitments and organized action capabilities. In the European context this implies that rather than seeing the degree and form of integration and European-level institution building as a functional necessity and a process where all are winners it is likely to be fruitful to study integration and disintegration as another case of tensions between order–change, unity–diversity, and center-building and local (nation-state) defense.

There are difficult trade-offs and balancing acts when it comes to system integration and component autonomy and discretion, with elements of intergovernmental, transnational, and supranational arrangements. At issue is the role of accountability processes in developing and maintaining political community and authority in spite of enduring diversity. The more discrepancies in basic structures between an existing component unit and a possible larger polity, and the more favored arrangements a basic unit has to give up, the less likely is support for integration (Brunsson and Olsen 1998: 31–4). A question is how accountability regimes may or may not contribute to European integration without weakening or destroying institutional arrangements and ways of governing that have great value and support in the component units. Another question is whether accountability processes contribute to orderly change and improved legitimacy.

The continent faces the old and still unanswered question of "whether societies of men are really capable or not of establishing good government from reflection and choice or whether they are forever destined to depend, for their political constitution, on accident and force" (Hamilton et al. 1964: 1). One answer is that the role of deliberate choice and intention varies over institutional contexts and that it changes over time. For example, the EU has had a series of major treaty revisions as well as incremental changes. Norway, a small and relatively homogeneous country, has had a large number of incremental reforms but never a major reform of its written constitution since 1814, and a standard argument has been that such processes are likely to create "unnecessary conflicts" (Chapter 5).

It is often observed that institutional arrangements rarely can be created and changed arbitrarily and instantaneously. It is difficult to change formal legal orders. It is even more difficult to change "living" institutional practices and informal rules and to achieve intended and desirable outcomes as a result of institutional changes (March and Olsen 1989, Olsen 2010). The political organization of Europe has been strongly affected by wars, civil wars, and revolutions, as well as by political compromises. There have been institutional leaps, discontinuities, and breakdowns. System adaption and local adaption are not always coordinated. Agents as well as principals have tried to learn from experience and adapt. But such processes are rarely perfect and neither are rule-following, competitive selection, imitation, diffusion, or any other processes of change (March 1981). However, accountability processes understood as decision making and as sense making call attention to two stylized processes: Change through deliberate constitutional choices and change through evolving historical practices.

Constitutional choices refer to great, transformative moments when an old political order is replaced by a new one. There is a new beginning or a new direction decided by a constituent power through a deliberate constitutive act. A constitutional convention may create new institutions and basic rules for orderly amendments. Or an assembly may write a text, which will be accepted or not by the demos through a popular referendum. The constituent power is, in both cases, the people. In a democracy, only the people can be the source of the normative order and the highest ranking standards of rule, creating and recreating the institutional boundaries within which government and politics are supposed to function in the future. Historically, such events have often been related to wars, socio-economic crises, and major disasters. European integration was, for example, triggered by a disastrous war and there have been several treaty-making conferences since the Treaty of Paris (the treaty establishing the European Coal and Steel Community, signed in 1951) and the Treaty of Rome (the treaty establishing the European Economic Community and EURATOM, signed in 1957). Changes in the EU's institutional order requiring unanimous decisions have, however, been difficult to agree upon for the elites and even more problematic to have accepted by citizens. A study of 14 European countries shows that not even the 2008 fiscal crisis led to major structural reforms in the public sector in most countries. Cutbacks and incremental reforms, more than major order-related reorganizations, were used to cope with the urgencies generated by the crisis and to restore fiscal balance. The crisis was used to justify rather than to instigate change. In other words, there was political rhetoric without concrete action (Randma-Liiv and Kickert 2016).

Change through constitutive acts requires decisions, either consensual or by a winning coalition that knows what it wants, understands how to get it, and controls the factors necessary to achieve the desired solution. Contemporary European political life seems more characterized by conflict, ambiguity, uncertainty, and limited control. There is no agreement about a road map (Chapter 5). The conditions for anticipating the future, long-term planning, and grand constitutional choices making the rules that should govern the future are largely absent.

Evolving historical practices refer to incremental change in rules and everyday practices and to ongoing discourses about what the common good and good governance mean and imply and what is a desirable political order: Normative and organizational principles; identities, common purposes, and dividing lines; the legitimate role of citizens and different types of power holders; and institutionalized ways of coping with conflicts and legitimately amending the existing order. These are issues that are not settled once and for all in democracies. Rather, a democratic ideal prescribes reflection, criticism, deliberation, account and reason giving, and attempts to persuade others as part of securing well-informed citizens and officials and identifying common purposes.

Efforts to create shared European understandings and assessments through accountability processes are complicated by the fact that history matters. There is path dependency and it is necessary to understand the historical processes through which competing patterns have been generated (Berger and Luckmann 1967: 54–5). In Europe, different historically developed national traditions are difficult to reconcile. There is considerable continuity in ideas about the proper political order among actors engaged in polity building. Different ideas of the polity reflect fundamental and persistent cleavages (Jachtenfuchs et al. 1998: 434). There are, furthermore, different traditions of more or less elevated public discourse and argumentation, and it is necessary to consider how accountability politics, as well as decision making processes in general, may involve expressive ceremonial behavior. Participants may employ myths that offer symbolic reassurance of control and good governance and narratives that unify citizens and create belief in a legitimate order. Or there may be hateful campaigns that exploit divisive myths and foster confrontation. In both cases, political talk and political action may be more or less tightly coupled and the implications will depend on the degree to which future public discourse will adhere to rules of civil public discourse.

While it may be tempting to assume that one (perfect) process governs orderly change, it is more realistic to assume that changes in political orders in compound polities are affected by a shifting mix of imperfect processes. As a consequence, I have argued that in contexts such as the contemporary European one, accountability theory must go beyond interpretations inspired by ideas about self-regulating competitive markets portraying orderly change as a result of competitive selection and a simple reflection of differences in the comparative functional efficiency of alternative institutional arrangements. An example is European integration explained in terms of increasing interdependencies, contact, and communication across national borders, which by necessity generates integration in terms of cooperation, coordination, and supranational institutions as a superior functional solution, in turn fostering cultural integration.

Accountability theory also has to go beyond assumptions about orderly change secured by predetermined principals and agents, rational legal hierarchical structures, and command and control processes. Certain ideas about structural choice—namely that principals deliberately design and reform political orders and accountability regimes and thereby achieve desired performance and outcomes—are problematic. It may be useful to look at how change processes are influenced by the fact that democracies are integrated by various degrees of we-feelings, shared beliefs and purposes, which makes majority decisions, hierarchical coercion, and incentives less important and mutual trust, commitments, and loyalty more relevant for orderly and legitimate institutional change.

Citizens are not without leverage. There are elements of governance by feedback and constitutional reforms have been stopped by citizens in Europe and elsewhere through referendum (Fossum 2016b). For example, the Convention on the Future of Europe was established by the European Council at the end of 2001. It was inspired by the Philadelphia Convention, and it was a result of several years of concern with the EU's democratic deficit and its legitimacy. The Treaty Establishing a Constitution for Europe (2004) was signed, but in 2005 France (54.9 percent to 45.1 percent) and the Netherlands (61.5 percent to 38.5 percent) voted against the draft European Constitution and it was never ratified. Neither did the Treaty of Lisbon, signed in December 2007 and entering into force two years later, or the following consolidated versions of the Treaty on European Union and the Treaty on the Functioning of the European Union (2012) solve the legitimacy problem.

The *implications* of referendums and popular opinions and behavior have, however, been affected by complex post-event processes, usually giving citizens limited influence. European citizens have on several occasions sent strong signals of anger and alienation. They have abandoned mainstream political parties and supported anti-establishment parties and protest movements.

They have used mass media and social media. They have gone on strike and taken to the streets. Still, the rulers of Europe have, to a limited degree, adapted to public opinion or been able to persuade the ruled. People's opposition to the view that "the way forward" implies more European integration, their feeling of being left out in the cold, and their discontent with the handling of different crises at the national and the European levels have not always been seen as reasonable reactions to reduced well-being and life chances. Rather, political leaders and commentators have frequently labeled protesters nationalist, populist, racist, and xenophobic, treating their concerns as attitudes to be combatted rather than problems to be solved. The existing gap between rulers and ruled in the EU has probably been widening.

In the EU, no-votes in referendums to treaty changes have typically been interpreted by many European political leaders as a result of voter ignorance or incompetence, sometimes going so far as to suggest that it is a mistake to allow ordinary people to vote on complex issues such as EU membership or treaty changes. Several times, a popular no-vote has resulted in minor modifications of the treaty proposal and new referendums that have given a "yes." In Norway, a majority of the people voted down proposals to join the EU in both 1972 and 1994, against the advice of the political establishment, and in the spring of 2016 surveys showed that more than 70 percent of the population was against Norwegian EU membership. Still, through a variety of processes Norway has become tightly integrated into many EU institutions and bound by decisions the country has no formal right to influence. Norwegians have since been wont to say that the "no" side won the day of the referendum but has lost every day since (Chapter 5).

The British "Brexit" referendum will provide another test of the implications of a popular no-vote. It is claimed that the decision is irreversible. But it seems more reasonable to conclude that what will actually follow—for the United Kingdom as well as for the EU—is rather uncertain and will depend on what political processes are triggered. There are competing interpretations of what is happening in Europe and contested visions of the future political organization of the continent and what processes to follow. Opinions are highly divided in both the UK and the EU, and there is a lack of political leadership. Some reiterate their commitment to an ever closer union, even if it will be smaller than the EU of today. Some advocate major reforms involving a return of powers to member states and intergovernmental cooperation rather than strong supranational institutions. Others simply want to dissolve the union.

Nevertheless, compared to earlier no-votes, the Brexit referendum seems to have made more political leaders conclude that there is something wrong with the functioning of the EU and not with the voters. The EU does not protect *all* its citizens well. There are losers as well as winners. There is mistrust and a crisis of confidence related to institutions and leaders and considerable skepticism towards more integration and stronger supranational institutions. Citizens' confidence and trust must be regained or more countries are likely to follow the Brexit example. There is a perceived need for consensus and common European solutions to a variety of cross-border challenges. There is also some agreement about non-operational goals related to peace, political stability, economic growth, employment, refugees, migration, terrorism, and climate, but little agreement about how such goals can be reconciled and achieved. There exist few agreed-upon solutions when it comes to the division of labor and powers among member states and the EU and between institutions at the same level of governance. Some give priority to more economic freedoms and less regulation, more market competition, and the need to win the trust of financial market actors. Others are more concerned with how individual socio-economic security and welfare rights can be protected and a democratic European identity and solidarity can be developed.

In sum, like constitutional choice and other orderly change processes, experiential learning, incremental adaptation, and evolving practices are less than perfect. Political life is often messy. Fluidity, inconsistencies, and contestations complicate the task of attributing responsibility and accountability, and uncertainty, ambiguity, and limited control by a center increase the space for accountability politics, for blame games, and for image management. At the European level, there is also a lack of shared institutions (civil society, public space, schools) for deliberating about the terms of political order and what the rules for living together should be. Institutions for forming citizens into "democrats" and "Europeans" with shared frames of interpretation are relatively weak or absent.

Incremental changes in practice often seem to come before changes in narratives and theories about constitutional choice (Olsen 2010), and the search for meaning, reassessments, and incremental changes in everyday practice can be both an alternative to and a precondition for change through constitutional acts. Sense-making processes with demands for explanations and justifications can create a "climate" of opinion which makes formal decisions and their successful implementation possible. But processes of communicative rationality and experiential learning creating rational institutional adaptation and enlightened citizens and officials are not guaranteed. A rapidly growing Public Relations (PR) industry and an increasing number of spin doctors make democratic ideals about enlightened public discourse difficult to achieve. It is often easier to manipulate accounts and statistics than to change practices and substantive outcomes (March 1984, 1987). For students of democratic accountability it may be useful to consider the scope of application for different models of change and in particular how they interact in different institutional contexts, rather than to assume one dominant process of orderly change.

Back to the Roots

Contemporary Europe offers a special context for studying the relations between democratic accountability, political order, and orderly change. Europe's history and institutions impact accountability processes as well as the shifting terms of political order and change. Nevertheless, the changing nature of the study object—namely the ongoing transformation of political association, organization, and agency—makes it important to re-examine and reassess the key ideas and assumptions of available interpretations of democratic accountability. Arguably, an era of transformation may open up for new understandings of issues that are difficult to study in periods of institutional continuity.

The political *association* of contemporary Europe is different from that of industrial-era Europe with its class identities and distributional conflicts. The industrial working class has shrunk along with its solidarities and associations, and there are new forms of poverty and deprivation. Several dividing lines compete with the dominant labor–capital cleavage of industrial society. The political *organization* of the continent has changed in several respects. The hegemonic role of the territorial nation-state has been challenged and European-level institutions of governance have been strengthened. There are new tensions between levels of governance and between institutional spheres, and there is reduced interest among citizens in traditional forms of political participation and representation. The conditions for political *agency* have been radically changed as Europe has lost its world hegemony. A new geopolitical landscape has changed Europe's power and role in the world. At both the European and national levels, new patterns of checks and balances beyond those envisioned by Montesquieu have evolved, and the power of class-based political parties and trade unions has been reduced.

A changing study object makes it difficult to comprehend democratic accountability, political order, and orderly change with available analytical frameworks. Much current theory building is based upon studies of an exceptional historical period in the Western world characterized by (relative) peace, economic growth, and considerable continuity in political identities and institutional arrangements—namely the post-World War II period. However, some of the assumptions on which existing approaches have been based cannot be taken for granted any more. For example, we can no longer assume that traditional democratic–representative institutions and their interrelationships will be capable of holding elected rulers, appointed officials, and resourceful interest groups accountable for their actions. There is a need for new understandings, concepts, and vocabulary regarding political life and the organization of government (Schmitter 2016), and accountability studies in an era of European transformations bring us back to the roots of political science.

Exploring how political association, organization, and agency affect and are affected by accountability processes brings up foundational and enduring issues regarding how and why individuals constitute themselves in political communities: How are forms of association characterized by different mixes of unity and diversity, providing different types of challenges for political institutions? How do differently organized institutional arrangements contribute to conflict resolution in ways consistent with democratic principles, and to reconciling order and change, unity and diversity? How is democratic agency fostered and maintained? What role does democratic accountability have in such processes? These are questions related to a basic democratic challenge: How is it possible to organize peaceful coexistence, cooperation, and conflict resolution among people with competing conceptions of the good society and good governance?

A key task of democratic institutions, accountability regimes included, is to transform a heterogeneous and pluralistic society into a viable political community based on principles and rules that have normative validity in themselves, beyond their specific policy outcomes, while sustaining the diversity essential for a community to endure in the long run. A democratic aspiration is to build and maintain shared purposes, trust, solidarity, and deserved legitimacy and allegiance for the political order while maintaining individual freedom and influence (Perry 1988: 180–2, March and Olsen 1989: 118, 126, 2006). The quintessence of democratic politics and governance is the construction and reconstruction of our lives together, our relationships with others, making order and civilized coexistence possible (Wildavsky 1987: 5). Politics and government involve coping with conflicts and building community, cooperation, and trust and maintaining unity in spite of the many forces that work towards division and disintegration (Lipset and Rokkan 1967: 46–8). Statecraft implies the ability to make and enforce collective decisions and sustain a political community in the face of enduring differences (Selznick 1992: 369).

A premise of this book has been that the routines of institutional accountability are important to such things. But it is not enough to analyze how accountability processes contribute to the routinized maintenance of an established democratic order within relatively stable, simple, and well-known situations. We need to understand the place of ideas about accountability in eras of institutional confusion and contestation and in dynamic, complex, and unknown situations.

These more complicated situations call attention to important features of democratic accountability. First, variations in the relations between democratic accountability and political association, organization, and agency are endogenous to democratic politics and government. They arise from the enduring tensions and conflicts that are central to democratic order. Second, accountability processes take place within both settled and unsettled orders. They can be both order maintaining and order transforming. Third, accountability involves sense making as well as decision making. Under some conditions, the processes allow separation of accountability talk and action. Fourth, accountability may attract public attention and involve mass mobilization or go on largely unnoticed by the public. Fifth, accountability processes may or may not foster new practices and ideas about political order, democratic government, and the role of rank-and-file citizens in political life. They may or may not foster democracy as a particular form of political community, organization, and governance and affect what democracy will mean and imply in the future.

References

Ackerman, B. 1993 (paperback ed.), *We the people. Foundations*. Cambridge, MA: Harvard University Press.

Alesina, A. and Cukierman, A. 1990, The politics of ambiguity. *Quarterly Journal of Economics* 105 (4): 829–50.

Allardt, E., Andrén, N., Friis, E.J., Gíslason, G., Nilson, S.S., Valen, H., Wendt, F., and Wisti, F. (eds) 1981, *Nordic Democracy. Ideas, Issues, and Institutions in Politics, Economy, Education, Social, and Cultural Affairs of Denmark, Finland, Iceland, Norway, and Sweden*. Copenhagen: Det danske selskab.

Amnå, E. and Ekman, J. 2014, Standby citizens: Diverse faces of political passivity. *European Political Science Review* 6 (2): 261–81.

Arnold, C., Sapir, E.V. and Zapryanova, G. 2012, Trust in the institutions of the European Union: A cross-country examination. In L. Beaudonnet and D. Di Mauro (eds): Beyond Euro-Skepticism: Understanding Attitudes towards the EU. *European Integration online Papers*, Special Mini-Issue 2, 16 (8), <http://eiop.or.at/eiop/texte/2012-008a.htm> (accessed 1 April, 2016).

Aucoin, P. and Heintzman, R. 2000, The dialectics of accountability for performance in public management reform. *International Review of Administrative Sciences* 66 (1): 45–55.

Azoulai, L. and Dehousse, R. 2012, The European Court of Justice and the legal dynamics of integration. In E. Jones, A. Menon, and S. Weatherill (eds): *The Oxford Handbook of the European Union*: 350–64. Oxford: Oxford University Press.

Ball, T.J. Farr and Hanson, R.L. (eds) 1989, *Political Innovation and Conceptual Change*. Cambridge: Cambridge University Press.

Barroso, J.M. 2010, Preface, European Commission 2010, Europe 2020. *A Strategy for Smart, Sustainable and Inclusive Growth*. Brussels 3.3 2010: COM(2010) 2020 final.

Barroso, J.M.D. 2013, *State of the Union Address 2013*, <http://europa.eu/rapid/press-release_SPEECH-13-684_en.htm> (accessed 12 September, 2013).

Barth, T.J. 1993, Constitutional subordinate autonomy. Serving multiple masters—a normative theory in practice. *Administration and Society* 25 (2): 160–82.

Bartolini, S. 2005, *Re-Structuring Europe: Centre Formation, System Building and Political Structuring between the Nation State and the European Union*. Oxford: Oxford University Press.

Battista, E., Setari, N. and Rossignol, E. 2014, *The Mind and Body of Europe: A New Narrative*. Luxemburg: Publication Office.

Bendix, R. (ed.) 1968, *State and Society*. Boston, MA: Little, Brown.

Benz, A., Harlow, C. and Papadopoulos, Y. (eds) 2007, Accountability in EU multilevel governance. *European Law Journal*, Special Issue 13 (4).

Berger, P.L. and Luckmann, T. 1967, *The Social Construction of Reality*. New York: Doubleday, Anchor Books.

Bickerton, C., Hodson, D. and Puetter, U. 2015, The new intergovernmentalism. *Journal of Common Market Studies* 53 (4): 703–22.

Biedenkopf, K., Geremek, B. and Michalski, K. 2004, The spiritual and cultural dimension of Europe. Concluding remarks. Printed in Europan Commission, Directorate-General for Research EUR 21360: 5–12, Luxemburg: Office for Official Publications of the European Communities.

Bogdanor, V. 1996, *Politics and the Constitution. Essays on British Government*. Aldershot: Dartmouth.

Boin, A. and Lodge, M. 2016, Designing resilient institutions for transboundary crisis management: A time for public administration. *Public Administration* 94 (2): 289–98.

Boin, A. and 't Hart, P. 2016, Foreword. In N. Schiffino, L. Taskin, C. Donis, and J. Raone (eds): *Organizing after Crisis. The Challenge of Learning*: 13–15. Brussels: Public Action.

Borowiak, C.T. 2011, *Accountability and Democracy. The Pitfalls and Promises of Popular Control*. Oxford: Oxford University Press.

Boussaguet, L. 2016, Participatory mechanisms as symbolic policy instruments? *Comparative European Politics* 14 (1): 107–24.

Bovens, M. 2007, Analysing and assessing accountability: A conceptual framework. *European Law Journal* 13 (4): 447–68.

Bovens, M. 2010, Two concepts of accountability: Accountability as virtue and as a mechanism. *West European Politics* 33 (5): 946–67.

Bovens, M., Schillemans, P. and 't Hart, P. 2008, Does public accountability work? *Public Administration* 86: 225–42.

Bovens, M., Curtin, D., and 't Hart, P. (eds) 2010, *The Real World of EU Accountability. What Deficit?* Oxford: Oxford University Press.

Bovens, M., Goodin, R.E. and Schillemans, T., (eds) 2014, *The Oxford Handbook of Public Accountability*. Oxford: Oxford University Press.

Brunsson, N. 1989, *The Organization of Hypocrisy. Talk, Decisions and Actions in Organizations*. Chichester: Wiley.

Brunsson, N. 2007, *The Consequences of Decision-Making*. Oxford: Oxford University Press.

Brunsson, N. and Olsen, J.P. 1993, *The Reforming Organization*. London: Routledge.

Brunsson, N. and Olsen, J.P. 1998, Organization theory: Thirty years of dismantling, and then...? In N. Brunsson and J.P. Olsen (eds): *Organizing Organizations*: 13–43. Bergen: Fagbokforlaget.

Busuioc, E.M. and Lodge, M. 2016, The reputational basis of public accountability. *Governance* 29 (2): 247–63.

Busuioc, M. 2010, *The Accountability of European Agencies. Legal Provisions and Ongoing Practices*. Delft: Eburon.

Busuioc, M. 2013. *European Agencies: Law and Practices of Accountability*, Oxford: Oxford University Press.

Busuioc, M., Curtin, D. and Groenleer, M. 2011, Agency growth between autonomy and accountability: The European Police Office as a "living institution." *Journal of European Public Policy* 18 (6): 848–67.

Busuioc, M., Groenleer, M. and Trondal, J. 2012, *The Agency Phenomenon in the European Union: Emergence, Institutionalisation and Everyday Decision-Making,* Manchester: Manchester University Press.

Caramani, D. 2004, *The Nationalization of Politics. The Formation of National Electorates and Party Systems in Western Europe*. Cambridge: Cambridge University Press.

Carpenter, D.P. 2001, *The Forging of Bureaucratic Autonomy*. Princeton, NJ: Princeton University Press.

Carrubba, C.J. and Clark, T.S. 2012, Rule creation in a political hierarchy. *American Political Science Review* 106 (3): 622–43.

Chamon, M. 2016, *Agencification* in the United States and Germany and what the EU might learn from it. *German Law Journal* 17 (2): 119–52.

Christensen, T. and Lægreid, P. 2005, Regulatory agencies. The challenges of balancing agency autonomy and political control. *Governance* 20: 499–520.

Christensen, T. and Lægreid, P. (eds) 2006, *Autonomy and Regulation. Coping with Agencies in the Modern State*. Cheltenham: Edward Elgar.

Christensen, T. and Lægreid, P. (eds) 2016, *The Ashgate Research Companion to Accountability and Welfare State Reforms in Europe*. Aldershot: Ashgate.

Cohen, M.D. and March, J.G. 1986 (2nd ed.), *Leadership and Ambiguity: The American College President*. Cambridge MA: Harvard Business Press.

Cohen, M.D., March, J.G. and Olsen, J.P. 1972, A garbage can model of organizational choice. *Administrative Science Quarterly* 17: 1–25.

Committee of Independent Experts 1999, First Report on Allegations regarding Fraud, Mismanagement and Nepotism in the European Commission, 15 March, <http://www.europarl.europa.eu/experts/9_en.htm> (accessed 17 March, 1999).

Connolly, W.E. 1987, *Politics and Ambiguity*. Madison: University of Wisconsin Press.

Considine, M. 2002, The end of the line? Accountable governance in the age of networks, partnerships, and joined-up services. *Governance* 15 (1): 21–40.

Cooper, I. 2016, The politicization of interparliamentary relations in the EU: Constructing and contesting the "Article 13 Conference" on economic governance. *Comparative European Politics* 14 (2): 196–214.

Costa, O., Jabco, N. Lequesne, C. and Magnette, P. (eds) 2003, The diffusion of democracy—emerging forms and norms of democratic control in the European Union. *Journal of European Public Policy* 10 (2): Special Issue.

Crick, B. 1982 (2nd ed.) [1962], *In Defence of Politics*. Harmondsworth: Penguin Books.

Crouch, C. 2011, *The Strange Non-Death of Neo-Liberalism*. Cambridge: Polity.

Crozier, M.J., Huntington, S.P. and Watanuki, J. 1975, *The Crisis of Democracy*. New York: New York University Press.

Curtin, D. 2007, Holding (quasi-)autonomous EU administrative actors to public account. *European Law Journal* 13 (4): 523–41.

Curtin, D. and Egeberg, M. (eds) 2008, Towards a new executive order in Europe? *West European Politics* 31 (4): Special Issue.

Curtin, D., Mair, P. and Papadopoulos, Y. 2010, Positioning accountability in European governance: An introduction. *West European Politics* 33 (5): 929–45.

Cyert, R.M. and March, J.G. 1963, *A Behavioral Theory of the Firm*. Englewood Cliffs, NJ: Prentice Hall. 2nd ed. 1992, Oxford: Basil Blackwell.

Dahl, R.A. 1961, *Who Governs. Democracy and Power in an American City*. New Haven, CT: Yale University Press.

Dahl, R.A. 1970, *After the Revolution. Authority in a Good Society*. New Haven, CT: Yale University Press.

Dahl, R.A. 1989, *Democracy and Its Critics*. New Haven, CT: Yale University Press.

Dahl, R.A. 1996, Thinking about democratic constitutions: Conclusions from democratic experience. *NOMOS* 38: 175–206.

Dahl, R.A. 1998, *On Democracy*. New Haven, CT: Yale University Press.

Dahl, R.A. and Lindblom, C.E. 1963 (paperback ed.) [1953], *Politics, Economics, and Welfare*. New York: Harper Torchbooks.

Dahlström, C., Peters, B.G. and Pierre, J. (eds) 2011, *Steering from the Centre. Strengthening Political Control in Western Democracies*. Toronto: University of Toronto Press.

Dahrendorf, R. 1988, *The Modern Social Conflict. An Essay on the Politics of Liberty*. London: Weidenfeld and Nicolson.

Dawson, M. 2015, The Euro crisis and its transformation of EU law and politics. In *The Governance Report 2015*. Hertie School of Governance: 41–68. Oxford: Oxford University Press.

Day, P. and Klein, R. 1987, *Accountabilities: Five Public Services*. London: Tavistock.

De Beauvoir, S. 1972 [1947], *The Ethics of Ambiguity*. Secaucus, NJ: Citadel Press.

Dehousse, R. 2015, The new supranationalism. Centre d'études européennes Sciences Po Paris. Paper prepared for presentation at the ECPR General Conference, Montreal, 26 August –9.

Deutsch, K.W. 1966, paperback ed. [1963], *The Nerves of Government. Models of Political Communication and Control*. New York: Free Press.

Dewey, J. 1927, *The Public and Its Problems*. Denver. CO: Allan Swallow.

DiEM25 2016, A Manifesto for Democratising Europe. Democracy in Europe Movement 2025, <http://diem25.org> (accessed 2 October, 2016).

Dogan, M. 2005, Erosion of confidence in thirty European democracies. *Comparative Sociology* 4 (1–2): 11–53.

Dubnick, M.J. 2005, Accountability and the promise of performance: In search of mechanisms. *Public Performance and Management Review* 28 (3): 376–417.

Dubnick, M.J. 2011, Move over Daniel: We need some "accountability space." *Administration and Society* 43: 704–16.

Easton, D. 1975, A reassessment of the concept of political support. *British Journal of Political Science* 5 (4): 435–57.

Egeberg, M. 2004, An organizational approach to European integration: Outline of a complementary perspective. *European Journal of Political Research* 43 (2): 199–219.

Egeberg, M. (ed.) 2006, *Multilevel Union Administration. The Transformation of Executive Politics in Europe*. London: Palgrave Macmillan.

Egeberg, M. 2009, Towards an organizational theory of international integration. In P.G. Roness and H. Sætren (eds): *Change and Continuity in Public Sector Organizations*. Bergen: Fagbokforlaget.

Egeberg, M. and Trondal, J. 2011, EU-level agencies: New executive centre formation or vehicles for national control. *Journal of European Public Policy* 18 (6): 868–87.

Egeberg, M. and Trondal, J. 2016, Agentification of the European Union administration. Connecting the dots. Oslo: TARN WP Series No. 1 and ARENA WP Series No. 3.

Egeberg, M., Trondal, J. and Vestlund, N.M. 2015, The quest for order. Unravelling the relationship between the European Commission and the European Union agencies. *Journal of European Public Policy* 22 (5): 609–29.

Eisenstadt, S.N. 1995, The order-maintaining and order-transforming dimensions of culture. Reprinted in S.N. Eisenstadt: *Power, Trust and Meaning*: 306–27. Chicago, IL: University of Chicago Press.

Eisenstadt, S. and Rokkan, S. (eds) 1973/1974: *Building States and Nations*, Vols I and II. Beverly Hills, CA: Sage.

Elazar, D.J. 1991 (paperback ed.), *Exploring Federalism*. Tuscaloosa: University of Alabama Press.

Elias, N. 1982 [1939], *The Civilizing Process. State Formation and Civilization*. Oxford: Basil Blackwell.

Elkin, S.L. and Soltan, K.E. (eds) 1999, *Citizens Competence and Democratic Institutions*. University Park: Pennsylvania State University Press.

Eriksen, E.O. 2005, Conclusion. From reflexive interaction to deliberative supranationalism? In E.O. Eriksen (ed.): *Making the European Polity. Reflexive Integration in the EU*: 253–70. Abingdon: Routledge.

Eriksen, E.O. and Fossum, J.E. (eds) 2014, *Det norske paradoks. Om Norges forhold til den Europeiske Union*. Oslo: Universitetsforlaget.

Eriksen, E.O., Fossum, J.E. and Menéndez, A. (eds) 2004, *Developing a Constitution for Europe*. London: Routledge.

Eriksson, A. 2016, MEPs explore new ways to monitor EU commissioners. Brussels, <https://euobserver.com/institutional/134442> (accessed 21 July, 2016).

Etzioni, A. 1964, *Modern Organizations*. Englewood Cliffs, NJ: Prentice-Hall.

EurActive 2014, Schäuble advocates separate Eurozone parliament, 28 January, <http://www.euroactive.com/section/future-en/news/schauble-advocates-separate-eurozone-parliament> (accessed 29 January, 2014).

European Commission 1992, From the Single Act to Maastricht and Beyond: The Means to Match Our Ambitions. Brussels: COM(92) final.

European Commission 2001, European Governance. A White Paper. Brussels: COM(428) final.

European Commission 2004, The Spiritual and Cultural Dimension of Europe. Reflection Group. Directorate-General for Research EUR 21360. Luxemburg: Office for Official Publications of the European Communities.

European Commission 2010, Europe 2020. A Strategy for Smart, Sustainable and Inclusive Growth. Brussels 3.3: COM(2020) final.

European Commission 2015, *Commission Work Program 2016. No Time for Business as Usual*. Communication from the Commission to the European Parliament, the Council, the European Economic and Social Committee and the Committee of the Regions. Strasbourg, October 27, COM(610) final.

European Council 2012, Treaty on Stability, Coordination and Governance in the Economic and Monetary Union, Brussels: (T/SCG/en).

Everson, M. and Joerges, C. 2012, Reconfiguring the politics–law relationship in the integration project through conflicts–law constitutionalism. *European Law Journal* 18 (5): 644–66.

Fabbrini, S. 2014, After the Euro Crisis: A New Paradigm on the Integration of Europe. Oslo: ARENA Working Paper 05/2014, <http://www.sv.uio.no/arena/english/research/publications/arena-publications/workingpapers/working-papers2014/wp5-14.xml> (accessed 2 October, 2016).

Fabbrini, S. 2015, *Which European Union? Europe after the Euro-Crisis*. Cambridge: Cambridge University Press.

Fabbrini, S. 2016, The constitutional conundrum of the European Union. *Journal of European Public Policy* 23 (1): 84–100.

Feldman, M.S. and March, J.G. 1981, Information in organizations as signal and symbol. *Administrative Science Quarterly* 26: 171–86.

Ferguson, Y.H. and Mansbach, R.W. 1996, *Polities. Authority, Identities and Change*. Columbia: University of South Carolina Press.

Festinger, L. 1957, *A Theory of Cognitive Dissonance*. Stanford, CA: Stanford University Press.

Fimreite, A.L., Lango, P. Lægreid, P. and Rykkja, L.H. 2014 (2nd ed.), *Organisering, samfunnssikkerhet og krisehåndtering*. Oslo: Universitetsforlaget.

Fisher, E. 2004, The European Union in the age of accountability. *Oxford Journal of Legal Studies* 24 (3): 495–515.

Fliegstein, N., Polyakova, A. and Sandholtz, W. 2012, European integration, nationalism and European identity. *Journal of Common Market Studies* 50: 106–22.

Flinders, M. 2011, Daring to be a Daniel: The pathology of politicized accountability in monitory democracy. *Administration and Society* 43 (5): 595–619.

Fossum, J.E. 2016a, Democracy and legitimacy in the EU: Challenges and options. Rome: Instituto Affari Internazionali working papers, 16 January.

Fossum, J.E. 2016b, Democratic federalization. Oslo: ARENA manuscript.

Fossum, J.E. and Menéndez, A.J. 2011, *The Constitution's Gift: A Constitutional Theory for a Democratic European Union*. Lanham: Rowman and Littlefield.

Frazer, N. 1992, Rethinking the public sphere: A contribution to a critique of actually existing democracy. In C. Calhoun (ed.): *Habermas and the Public Sphere*: 109–42. Cambridge MA: MIT Press.

Freeman, G.P. 2006, Politics and mass immigration. In R.E. Goodin and C. Tilly (eds): *The Oxford Handbook of Contextual Analysis*: 636–48. Oxford: Oxford University Press.

Frey-Wouters, E. 1965, The progress of European integration. *World Politics* 17 (3): 460–77.

Friedrich, C.J. 1942, *The New Belief in the Common Man*. Brattleboro, VT: Vermont Publishing Company.

Friedrich, C.J. 1950 (revised ed.). *Constitutional Government and Democracy: Theory and Practice in Europe and America*. Boston, MA: Ginn and Company.

Fukuyama, F. 2014, *Political Order and Political Decay: From the Industrial Revolution to the Globalization of Democracy*. New York: Farrar, Straus and Giroux.

Fung, A. 2001, Accountable autonomy: Toward empowered deliberation in Chicago schools and policing. *Politics and Society* 29 (1): 73–103.

Furnham, A. and Marks, J. 2013, Tolerance of ambiguity: A review of recent literature. *Psychology* 4 (9): 717–28.

Gailmard, S. 2014, Accountability and principal–agent theory. In M. Bovens, R.E. Goodin, and T. Schillemans (eds), *The Oxford Handbook of Public Accountability*: 90–105. Oxford: Oxford University Press.

Galston, W.A. 2010, Realism in political theory. *European Journal of Political Theory* 9 (4): 385–411.

Gamson, W.A. 1968, *Power and Discontent*. Homewood, IL: Dorsey Press.

Gaus, J.M. 1950, Trends in the theory of public administration. *Public Administration Review* 10 (3): 161–8.

Gilmour, R.S. and Jensen, L.S. 1998, Reinventing government accountability: Public functions, privatization, and the meaning of "state action." *Public Administration Review* 58 (3): 247–58.

Goldoni, M. 2012, Two internal critiques of political constitutionalism. *International Journal of Constitutional Law* 10 (4): 926–49.

Goodin, R.E. 1982, *Political Theory and Public Policy*. Chicago, IL: University of Chicago Press.

Goodin, R.E. 2007, Enfranchising all affected interests, and its alternatives. *Philosophy and Public Affairs* 35 (1): 40–68.

Goodin, R.E. 2008, *Innovating Democracy. Democratic Theory and Practice after the Deliberative Turn*. Oxford: Oxford University Press.

Goodin, R.E. 2016, Reasons for Reason-Giving. Canberra: School of Philosophy, Australian National University: manuscript.

Gormley, W.T., Jr. and Weimer, D.L. 1999, *Organizational Report Cards*. Cambridge, MA: Harvard University Press.

Grant, R.W. and Keohane, R.O. 2005, Accountability and abuses of power in world politics. *American Political Science Review* 99 (1): 29–43.

Gustavsson, S., Karlsson, C. and Persson, T. (eds) 2009, *The Illusion of Accountability in the European Union*. London: Routledge.

Haas, E.B. 1968, 2nd ed. [1958], *The Uniting of Europe: Political, Social and Economic Forces 1950–1957*. Stanford, CA: Stanford University Press.

Habermas, J. 1996a, *Between Facts and Norms*. Cambridge, MA: MIT Press.

Habermas, J. 1996b, The European nation state. Its achievements and its limitations. On the past and future of sovereignty and citizenship. *Ratio Juris* 9 (2): 125–37.

Habermas, J. 1998, The European nation-state: On the past and future of sovereignty and citizenship. In C. Cronin and P. de Greiff (eds): *The Inclusion of the Other*: 105–27. Cambridge, MA: MIT Press.

Habermas, J. 2001, Constitutional democracy. A paradoxical union of contradictory principles? *Political Theory* 29 (6): 766–81.

Halachmi, A. 2014, Accountability overload. In M. Bovens, R.E. Goodin, and T. Schillemans (eds), *The Oxford Handbook of Public Accountability*: 560–73. Oxford: Oxford University Press.

Hall, J.A. 2004, The politics of modernity. In F. Engelstad and Ø. Østerud (eds): *Power and Democracy. Critical Interventions*: 131–50. Aldershot: Ashgate.

Hamilton, A., Jay, J. and Madison, J. 1964 [1787], *The Federalist Papers*. New York: Pocket Books, Simon and Schuster.

Hanson, R.L. 1989, Democracy. In T. Ball, J. Farr, and R.L. Hanson (eds): *Political Innovation and Conceptual Change*: 68–89. Cambridge: Cambridge University Press.

Harlow, C. and Rawlings, R. 2007, Promoting accountability in multilevel governance: A network approach. *European Law Journal* 13 (4): 542–62.

Harmon, M.M. 1995, *Responsibility as Paradox. A Critique of Rational Discourse on Government*. Thousand Oaks, CA: Sage.

Hay, C. and Stoker, G. 2009, Revitalising politics: Have we lost the plot? *Representation* 45 (3): 225–36.

Heater, D. 1992, *The Idea of European Unity*. Leicester: Leicester University Press.

Heider, F. 1958, *The Psychology of Interpersonal Relations*. New York: John Wiley.

Held, D. 2004, Democratic accountability and political effectiveness from a cosmopolitan perspective. *Government and Opposition* 39 (2): 364–91.

Hillion, C. 2015, Accession and withdrawal in the law of the European Union. In A. Arnull and D. Chalmers (eds): *The Oxford Handbook of European Union Law*: 126–52. Oxford: Oxford University Press.

Hirschl, R. 2004, The political origins of the New Constitutionalism. *Indiana Journal of Global Legal Studies* 11 (1): 71–108.

Hobolt, S.B. 2012, Citizens' satisfaction with democracy in the European Union. *Journal of Common Market Studies* 50: 88–105.

Hobsbawm, E.J. 1992 (2nd. ed.), *Nation and Nationalism since 1780*. Cambridge: Cambridge University Press.

Holmberg, S. and Rothstein, B. (eds) 2012, *Good Government. The Relevance of Political Science*. Cheltenham: Edward Elgar.

Hood, C. 1999, The garbage can model of organization: Describing a condition or a prescriptive design principle? In M. Egeberg and P. Lægreid (eds): *Organizing Political Institutions*: 59–78. Oslo: Scandinavian University Press.

Hood, C. 2014, Accountability and blame-avoidance. In M. Bovens, R.E. Goodin, and T. Schillemans (eds), *The Oxford Handbook of Public Accountability*: 603–16. Oxford: Oxford University Press.

Hooghe, L. and Marks, G. 2001, *Multi-Level Governance and European Integration*. Lanham: Rowman and Littlefield.

Hooghe, L. and Marks, G. 2009, A postfunctionalist theory of European integration: From permissive consensus to constraining dissensus. *British Journal of Political Science* 39 (1): 1–23.

Huber, J. and Shipan, C. 2002, *Deliberate Discretion? The Institutional Foundations of Bureaucratic Autonomy*. New York: Cambridge University Press.

Hutchings, V.L. 2005, *Public Opinion and Democratic Accountability: How Citizens Learn about Politics*. Princeton, NJ: Princeton University Press.

Isiksel, T. 2013, Citizens of a new agora: Postnational citizenship and international economic institutions. In W. Maas (ed.): *Multilevel Citizenship*: 184–202, 261–71. Philadelphia: University of Pennsylvania Press.

Jachtenfuchs, M., Diez, T. and Jung, S. 1998, Which Europe? Conflicting models of a legitimate European political order. *European Journal of International Relations* 4 (4): 409–55.

Jenson, J. 2007, The European Union's citizenship regime. Creating norms and building practices. *Comparative European Politics* 5: 53–69.

Joerges, C. 2010, *Rechtsstaat* and social Europe: How a classical tension resurfaces in the European integration process. *Comparative Sociology* 9: 65–85.

Joint Communiqué 2016, Charting the way ahead. An EU Founding Member's Initiative on Strengthening Cohesion in the European Union, September 2, <http://www.esteri.it.mae/it/sala_stampa/archivionotizie/communicat/2016/02/joint-communique-charting-the-way.html> (accessed 10 February 2016).

Jones, E. 2012, Identity and solidarity. In E. Jones, A. Menon, and S. Weatherill (eds): *The Oxford Handbook of the European Union*: 690–702. Oxford: Oxford University Press.

Kaiser, W. 2015, Clash of cultures: Two milieus in the European Union's "A New Narrative for Europe" project. *Journal of Contemporary European Studies* 23 (2): 364–77.

Karsten, N. 2015, Scrutinize me, please! The drivers, manifestations and implications of accountability-seeking behaviour. *Public Administration* 93 (3): 684–99.

Keane, J. 2009, *The Life and Death of Democracy*. London: Simon and Schuster.

Klijn, E.H. and Koppenjan, J.F.M. 2014, Accountable networks. In M. Bovens, R.E. Goodin, and T. Schillemans (eds), *The Oxford Handbook of Public Accountability*: 242–57. Oxford: Oxford University Press.

Klinger, D.E., Nalbandian, J. and Romzek, B.S. 2001, Politics, administration, and markets. Conflicting expectations and accountability. *American Review of Public Administration* 32 (2): 117–44.

Klosko, G. 2011, Political obligation. In G. Klosko (ed.): *The Oxford Handbook of the History of Political Philosophy*: 712–24. Oxford: Oxford University Press.

Kohler-Koch, B. 2005, European governance and system integration. Mannheim: European Governance papers, <http://www.edoc.vifapol.de/opus/volltexte/2011/2453/pdf/egp_connex_C_05_01.pdf> (accessed November 16, 2006).

Kohler-Koch, B. and Rittberger, B. (eds) 2007, *Debating the Democratic Legitimacy of the European Union*. Lanham, MD: Rowman and Littlefield.

Koppell, J.G.S. 2005, Pathologies of accountability. ICANN and the challenge of "multiple accountabilities disorder." *Public Administration Review* 65 (1): 94–108.

Kratochwil, F. 2009, Has the "Rule of law" become a "rule of lawyers"? In G. Palombella and N. Walker (eds): *Relocating the Rule of Law*: 171–96. Oxford and Portland, OR: Hart Publishing.

Kröger, S. and Bellamy, R. 2016, Beyond the constraining dissensus: The role of national parliaments in domesticating and normalising the politicization of European integration. *Comparative European Politics* 14 (2): 131–53.

Kumm, M. 2007, Institutionalising Socratic contestation: The rationalist human rights paradigm, legitimate authority and the point of judicial review. *European Journal of International Law* 1 (2): 1–32.

Lægreid, P. 2014, Accountability and the New Public Management. In M. Bovens, R.E. Goodin, and T. Schillemans (eds), *The Oxford Handbook of Public Accountability*: 324–38. Oxford: Oxford University Press.

Lægreid, P. and Neby, J.P. 2016, Gaming, accountability and trust: DRGs and activity-based funding in Norway. *Financial Accountability and Management* 32 (1): 57–79.

Lægreid, P. and Olsen, J.P. 1984, Top civil servants in Norway: Key players—on different teams. In E. Suleiman (ed.): *Bureaucracy and Policy Making*: 206–41. New York: Holmes and Meier.

Lægreid, P. and Verhoest, K. 2010, *Governance of Public Sector Organizations: Proliferation, Autonomy and Performance*. London: Palgrave MacMillan.

Laffan, B. 2003, Auditing and accountability in the European Union. *Journal of European Public Policy* 10 (5): 762–77.

Landau, M. 1969, Redundancy, rationality, and the problem of duplication and overlap. *Public Administration Review* 29 (4): 346–58.

Lango, P., Lægreid, P. and Rykkja, L.H. 2014, Etter 22. juli. Justis- og beredskapsdepartementets ansvar for samfunnssikkerheten. In A.L. Fimreite, P. Lango, P. Lægreid, and H. Rykkja (eds): *Organisering av samfunnssikkerhet og krisehåndtering* (2nd ed.): 60–76. Oslo: Universitetsforlaget.

Leazes, F.J., Jr. 1987, *Accountability and the Business State. The Structure of Federal Corporations*. New York: Praeger.

Lefkofridi, Z. and Schmitter, P.C. 2015, Transcending or descending? European integration in times of crisis. *European Political Science Review* 7 (1): 3–22.

Lerner, J.S. and Tetlock, P.E. 1999, Accounting for the effects of accountability. *Psychological Bulletin* 25 (2): 255–75.

Leuffen, D., Rittberger, B. and Schimmelfennig, P. 2013, *Differentiated Integration. Explaining Variance in the European Union*. Basingstoke: Palgrave Macmillan.

Lewin, L. 2007, *Democratic Accountability. Why Choice in Politics Is Both Possible and Necessary*. Cambridge, MA: Harvard University Press.

Lindblom, C.E. 1965, *The Intelligence of Democracy*. New York: Free Press.

Lipset, S.M. 1963, *Political Man. The Social Basis of Politics*. Garden City, NY: Doubleday, Anchor Books.

Lipset, S.M. and Rokkan, S. 1967, Cleavage structures, party systems, and voter alignments: An introduction. In S.M. Lipset and S. Rokkan (eds): *Party Systems and Voters Alignments*: 1–64. New York: Free Press.

Lipset, S.M. and Wolin, S.S. (eds) 1965, *The Berkeley Student Revolt: Facts and Interpretations*. Garden City, NY: Doubleday, Anchor Books.

Lomi, A. and Harrison, J.R. (eds) 2012, *The Garbage Can Model of Organizational Choice: Looking Forward at Forty*. Research in the Sociology of Organizations 36. Also Bingley: Emerald Books.

Lord, C. and Pollak, J. 2010, Representation and accountability: Communicating tubes? *Western European Politics* 33 (5): 968–88.

Lupia, A. and McCubbins, M.D. 1994, Learning from oversight: Fire alarms and police patrols reconstructed. *Journal of Economics, Law and Organization* 10 (1): 96–125.

Lupia, A. and McCubbins, M.D. 2000, Representation or abdication? How citizens use institutions to help delegation succeed. *European Journal of Political Research* 37: 291–307.

MacIntyre, A. 1988, *Whose Justice? Which Rationality?* Notre Dame, IN: University of Notre Dame Press.

Magnette, P. 2000, Towards "accountable independence"? Parliamentary controls of the European Central Bank and the rise of a new democratic model. *European Law Journal* 6 (4): 326–40.

Mair, P. 2007, Political opposition and the European Union. *Government and Opposition* 42 (2): 1–17.

Majone, G. 1998, Europe's "democratic deficit": The question of standards. *European Law Journal* 4 (1): 5–28.

Majone, G. 2014 From regulatory state to a democratic default. *Journal of Common Market Studies* 52 (6): 1216–23.

Manning, M. 2004, Torture and the politics of ambiguity, <http://www.project-syndicate.org/commentary/torture-and-the-politics-of-ambiguity> (accessed 21 August, 2012).

March, J.G. 1981, Footnotes to organizational change. *Administrative Science Quarterly* 26 (4): 563–77.

March, J.G. 1984, How we talk and how we act: Administrative theory and administrative life. In T.J. Sergiovanni and J.E. Corbally (eds): *Leadership and Organizational Cultures*: 18–35. Urbana: University of Illinois Press.

March, J.G. 1987, Ambiguity and accounting: The elusive link between information and decision making. *Accounting, Organizations, and Society* 12: 153–68.

March, J.G. 1994, *A Primer of Decision Making: How Decisions Happen*. New York: Free Press.

March, J.G. 1999, A learning perspective on the network dynamics of institutional integration. In M. Egeberg and P. Lægreid (eds): *Organizing Political Institutions*: 129–55. Oslo: Scandinavian University Press.

March, J.G. 2010, *The Ambiguities of Experience*. Ithaca, NY: Cornell University Press.

March, J.G. 2015, Do the mistakes lie in decision makers or in economics? In S. Rangan (ed.): *Performance and Progress*: 28–37. Oxford: Oxford University Press.

March, J.G. and Olsen, J.P. 1975, The uncertainty of the past. Organizational learning under ambiguity. *European Journal of Political Research* 3: 147–71.

March, J.G. and Olsen, J.P. 1976, *Ambiguity and Choice in Organizations*. Bergen: Universitetsforlaget.

March, J.G. and Olsen, J.P. 1983, Organizing political life: What administrative reorganization tells us about government. *American Political Science Review* 77 (2): 281–96.

March, J.G. and Olsen, J.P. 1989, *Rediscovering Institutions. The Organizational Basis of Politics*. New York: Free Press.

March, J.G. and Olsen, J.P. 1995, *Democratic Governance*. New York: Free Press.

March, J.G. and Olsen, J.P. 1998, The institutional dynamics of international political orders. *International Organization* 52 (4): 943–69.

March, J.G. and Olsen, J.P. 2006, Elaborating the "New Institutionalism." In R.A.W. Rhodes, S. Binder, and B. Rockman (eds): *The Oxford Handbook of Political Institutions*: 3–20. Oxford: Oxford University Press.

March, J.G. and Simon, H.A. 1958, *Organizations*. New York: Wiley.

March, J.G. and Weissinger-Baylon, R. (eds) 1986, *Ambiguity and Command. Organizational Perspectives on Military Decision Making*. Marshfield: Pitman.

Mattila, M. and Raunio, T. 2012, Drifting further apart: National parties and their electorates on the EU dimension. *West European Politics* 35 (3): 589–606.

Mendez, C. and Bachtler, J. 2011, Administrative reform and unintended consequences: An assessment of the EU cohesion policy "audit explosion." *Journal of European Public Policy* 18 (5): 746–65.

Menéndez, A.J. 2013, The existential crisis of the European Union. *German Law Journal* 14 (5): 453–525.

Menéndez, A.J. 2014, Editorial: A European Union in constitutional mutation? *European Law Journal* 20 (2): 127–41.

Mény, Y. 2012, Conclusion: A voyage to the unknown. *Journal of Common Market Studies* 50: 154–64.

Meyer, J.W. and Rowan, B. 1977, Institutionalized organizations: Formal structure as myth and ceremony. *American Journal of Sociology* 83: 340–63.

Michalsen, D. 2014, Grunnlovens nye verdiparagraf §2. *Tidsskrift for Rettsvitenskap* 127 (2): 206–34.

Michels, A. and Meijer, A. 2008, Safeguarding public accountability in horizontal government. *Public Management Review* 10 (2): 165–73.

Mill, J.S. 1956 [1859], *On Liberty*. Indianapolis, IN: Bobbs-Merrill.

Mill, J.S. 1962 [1861], *Considerations on Representative Government*. South Bend, IN: Gateway Editions.

Miller, G.J. 2005, The political evolution of principal–agent models. *Annual Review of Political Science* 8: 203–25.

Moe, T.M. 1990, Political institutions: The neglected side of the story. *Journal of Law, Economics, and Organization* 6: 213–66.

Moe, T.M. 1991, Politics and the theory of organization. *Journal of Law, Economics, and Organization* 7: 106–29.

Moe, T.M. and Caldwell, M. 1994, The institutional foundation of democratic government: A comparison of presidential and parliamentary systems. *Journal of Institutional and Theoretical Economics* 150 (1): 171–95.

Molander, A., Grimen, H. and Eriksen, E.O. 2012, Professional discretion and accountability in the welfare state. *Journal of Applied Philosophy* 29 (3): 214–30.

Moncrieffe, J.M. 1998, Reconceptualizing political accountability. *International Political Science Review* 19 (4): 387–406.

Moravcsik, A. 2004, Is there a "democratic deficit" in world politics? A framework for analysis. *Government and Opposition* 39 (2): 336–63.

Mouffe, C. 2005, Democratic citizenship and the political community. In C. Mouffe: *The Return of the Political*: 60–73. London: Verso.

Mulgan, R. 2000, "Accountability": An ever-expanding concept? *Public Administration* 78 (3): 555–73.

Näsström, S. 2011, The challenge of the all-affected principle. *Political Studies* 59: 116–34.

Nielsen, N. 2016a, TTIP investor court illegal, say German judges, <https://euobserver.com/economic/132142> (accessed 5 February, 2016).

Nielsen, N. 2016b, EU defends TTIP investor court after German backlash, <https://euobserver.com/economic/132295> (accessed February 9, 2016).

NOU 2003, 19, *Makt og demokrati. Sluttrapport fra Makt- og demokratiutredningen (1998–2003).*

NOU 2012, 2, *Utenfor og innenfor. Norges avtaler med EU.*

NOU 2012, 14, *Rapport fra 22. juli-kommisjonen.*

Olsen, J.P. 1976, The process of interpreting organizational history. In J.G. March and J.P. Olsen: *Ambiguity and Choice in Organizations*: 338–50. Bergen: Universitetsforlaget.

Olsen, J.P. 1978, *Politisk organisering*. Bergen: Universitetsforlaget.

Olsen, J.P. 1990, *Demokrati på svenska*. Stockholm: Carlssons.

Olsen, J.P. 1991, Political science and organization theory. Parallel agendas but mutual disregard. In R.M. Czada and A. Windhoff-Héritier (eds): *Political Choice: Institutions, Rules and the Limits of Rationality*: 87–119. Frankfurt am Main: Campus Verlag.

Olsen, J.P. 2003, Coping with conflicts at constitutional moments. *Industrial and Corporate Change* 12: 815–42.

Olsen, J.P. 2007, *Europe in Search of Political Order. An Institutional Perspective on Unity/Diversity, Citizen/Their Helpers, Democratic Design/Historical Drift, and the Co-existence of Orders*. Oxford: Oxford University Press.

Olsen, J.P. 2008, Explorations in institutions and logics of appropriateness. An introductory essay. In J.G. March: *Explorations in Organizations*: 191–202. Stanford, CA: Stanford Business Books.

Olsen, J.P. 2009a, Change and continuity: An institutional approach to institutions of democratic government. *European Political Science Review* 1 (1): 3–32. Reprinted in P.W Ingraham and J. Pierre (eds) 2010, *Comparative Administrative Change and Reform: Lessons Learned*: 15–47. Montreal and Kingston: McGill-Queen's University Press.

Olsen, J.P. 2009b, Democratic government, institutional autonomy and the dynamics of change. *West European Politics* 32 (3): 439–65.

Olsen, J.P. 2010, *Governing Through Institution Building. Institutional Theory and Recent European Experiments in Democratic Organization*. Oxford: Oxford University Press.

Olsen, J.P. 2013, The institutional basis of democratic accountability. *West European Politics* 36 (3): 447–73.

Olsen, J.P. 2014a, *Folkestyrets varige spenninger*. Oslo: Universitetsforlaget.

Olsen, J.P. 2014b, Accountability and ambiguity. In M. Bovens, R.E. Goodin, and T. Schillemans (eds), *The Oxford Handbook of Public Accountability*: 106–23. Oxford: Oxford University Press.

Olsen, J.P. 2015a, Democratic order, autonomy and accountability. *Governance* 28 (4): 425–40.

Olsen, J.P. 2015b, Et demokratiprosjekt? Grunnlovsjubileet og folkestyrets organisatoriske basis. *Norsk Statsvitenskapelig Tidsskrift* 31 (2): 83–117.

Olsen, J.P. 2016, Democratic accountability and the terms of political order. *European Political Science Review*, doi:10.1017/S1755773916000084.

Orator, A. 2016, Agencification by stealth: On the eroding constitutional bases to access the establishment and empowerment of EU agencies. Oslo: TARN Workshop, Arena, 31 January.

Orbuch, T.L. 1997, People's accounts count: The sociology of accounts. *Annual Review of Sociology* 23: 455–78.

Orren, K. and Skowronek, S. 2004, *The Search for American Political Development*. Cambridge: Cambridge University Press.

Osborne, F. and Gaebler, T. 1992. *Reinventing Government*. Reading, MA: Addison-Wesley.

Østerud, Ø., Engelstad, T. and Selle, P. 2003, *Makten og demokratiet. En sluttbok fra Makt- og demokratiutredningen*. Oslo: Gyldendal.

Page, B.I. 1976, The theory of political ambiguity. *American Political Science Review* 70 (3): 742–52.

Papadopoulos, Y. 2010, Accountability and multi-level governance: More accountability. Less democracy? *West European Politics* 33 (5): 1030–49.

Papadopoulos, Y. 2013, *Democracy in Crisis? Politics, Governance and Policy*. Houndmills: Palgrave Macmillan.

Perry, M.J. 1988, *Morality, Politics and Law*. Oxford: Oxford University Press.

Peters, B.G. and Pierre, J. (eds) 2012 (2nd ed.), *The Sage Handbook of Public Administration*. London: Sage.

Philp, M. 2009, Delimiting democratic accountability. *Political Studies* 57: 28–53.

Philp, M. 2010, What is to be done? Political theory and theoretical realism. *European Journal of Political Theory* 9 (4): 466–84.

Pierre, J. 2009, Reinventing governance, reinventing democracy. *Policy and Politics* 37: 591–609.

Pitkin, H.F. 1972 [1967], *The Concept of Representation*. Berkeley: University of California Press.

Pollitt, C. 2006, Performance management in practice: A comparative study of executive agencies. *Journal of Public Administration Research and Theory* 16: 25–44.

Pollitt, C. and Hupe, P. 2011, Talking about government. The role of magic concepts. *Public Management Review* 13 (5): 641–58.

Pollitt, C. and Summa, H. 1997, Reflexive watchdogs? How supreme audit institutions account for themselves. *Public Administration* 75 (Summer): 313–36.

Porter-O'Grady, T., Hawkins, M.A. and Parker, M.L. 1997, *Whole-Systems Shared Governance: Architecture for Integration*. Gaithersburg MD: Aspen Publishers.

Power, M. 1994, *The Audit Explosion*. London: Demos.

Preuss, U.K. 1996, Prospects of a constitution of Europe. *Constellations* 3 (2): 209–24.

Przeworski, A., Stokes, A.T. and Manin, B. (eds) 1999, *Democracy, Accountability, and Representation*. Cambridge: Cambridge University Press.

Randma-Liiv, T. and Kickert, W. 2016, The impact of the fiscal crisis on public administration reforms: Comparison of 14 European countries. *Journal of Comparative Policy Analysis*, <http://dx.doi.org/10.1080/13876988.2015.1129737> (accessed April 11, 2016).

Rasmussen, M. 2008, The origins of a legal revolution. The early history of the European Court of Justice. *Journal of European Integration History* 14 (2): 77–98.

Reichborn-Kjennerud, K. 2013, Political accountability and performance audit: The case of the auditor general in Norway. *Public Administration* 91 (3): 680–95.

Resodihardjo, S.L., Carroll, B.J. van Eijk, C.J.A. and Maris, S. 2016, Why traditional responses to blame games fail: The importance of context, rituals, and sub-blame games in the face of raves gone wrong. *Public Administration* 94 (2): 350–63.

Richter, M. 1995, *The History of Political and Social Concepts. A Critical Introduction*. New York and Oxford: Oxford University Press.

Roberts, A. 2017, *Four Crises of American Democracy: Representation, Mastery, Discipline, Anticipation*. Oxford: Oxford University Press.

Roccas, S., Sagiv, L. Schwartz, S. Halevy, N. and Eidelson, R. 2008, Toward a unifying model of identification with groups: Integrating theoretical perspectives. *Personality and Social Psychology Review* 12 (3): 280–306.

Rokkan, S. 1966, Norway: Numerical democracy and corporate pluralism. In R.A. Dahl (ed.): *Political Oppositions in Western Democracies*: 70–115. New Haven, CT: Yale University Press.

Rokkan, S. 1999, *State Formation, Nation-Building and Mass Politics in Europe. The Theory of Stein Rokkan* (edited by P. Flora with S. Kuhnle and D. Urwin). Oxford: Oxford University Press.

Rokkan, S. and Urwin, D. 1983, *Economy, Territory, Identity: Politics of West European Peripheries*. London: Sage.

Romzek, B.S. 2000, Dynamics of public sector accountability in an era of reform. *International Review of Administrative Sciences* 66: 21–44.

Rose, R. 2013, *Representing Europeans: A Pragmatic Approach*. Oxford: Oxford University Press.

Rothstein, B. 2011, *The Quality of Government. Corruption, Social Trust and Inequality in International Perspective*. Chicago, IL: University of Chicago Press.

Rubenstein, J. 2007, Accountability in an unequal world. *Journal of Politics* 69 (3): 616–32.

Rudolph, T.J. 2003, Institutional context and the assignment of political responsibility. *Journal of Politics* 65 (1): 190–215.

Sabel, C.F. and Zeitlin, J. (eds) 2010, *Experimentalist Governance in the European Union*. Oxford: Oxford University Press.

Saint-Martin, D. 2000, *Building the New Managerialist State*. Oxford: Oxford University Press.

Saint-Martin, D. 2001, How the reinventing government movement in public administration was exported from the US to other countries. *International Journal of Public Administration* 24 (6): 573–604.

Sartori, G. 1987, *The Theory of Democracy Revisited*. Chatham, NJ: Chatham House Publishers.

Saward, M. 2006, The representative claim. *Contemporary Political Theory* 5: 297–318.

Scharpf, F.W. 1999, *Governing in Europe. Effective and Democratic*. Oxford: Oxford University Press.

Scharpf, F.W. 2010, The asymmetry of European integration, or why the EU cannot be a "social market economy." *Socio-Economic Review* 8: 211–50.

Scharpf, F.W. 2015, After the crash: A perspective on multilevel European democracy. *European Law Journal* 21 (3): 384–405.

Schattschneider, E.E. 1960, *The Semi-Sovereign People*. New York: Holt, Rinehard, and Winston.

Schillemans, T. 2008, Accountability in the shadow of hierarchy: The horizontal accountability of agencies. *Public Organization Review* 8 (2): 179–95.

Schillemans, T. 2013, Moving beyond the clash of interests. On stewardship theory and the relationships between central government departments and public agencies. *Public Management Review* 15 (4): 541–62.

Schillemans, T. and Busuioc, M. 2014, Predicting public sector accountability: From agency drift to forum drift. *Journal of Public Administration Research and Theory* 25 (1): 191–215.

Schimmelfennig, F. 2015, What's the news in "New Intergovernmentalism"? A critique of Bickerton, Hodson and Puetter. *Journal of Common Market Studies* 53 (4): 723–30.

Schmidt, V.A. 2006, *Democracy in Europe*. Oxford: Oxford University Press.

Schmidt, V.A. 2007, *The EU and National Politics*. Oxford: Oxford University Press.

Schmitt, C. 1976 [1927], *The Concept of the Political*. New Brunswick, NJ: Rutgers University Press.

Schmitter, P.C. 1996, If the nation-state were to wither away in Europe, what might replace it? In S. Gustavsson and L. Lewin (eds): *The Future of the Nation-State*: 211–44. London: Routledge.

Schmitter, P.C. 2000, *How to Democratize the European Union... and why Bother?* Lanham: Rowman and Littlefield.

Schmitter, P.C. 2016, Politics as a Science (aka Politology), <http://www.eui.eu/Documents/DepartmentsCentres/SPS/Profiles/Schmitter/Politics-as-a-science.pdf> (accessed October 25, 2016).

Schmitter, P.C. and Lefkofridi, Z. 2016, Neo-functionalism as a theory of disintegration. *Chinese Political Science Review*, doi: 10.1007/s41111-016-0012-4.

Searle, J.R. 1995, *The Construction of Social Reality*. London: Penguin.

Sejersted, F. 2005, *Sosialdemokratiets tidsalder. Norge og Sverige i det 20. århundre*. Oslo: Pax.

Sejersted, F. 2013, Det elastiske panser. Om utviklingen av den norske statsforfatningen 1814–2014. In E. Holmøyvik (ed.): *Tolkingar av Grunnlova. Om forfatningsutviklinga 1814–2014*: 35–109. Oslo: Pax Forlag.

Sejersted, F. 2014, Ny paragraf, gammel regel. *Tidsskrift for Rettsvitenskap* 127 (2): 235–67.

Selle, P. and Østerud, Ø. 2006, The eroding of representative democracy in Norway. *Journal of European Public Policy* 13 (4): 551–68.

Selznick, P. 1957, *Leadership in Administration. A Sociological Interpretation*. New York: Harper and Row.

Selznick, P. 1992, *The Moral Commonwealth. Social Theory and the Compromise of Community*. Berkeley: University of California Press.

Shapiro, M. 2008, Law and politics: The problem of boundaries. In K.E. Whittington, R.D. Kelemen, and G.A. Caldeira (eds): *The Oxford Handbook of Law and Politics*: 767–74. Oxford: Oxford University Press.

Shapiro, S.P. 2005, Agency theory. *Annual Review of Sociology* 31: 263–84.

Shaw, J. 1996, European Union legal studies in crisis? Towards a new dynamic. *Oxford Journal of Legal Studies* 16 (2): 231–53.

Shepsle, K.A. 1972, The strategy of ambiguity: Uncertainty and electoral competition. *American Political Science Review* 66 (2): 555–68.

Shklar, J.N. 1990, *The Faces of Injustice*. New Haven, CT: Yale University Press.

Simon, H.A. 1953, The birth of an organization: The Economic Cooperation Administration. *Public Administration Review* 13: 227–36.

Simon, H.A. 1957 (2nd ed.), *Administrative Behavior*. New York: Free Press.

Somek, A. 2013, What is a political union? *German Law Journal* 14 (5): 561–80.

Spinelli Group 2013, *A Fundamental Law of the European Union*. Gütersloh: Verlag Bertelsmann Stiftung.

Stone, B. 1995, Administrative accountability in the "Westminster" democracies: Towards a new conceptual framework. *Governance* 8 (4): 505–26.

Stone Sweet, A. 2007, The juridical coup d'état and the problem of authority. *German Law Journal* 8: 915–28.

Stratham, P. and Trenz, H.-J. 2013, *The Politicization of Europe. Contesting the Constitution in the Mass Media*. London: Routledge.

Streeck, W. 2014, *Buying Time: The Delayed Crisis of Capitalism*. London: Verso.

Strøm, K. 2000, Delegation and accountability in parliamentary democracies. *European Journal of Political Research* 37: 261–89.

Strøm, K., Müller, W.C. and Bergman, T. (eds) 2003, *Delegation and Accountability in Parliamentary Democracies*. Oxford: Oxford University Press.

Strømsnes, K. 2003, *Folkets makt. Medborgerskap, demokrati, deltakelse*. Oslo: Gyldendal Akademisk.

Svara, J.H. 1999, Complementarity of politics and administration as a legitimate alternative to the dichotomy model. *Administration and Society* 30 (6): 676–705.

Szczerbiak, A. and Taggart, P. 2008, *Opposing Europe? The Comparative Party Politics of Euroscepticism*. Oxford: Oxford University Press.

Teffer, P. 2016, MEPs stake claim to be EU investigators, <https://euobserver.com/institutional/133742> (accessed June 9, 2016).

Tetlock, P.E. 1992, The impact of accountability on judgement and choice: Toward a social contingency model. *Advances in Experimental Psychology* 25: 331–76.

Thatcher, M. and Stone Sweet, A. 2002, Theory and practice of delegation to non-majoritarian institutions. *West European Politics* 25 (1): 1–22.

Thompson, D.F. 1987, *Political Ethics and Public Office*. Cambridge, MA: Harvard University Press.

Tilly, C. 1975, Reflections on the history of European state-making. In C. Tilly (ed.): *The Formation of National States in Europe*: 3–83. Princeton, NJ: Princeton University Press.

Tranvik, T. and Selle, P. 2003, *Farvel til folkestyret? Nasjonalstaten og de nye nettverkene*. Oslo: Gyldendal Akademisk.

Trichet, J.-C. 2013, Improving European democratic accountability: Towards an economic and fiscal federation by exception, <http://institute.eib.org/wp-content/uploads/2013/10/TrichetArticleFinal2.pdf> (accessed 4 June, 2014).

Trondal, J. 2010, *An Emergent European Executive Order*. Oxford: Oxford University Press.

Usherwood, S. 2013, The shifting focus of opposition to the European Union. *Journal of Contemporary European Research* 9 (2): 279–96.

Van Thiel, S., Verhoest, K. Bouckaert, S.G. and Lægreid, P. (eds) 2012, Lessons and recommendations for the practice of agencification. In K. Verhoest, S. Van Thiel, G. Bouckaert, and P. Lægreid (eds) *Government Agencies. Practices and Lessons from 30 Countries*: 413–39. Houndmills: Palgrave Macmillan.

Varoufakis, Y. 2016, The EU no longer serves the people—democracy demands a new beginning. *Guardian*, 5 February.

Verhey, L., Broeksteeg, H. and Van den Driessche, I. (eds) 2008, *Political Accountability in Europe: Which Way Forward. A Traditional Concept of Parliamentary Democracy in a EU Context.* Groningen: Europa Law Publishing.

Verhoest, K., Peters, B.C. Bouckaert, G. and Verschuere, B. 2004, The study of organizational autonomy: A conceptual overview. *Public Administration and Development* 24 (2): 101–18.

Verhoest, K., Van Thiel, S. Bouckaert, G. and Lægreid, P. (eds) 2012, *Government Agencies. Practices and Lessons from 30 Countries*. Houndmills: Palgrave Macmillan.

Vibert, F. 2007, *The Rise of the Unelected. Democracy and the New Separation of Powers.* Cambridge: Cambridge University Press.

Walzer, M. 1984, The resources of American liberalism: Liberalism and the art of separation. *Political Theory* 12: 315–30.

Warleigh, A. 2002, Towards network democracy. The potential of flexible integration. In M. Farrell, S. Fella, and N. Newman (eds): *European Integration in the 21st Century. Unity and Diversity*: 101–18. London: Sage.

Warren, M.E. 2011, Democracy. In G. Klosko (ed.): *The Oxford Handbook of the History of Political Philosophy*: 517–29. Oxford: Oxford University Press.

Waterman, R.W. and Meier, K.J. 1998, Principal–agent models: An expansion? *Journal of Public Administration Research and Theory* 8 (2): 173–202.

Weber, M. 1970, Politics as a vocation. In H.H. Gerth and C. Wright Mills (eds): *From Max Weber*: 7–128. London: Routledge and Kegan Paul.

Weber, M. 1978, *Economy and Society*. Edited by G. Roth and C. Wittich. Berkeley: University of California Press.

Wehberg, H. 1959, Pacta sunt servanda. *American Journal of International Law* 53 (4): 775–86.

Weick, K.E., Sutcliffe, K.M. and Obstfeld, D. 2005, Organizing and the process of sensemaking. *Organization Science* 16 (4): 409–21.

Weiler, J.H.H. 1996, European neo-constitutionalism: In search of foundations for the European constitutional order. In R. Bellamy and D. Castiglione (eds): *Constitutionalism in Transition: European and Theoretical Perspectives*: 105–21. Oxford: Blackwell.

Weiler, J.H.H. 2012, Europe in crisis—on "political Messianism," "legitimacy" and "the rule of law." *Singapore Journal of Legal Studies*. December: 248–68.

Whelan, C.T. and B. Maître 2009, Europeanization of inequality and European reference groups. *Journal of European Social Policy* 19 (2): 117–30.

Wildavsky, A. 1987, Choosing preferences by constructing institutions: A cultural theory of preference formation. *American Political Science Review* 81: 3–22.

Wille, A. 2010, The European Commission's accountability paradox. In M. Bovens, D. Curtin, and P. 't Hart (eds), *The Real World of EU Accountability. What Deficit?*: 63–86. Oxford: Oxford University Press.

Wille, A. 2013, *The Normalization of the European Commission. Politics and Bureaucracy in the EU Executive*. Oxford: Oxford University Press.

Wolin, S.S. 1960, *Politics and Vision. Continuity and Innovation in Western Political Thought*. Boston: Little, Brown.

Wright, T. 2015, The politics of accountability. In M. Elliot and D. Feldman (eds): *The Cambridge Companion to Public Law*: 96–115. Cambridge: Cambridge University Press.

Zalan, E. 2016, EU commission under fire over Barroso bank job. Brussels, July 11, <https://euobserver.com/institutional/134297> (accessed 12 July, 2016).

Index